D0090648

Broke

ALSO BY JODIE ADAMS KIRSHNER

International Bankruptcy:
The Challenge of Insolvency in a Global Economy

Broke

Hardship and Resilience in a City of Broken Promises

Jodie Adams Kirshner

St. Martin's Press
New York

First published in the United States by St. Martin's Press, an imprint of
St. Martin's Publishing Group

Although this is a work of nonfiction, the names and some identifying charac-
teristics of certain individuals and companies have been changed to protect their
privacy, and some of the scenes have been reconstructed based on how some of the
people described them to the author.

www.stmartins.com

Design by Meryl Sussman Levavi

Library of Congress Cataloging-in-Publication Data

Names: Kirshner, Jodie Adams, author.
Title: Broke : hardship and resilience in a city of broken promises / Jodie
    Adams Kirshner.
Description: First edition. | New York : St. Martin's Press, [2019] |
    Includes bibliographical references and index.
Identifiers: LCCN 2019024268 | ISBN 9781250220639 (hardcover) | ISBN
    9781250237125 (ebook)
Subjects: LCSH: Bankruptcy—Michigan—Detroit. | Urban
    poor—Michigan—Detroit.
Classification: LCC HG3767.M5 K57 2019 | DDC 336.3/680977434—dc23
LC record available at https://lccn.loc.gov/2019024268

Our books may be purchased in bulk for promotional, educational, or business
use. Please contact your local bookseller or the Macmillan Corporate and
Premium Sales Department at 1-800-221-7945, extension 5442, or by email at
MacmillanSpecialMarkets@macmillan.com.

First Edition: November 2019

10 9 8 7 6 5 4 3 2 1

To the People of Detroit

Contents

Foreword

Detroit vs. Everybody

Detroit, Michigan, reigned for a long spell in the American imagination as the quintessential industrial American city. It was a city on the go, literally, with its commercial wheels spun by a booming economy fed by a smoothly running automobile industry. From 1914, when Henry Ford doubled the wages of his employees and offered them an unheard of $5.00 a day, to the mid-1970s, when a series of gasoline crises fueled the economy for foreign cars, Detroit was a model of American enterprise tied to an enormous cultural vitality. The artistic fertility of the city was best embodied in Berry Gordy's Motown Records, whose artistic production was modeled, intriguingly enough, on the assembly lines that manufactured the city's fantastic cars. Even though the prosperity was never spread equally among the races, the plentiful work on the assembly line helped, if not to democratize capital, then at least to catapult thousands of black families into the middle class.

But while pockets of black communities flourished economically, overall political progress flagged. Automobile factories, which were converted into manufacturers of materials for the Second World War, drew nearly half a million people to the city between 1940 and 1943. Many of the migrants were white southerners who rolled into the city with a Jim Crow outlook, including deep-seated bigotry against blacks and shop-worn stereotypes of Negro life. Many black folk came too—my father and, much later, my mother among them—setting up fraught competition for jobs between blacks and whites. The booming economy absorbed much of the friction, and offset, to a degree, black political marginalization and de facto disenfranchisement, but the underlying tension sparked a race riot in 1943.

Nearly a quarter century later, in 1967, when another riot and rebellion jumped off, the city's morale and fortunes plummeted dramatically. White folk fled even faster to surrounding suburbs and collar counties, leaving Detroit to become, as it had been becoming for more than a decade, a black Mecca, and then, afterward, a black hole that crushed the city's economic life through deindustrialization and white flight. The election of Coleman Young, the city's first black mayor, in 1974, showcased the striking contrast between evolving black political power and collective white resentment.

As Detroit got blacker and blacker, its economic prospects got bleaker and bleaker. Nationally, service industries supplanted manufacturing bases in a postindustrial surge that led, in relatively quick succession, to structural shifts in the economy, to the sputtering of the automobile industry—which, presaging the fate of the city itself, saw Chrysler and GM declare bankruptcy in 2009—to the city's credit rating sliding into junk territory. At the same time, the city's colorful and controversial young black mayor, Kwame Kilpatrick, succumbed to political self-destruction, the city's economy underwent further restructuring, and later, the automobile industry was bailed out by President Obama. But, perhaps most fatefully, ignominiously, and to many, unjustly, Governor Rick Snyder, embracing a jilting neoliberal politic, plunged Detroit into bankruptcy, making even more precarious the political and economic standing of its mostly black citizens. In so many ways, as Jodie Adams Kirshner says in the title of this arresting and affecting book, the city was just plain broke.

Broke exposes our stark neoliberal nightmare for what it truly is—a socially depraved ideology that touts the free market as the ultimate solution for the various problems that it helps to create, including shifts in the auto industry, automation's impact on labor, and the housing and mortgage crises. Too often critics and analysts find false consolation in data to grapple with these economic trends and troubles. To be blunt, many of us are enamored with statistics. A more dramatic analytical framework and a far more compelling moral response are required. *Broke*'s narrative offers just that. Its case-study style snatches off the convoluted cloak of data to reveal the deep and personal scarring of an American urban community deliberately placed in a spiral of economic despair.

Detroit's economic woes are not exclusively the result of political mismanagement. To be sure, that narrative is easier to digest than one that highlights the urban impact of post-industrialization, outsourcing, and the systematic privatization of public education. Those problems are real and have contributed to Detroit's unique situation. *Broke* is at its thrilling best when it usefully mines the real-life experiences of Detroit's gritty residents; it shines brightly when it depicts how residents are directly impacted by laws and policies that are crafted well beyond their municipal purview.

At times, *Broke* seems to be all about telling these individual stories—how Charles, Lola, or Miles wrestles with debilitating economic circumstances. At other times, *Broke* surveys the financial crises of a city under assault by shifting economic paradigms and predatory developers and their political enablers. But in the end, *Broke* isn't about how any of the enduring protagonists of Detroit are cash poor. Nor is it about the chronic financial woes of a city in intermittent financial disarray. *Broke* is about how the entire system of governance itself is "broke."

Kirshner persuasively argues that the bankruptcy option for cities is a relatively new one, and a strategy that has largely proved ineffective. The option became viable in the late 1970s after federal, and by extension state, assistance to cities peaked. In 2013 Detroit became "the largest American city ever to enter bankruptcy." More than 70 cities have followed that course since 2007. This isn't merely a Detroit problem, but, as Kirshner makes abundantly clear, one that looms large for dozens of other mostly urban communities vulnerable to a violent economic seizure and financial takeover. As it has done in other industrial pursuits, Detroit has sadly pioneered a troubling trend. The Motor City is a harbinger of the trauma to come.

Federal and state governments, agencies, and policies are just as responsible for the crisis in the American city as any local or city government. In the case of Detroit, federal and state governments, Republican and Democratic alike, have colluded to systematically defund and underfund the once teeming metropolis. It is an unquestionably tragic entry in the ledger of America's vexed history with its urban centers. For example, in 2000, John Engler—the near Dickensian governor of Michigan who promoted an agenda of supply-side property tax cuts, privatization of state services, a hike in sales tax, and welfare and educational reform—ended the requirement for city workers to live within the city's limits. This had an immediate and deleterious impact on Detroit and its capacity to sustain its eroding tax base. At the same time, in a bitter irony, it subsidized the suburbs of Detroit from the new economy jobs in the 5 percent of Detroit that was in full recovery. To make matters worse, years later, neither Republican governor Rick Snyder nor Democratic president Barack Obama offered to bail out Detroit.

A couple of burning questions, however, must be answered: How can the same government entities that were responsible for Detroit's malaise experience a change of heart and direction? How might they apply morally informed policy initiatives to address the problems that underwrite the fall of the American city? *Broke* will hopefully foster enthusiasm to grapple with these issues, especially as the stakes grow ever higher.

There is a great need, especially in our racially amnesiac Trump era, to recall and wrestle with the racial forces that crowd our historical landscape. For instance, the history of the transition from legal housing discrimination and racial deed restrictions to the subprime mortgage crisis, which deliberately targeted African American homeowners, is labyrinthine. But *Broke* tells it brilliantly. Kirshner draws a nearly straight line from American politics and policy into the heart of the black American dream of homeownership.

The central, trenchant, undeniable argument of *Broke* is clear: Bankruptcy is neither a fiscally responsible nor a morally irresistible response to the myriad challenges faced by the modern American city. Some may prefer to blame the corruption of black political power for the blight of Detroit instead of economic malaise and a deeply entrenched racism that scorns black populations and sees them as their own worst enemies. But after reading the poignant, heartbreaking, defiant pages of *Broke*, no one should question the need for a moral referendum on how policy is created in and for urban America.

MICHAEL ERIC DYSON

Prologue

Springtime in Detroit

Miles strode through the streets of Detroit, long-legged and focused, carrying a cup of keys to all the houses he contracted and an envelope of charge cards to cover construction supplies. He had reached his mid-30s with experience and skills and a reputation as a guy who handled stuff, on budget and on schedule. People called to ask for him by name, and he turned down small jobs.

He had "the contacts, the contracts," he said, the words tripping off his tongue like a beatbox poet's. "Detroit's a good thing when it's going good." And back then, in the mid-2000s, it was: The city seemed on a tear, with new theaters and sports stadiums and a resurgence in manufacturing. His house, a two-family frame house on Belvidere Street he bought when he turned 19, sat on a block that had two- and three-story houses with homeowners inside and furnished front porches out front. The American Dream seemed firmly within his grasp, wealth one investment away. He planned to buy a second house and become a landlord.

Television ads and billboards and even casual conversations described the quick cash to be attained in the mortgage market. When a mortgage lender offered Miles a loan against his house, he took it. On a day so cold that it bit at his skin he made a down payment on a second house a few blocks south on Belvidere, a small single-family bungalow. When the temperature rose high enough, he worked hard installing toilets and sinks at the new house, replacing the kitchen cabinets, and painting the exterior white with red trim. Then he woke up to a phone call from a neighbor: The house had burned down.

As the year 2008 bore down he sensed his work slowing and more people competing for construction work. Instead of contracting whole houses, now he only got requests for repairs. His first house on Belvidere Street was developing leaks, damaging the roof and the foundation, while the interest rate on his reverse mortgage climbed. He had a tenant, but the tenant got shot trying to stop a carjacking. Then the tenant saw bills from the mortgage servicer for mounting delinquency fees and stopped paying rent.

Miles hung on to the house until January 2012, when the lender foreclosed on it. Miles had to move out, under a winter sky the color of pearls, and a few days later scrappers arrived to steal any copper wiring or other metals. Within a week the house had crumbled. As winter progressed the street steadily accumulated vacant and deteriorated houses.

Miles said he had a devil on his shoulder, testing his faith. A friend's aunt gave him her house on Rowe Street, a 10-minute drive north of Belvidere in the Osborn neighborhood of Detroit, a poorer area hit hard by mortgage foreclosure. On Rowe Street the houses packed together up to the frozen sidewalk, and illegal dumping littered the puddled edges of the street.

This house had also burned, and the woman planned to use a payment from her insurance policy to leave Detroit. Though the house kept the snow and rain off Miles, the cost of making it livable seemed insurmountable, and in spite of his height and serious demeanor, he felt unsafe there. His daughter, a freshman in high school, could not stay with him. The man who lived across the street got shot one night and died.

Miles scoped newspaper ads and found a faux-Tudor house he liked further east, on Rosemary Street, offered by an investment company called Detroit Progress LLC. Detroit Progress had listings for hundreds of houses for sale, and Miles had seen the company's signs around town. He liked the house on Rosemary because it was brick and bigger than it looked from outside, and the block seemed quiet. In 2007 the house had gone through mortgage foreclosure and then in 2012 entered tax foreclosure. In the county tax foreclosure auction that year Detroit Progress had won 100 tax-foreclosed properties. Now the company sought to flip the Rosemary Street house for $4,000 plus any unpaid property taxes, more than five times as much as the company had bid to win it.

Miles viewed the house and saw its decrepitude, but by then lots of Detroit houses looked as bad, and he thought he had the skills to fix it. Thieves had stolen the furnace and all the piping, holes pocked the roof, and smoke damage on the walls gave the impression of mold spores. He asked an acquaintance whose voice he thought sounded white to negotiate for him by phone. The asking price for the house dropped by a third, and Miles drove downtown through heavy snow to check the property records. The records showed more than twice the price of the house in outstanding 2013 property taxes, but he decided to buy it anyway. He carried his belongings over at six in the morning and twelve at night in darkness so that no one would see him and try to steal them. He did not have much to bring to Rosemary Street: his tools, a vinyl sofa, two lamps with no shades, a low glass table, one dining room–style chair, and a mattress. When he finished, he boarded up the front door of his old Rowe Street house and parked a neighbor's spare truck in the iced-over driveway. A few days later the truck caught fire and burned the side of the house. Soon afterward the roof fell in.

Miles had not found much construction work since the financial crisis intensified, but he thought he could manage the costs of his new house. He had been fending for himself for years in a city now seven months into bankruptcy, but people were telling him, "Detroit's coming up—Detroit's moving," and he believed his life might become easier. He did not know that he would soon find himself fighting for his fourth house, barred from driving, and dogged by criminal charges brought against him 14 years earlier.

* * *

Detroit entered bankruptcy in July 2013 after a state-appointed emergency manager displaced local elected officials from power and chose not to pay $300 million due on the city's debt. Bankruptcy offered a process in which the emergency manager could negotiate modifications to the debt without having to pay creditors during the negotiations.

In bankruptcy, when a majority of creditors support a re-structuring plan, the plan binds every creditor. Outside bankruptcy even one creditor can undermine the restructuring plan by insisting on a better deal for itself. Such a plan generally includes lower debt payments, which free a city from spending as much money servicing the debt, and further savings from shrinking the size of the public workforce, cutting services, and selling city-owned assets.

Seventeen months and nearly $180 million in fees and

costs later, Detroit emerged from bankruptcy having cut some municipal workers' pensions nearly 7 percent, paid a financial creditor 13 cents on every dollar it was due, and obtained $325 million in new loans. In lengthy and often fraught negotiations at the local bankruptcy court downtown, the city had balanced its budget and gained ideas for generating new money to fund essential services.

Yet Detroit still faced the squeeze of population decline and widespread poverty that eroded its tax base and overburdened its public welfare programs. It still received limited help from the federal and state governments and had no clear path to population growth or new jobs. Bankruptcy could not provide new remedies against financial problems. It could not directly reverse the population loss, employment loss, or property value loss that contributed to the shrinking tax base, nor could bankruptcy bring back lost federal and state support to offset pressures on public welfare.

For months Detroit's problems headlined national news. Following that, how could the city attract people and businesses? If any new investment occurred, how would it affect existing residents? No one knew the extent to which a courtroom bankruptcy process in a large American city could spur solutions to deep-seated structural problems, many the result of poverty, race, and power inequities.

* * *

No one knew in part because for decades cities hardly ever went bankrupt. Until the Great Depression bankruptcy procedures did not even exist for cities, and between 1970 and 2007 only three cities entered bankruptcy. Those cities had smaller populations than Detroit and used the bankruptcy process to address isolated setbacks like the loss of a large lawsuit or a natural disaster.

Historically, instead of declaring bankruptcy, cities received more support from higher levels of government. In 1944 Franklin Delano Roosevelt touted in a fireside chat the interdependency of "all groups and sections of the population of America" and proposed a second bill of rights that committed the federal government to the provision of good jobs, housing, and education. In 1966, after the Great Society programs directed further federal aid to cities, Robert Kennedy testified before Congress, "To speak of the urban condition . . . is to speak of the condition of American life. To improve the cities means to improve the life of the American people." In 1975 New York State advanced money to New York City and helped the city by backing local bonds with state tax revenues. In 1978 after Cleveland defaulted on some debt, Ohio lent it money.

But as voters moved to the South, the West, and city suburbs, politics changed. Assistance to cities peaked in 1978, the same year Jimmy Carter said in his State of the Union address, "Government cannot eliminate poverty or provide a bountiful economy or reduce inflation or save our cities or cure illiteracy or provide energy." Between 1980 and 1988, during Reagan's presidency, total intergovernmental aid to cities fell by half.

Mandatory balanced budget rules forced states to reduce funding to cities. Lacking support from federal and state governments to meet urgent obligations, cities turned to the bond markets, subjecting themselves to market volatility. The recent financial crisis revealed the unsustainable position of cities that resulted from the risk and leverage they acquired. During the crisis governmental support continued to fall, leaving cities without a buffer against the market downturn.

Meanwhile demands for social services in cities increased.

In order to maintain solvency cities turned to the limited options available to them: reducing services, raising taxes and user fees, borrowing more money by issuing municipal bonds, and competing for private investment by offering tax deals and incentives to companies. Not all cities had the capacity to stabilize their budgets through these actions.

Bankruptcy offered federal and state governments a way to avoid bailing out the cities that lacked the capacity. Politicians branded municipal budget shortfalls as the fault of entitled municipal workers and retirees and reckless borrowing by municipal leaders. In 2012 Stockton, California, became the then-largest city to file for bankruptcy, and the bankruptcy process rewrote Stockton's union contracts. By the end of 2012 three more California cities had filed for bankruptcy, and nine more had declared financial emergencies.

In 2013 Detroit broke Stockton's record and assumed the mantle of the largest city ever to enter bankruptcy. Detroit became emblematic. The problems Detroit confronted paralleled problems in many other American cities. Though a few unique cities have attracted the optimal industries and population to win the spoils of the modern economy, many cities have failed to manage persistent unemployment, stagnant wages, and rising inequality. Without outside help from their state and local governments, more than 70 American municipalities since 2007 have entered bankruptcy and been forced to write down their debt on their own. Several hundred more cities now struggle on the brink of default and are shrinking public payrolls, cutting services, and selling public lands. Cities have suffered the brunt of mortgage foreclosures and declining property values and have generally been home to the largest numbers of poor and marginalized Americans, those most dependent on public services.

Detroit's bankruptcy offered an opportunity to test whether bankruptcy could affect cuts to cities' pension obligations. Many states' constitutions, including Michigan's, protected pension contracts against modifications, but federal bankruptcy law allowed any contract to be changed during bankruptcy. In one of the few rulings in the case the Detroit bankruptcy judge found federal bankruptcy law could supersede state pension protections.

Through bankruptcy's exclusive focus on cities' culpability for fiscal crisis, its lack of attention to the people affected, and its implicit demand for cities to solve "their" problems on their own, we have overestimated the ability of cities and their residents to combat powerful forces like automation, suburbanization, the recent financial crisis, and deindustrialization. We have underestimated the resources and tools necessary to change the trajectory of cities and the importance of sustainable cities. We have neglected our fellow citizens, who have been forced to endure reduced services, high taxes, and insufficient human investment.

Broke follows seven Detroiters as they navigate life during and after their city goes bankrupt. Some of them are lifelong residents navigating the city's real estate market, school system, and job market; some are outsiders attempting to capitalize on foreclosed properties or start small businesses. None has received the attention and aid that he or she needs in order to flourish.

A majority of Americans live in cities. Cities provide the economic engine of America and are a depository of its culture. The country cannot prosper if its cities are decaying. Stabilizing cities' futures seems to depend not on bankruptcy but on expanding opportunity for individual urban residents.

Though Detroit is often described in terms of the population that it has lost, more than 700,000 people still live there, persevering in the face of high taxes, struggling schools, and scarce jobs. The people in Detroit, more than 35 percent of whom fall below the poverty line, are bravely making do. Their future holds a mirror to America's.

Protagonists

=

Miles: Mid-40s. African American construction worker with a tenuous hold on his house and an intrusive past.

Charles: Early 50s. African American Morningside resident with remnants of auto industry wealth, ready to give up on Detroit.

Robin: Late 40s. White property developer from Los Angeles.

Reggie: Mid-40s. African American land contract homebuyer.

Cindy: Early 60s. White, lifelong Brightmoor resident, active in community renewal organization.

Joe: Early 50s. White New Jersey tree surgeon and Detroit entrepreneur.

Lola: Mid-20s. African American, college-educated single mother seeking better work.

Part One

Bankruptcy

I

Emergency Management

AUTUMN 2016 / WINTER 2013

Miles's friend Charles lit a tank of propane gas to fuel a hot plate in the two-story house where he grew up. The hot plate sat in the kitchen next to an unused old stove stacked with oatmeal, salt, cereal, and other staples. It was morning in the fall of 2016, nearly two years after Detroit exited bankruptcy. The autumn sun had risen late, carrying a sharp chill, and Charles used a headlamp to see the eggs and bacon that he was cooking.

A small, stooped 54-year-old man, he had an appealing sweetness about him. His clothes looked a little too big, his mouth slightly twisted from oral cancer and framed by a neatly trimmed graying beard. He walked into the dining room and set his breakfast plate down on the mahogany dining table, underneath a dusty crystal chandelier. White-painted trim set off the ochre walls, which had stained and peeled over the years. Near the chandelier an open gash yawned across the ceiling. As he ate his eggs Charles stared into the detritus of the years his family had spent in the house, in Detroit's Morningside neighborhood. The china cabinet with gold-leafed porcelain platters behind glass windows had belonged to his family since before he was born.

Finished with the eggs, he crossed to the window and opened the blinds to let in any light the dull day could provide. If he craned his neck he could see Mack Avenue and into the suburb of Grosse Pointe Park, with its sweeping lawns and lakefront park open only to residents. But first he had to look past sagging porches, garbage on the street, and the old Top Video Superstore, which had closed 11 years earlier. Grosse Pointe Park had a population even more white than Detroit's was black, and its median household income of nearly $115,000 dwarfed Detroit's of under $25,000. Tensions between the city and the suburb had historically run high, with the suburb using statues and barricades to strengthen the border dividing them.

"Enough is enough," Charles said sadly. He had expected greatness in life, then grown increasingly disappointed. At community college he studied political science, then found jobs installing swimming pools at suburban houses. After moving away from Detroit several times, he moved back when his aging parents needed his help. Though he still did odd construction jobs, now he just wanted to look after his 90-year-old widowed mother, who suffered from Alzheimer's disease, in his family's house. But his half sister had recently moved their mother to her own family's house in Alaska and transferred their mother's remaining assets into her own name as guardian.

Charles missed his mother. He missed sharing meals with her, and he missed going to bed downstairs in the family house knowing that she slept upstairs. If "baddies" broke in, he had told her, they would have to deal with him first. To get his mother back he flew to Alaska.

While he was away someone squatted in the house. When Charles returned, alone, the man thanked him and departed, leaving Charles with the squatter's high utility bills. Stubbornly, Charles refused to cover someone else's electricity, heat, and hot water. Instead he bought the kerosene lamps and propane burners.

He tried to cheer himself by applying poetry to his situation. He joked frequently in his richly timbered voice, playing on the subtleties of language with lines like "it was highway robbery, except that it took place on the sidewalk" and flashing an impish smile. On cold days he wore a black fur hat the size of a dinner plate paired with a trench coat. But he was fending for himself alone in the house, bereft of his mother and without heat or electricity, and he did not know how much longer he could bear to stay.

* * *

Charles remembered Morningside when his family moved in as "almost just perfect." Back then it was a middle-class, flourishing neighborhood. Professors and policemen, old and young people, lived there together. They owned their own homes and regularly cut the grass and shoveled the snow. They even watered the grass.

The Morningside house represented the success Charles's family found in Detroit. In the late 1930s Charles's father migrated from Mississippi, joining other African Americans abandoning the South for flourishing northern industrial cities. Detroit had grown fat off the automobile, and as World War II began, Charles's father and other new arrivals helped fuel the city's shift from manufacturing cars to manufacturing tanks and bombers. With just 2 percent of the country's population, the city supplied 10 percent of the war's provisions.

Charles's father found work at the Budd Wheel factory, which produced wheels for the Big Three auto companies, brake components, and later the body of the Ford Thunderbird. Budd patented an all-steel military wheel, and Budd employees stamped sheet metal into railcars and World War II artillery shells. More than 8,000 people worked at the Detroit factory. The campus spanned 86 acres, and the main building replicated Philadelphia's Independence Hall.

Though Detroit offered opportunities for African American arrivals, newcomers like Charles's father suffered discrimination and poor living conditions. Contact between blacks and whites sparked race riots, strikes, protests, and cross burnings. African Americans could not access federally insured loans, and racial deed restrictions further blocked them from most neighborhoods. Urban redevelopment projects under the banner of slum clearance razed many open neighborhoods, increasing housing shortages and driving up rents.

Despite this, Charles's mother moved to Detroit from Texas and met Charles's father. After marrying, Charles's parents moved to the east side, four blocks from the sprawling Chrysler plant. The Supreme Court had found racial deed restrictions unenforceable, and African Americans in Detroit could suddenly buy nicer homes. African American families began moving from central ghettos into formerly all-white neighborhoods, catapulting housing to the forefront of civil rights battles. As the racial frontier in the city pushed outward, white residents began to leave. Detroit was becoming a hub for civil rights activism and black nationalism, much of it centered around African American churches. Block-busting real estate agents hired African Americans to parade through white neighborhoods, and many white homeowners, wary of declining property values, sold their properties at discounts to the agents. The agents flipped the same properties at steep markups to African Americans, who generally could not obtain mortgages.

Years later, to clear a site for a new, smaller Chrysler plant, Detroit officials acquired more than 20 residential blocks and demolished the houses on them, including the home where Charles's family was living. The city paid his family buyout money, and the family used it, along with savings, to buy the house in Morningside for cash.

* * *

In spite of how far the neighborhood had fallen, Charles still felt proud of all his family had achieved when they moved. He boasted, standing a little taller, that as a child he had the opportunity to be anything he wanted to be. In those days his father planned to live in the house forever and rarely took the family to visit what remained of the old neighborhood. He celebrated his new circumstances by planting a rosebush in the backyard.

In the evenings when Charles's father returned home from the factory, he read the newspaper aloud to Charles and taught him about the history of their city and the importance of knowing about changes taking place. By the 1950s the story of Detroit as a boomtown had reversed, which threatened to affect the family's way of life. Advances in automation increased productivity and reduced employment. Transportation and communication costs fell, and auto companies faced new competition from overseas. Detroit's central location near rail, river, and resources no longer offered as much advantage, and the auto companies began to relocate their remaining factories to save money and escape regulation. In the face of global shifts, the city's industrial spine was crumbling.

Charles's father explained how each manufacturing job that disappeared chipped away at Detroit's budget, and federal policies reinforced the city's decline. Federally insured mortgages for whites only and federal highway subsidies encouraged further white migration to the suburbs, entrenching segregation and aggravating the city's economic difficulties. As the city lost tax revenues and state financial contributions tied to population, it suffered repeated severe recessions throughout the 1950s. The fortunes of the auto industry rose and fell on consumer demand, and the city weathered economic downturns poorly. The auto companies laid off additional workers and more factories closed. The financial problems cemented the concentration of an increasingly poor, non-white population in the city.

Looking back, Charles noticed how the trajectory of Budd Wheel, where his father worked, paralleled the trajectory of his neighborhood. In the late 1970s a German steel conglomerate bought Budd and continued operating the plant. The neighborhood remained peaceful and middle-class. In 2000 the governor ended a requirement for city workers to live within the city limits, and Charles gradually felt the neighborhood unravel. By 2007 only 350 people still worked at the Budd plant. The German conglomerate restructured and then shut the plant down, shipping the metal-stamping presses from Detroit to Mexico.

In 2007, when Charles reached his 40s, his father passed away. As the baby of the family, Charles took charge of the household. He and his mother watched as their neighbors began to leave Detroit: Some moved to the suburbs, and some moved out of state. The state trooper who lived across the street transplanted his family to the suburbs after someone harassed his wife while she was jogging. Between 2000 and 2010 Morningside lost 27 percent of its population, somewhat more than Detroit's average. Foreclosure brought one in six Morningside properties into city ownership.

The Budd company, meanwhile, entered bankruptcy in 2012 and sold its remaining operations to a New York private equity company. The trooper and his wife still sometimes drove in from the suburbs to see how the neighborhood was changing. When he saw them, Charles skipped outside happily and waved.

* * *

As Charles surveyed his neighborhood, across the country Robin was taking a series of phone calls from his office in Los Angeles. That morning a rental property Robin owned in Detroit had burned down, and he was trying to determine what had gone wrong. Another tenant had recently left in the middle of the night and taken the hot water heater with him. Robin instructed his team in Detroit to scrutinize prospective tenants more closely and do whatever was required to recoup the full cost of the water heater: collection agency, garnishment, or seizure.

Though he talked tough, he looked more like a Los Angeles filmmaker than a Detroit property developer. He wore black and kept an electronic cigarette constantly pressed to his lips. His hair brushed against his shoulders, and his beard grew to his collarbone. He spoke in complete sentences that encouraged his listeners to imagine a world of color and possibility. In Los Angeles his office looked out on a parking lot that hugged a low-slung white concrete building, the original office of the Walt Disney company, and today the building seemed to glow against the backdrop of a cloudless California sky. From here, a world away from the hollowed-out buildings in many of Detroit's neighborhoods, Robin considered Detroit.

He found the city "magical." "It's just the sharing there,

the journey every time," he said, tucking back his long hair. Though he lived in Los Angeles so that his son could attend a local private school, Robin felt that for the right person Detroit was the most desirable city in the country. The people he met there at bars and at galleries had come to the city expressly to reinvent themselves. Real estate was inexpensive, and it seemed easy for them to pursue creative endeavors there.

Robin, however, did business with a different kind of tenant. He oversaw a portfolio of about 50 Detroit properties that he primarily rented to working-poor African Americans. He advertised the properties online, and potential tenants mostly viewed the ads on their cell phones. Few of them had Internet or home computers. He sought out people he thought would pay rent on time and not kick holes in walls, and he reviewed his applicants' criminal and eviction histories, trying to mask his artistic, Californian demeanor and seem stern. He ignored their credit scores because bad credit would have disqualified nearly everyone who applied.

Still, Robin felt he related to his tenants because he had grown up poor in Washington State. His father supported a wife and five children on the money he earned as a diesel mechanic. To get by, the family hunted deer and elk and canned pickles and berries. They had an acre of land around their house to cultivate, but Robin thought Detroit felt just as rural.

Robin's circumstances had improved through education and his entry into real estate. When he traveled to Detroit he stayed in the upstairs apartment of a big yellow house in the West Village neighborhood. A stable, historically upper-middle-class area close to downtown, the West Village had a reputation for eclectic architecture and new businesses like a vegan soul food restaurant. When he spent time there he liked to drive over to a 100-year-old Russian-Jewish bathhouse called the Schvitz, where people heated rocks over flames, then threw water and tea on the rocks to generate steam. Robin told people they should always come to Detroit with a bathing suit.

* * *

"What are you doing?" friends had demanded when Robin first bought Detroit properties in 2007. His first year investing there he could not even find a property underwriter willing to sell him insurance. But he pointed out fine construction to his friends—the municipal electrical boxes to him looked like churches—and talked in the bravura style of Hollywood about how the city would improve.

State politicians, however, saw reasons for concern about the city's future. In January 2011 Republican businessman Rick Snyder became the governor of Michigan. Eyeing Detroit and the still powerful unions operating there, he and Republican legislators pushed for a new law to expand the power of emergency managers. Emergency managers in Michigan already held authority to assume financial control of cities and enter the cities into bankruptcy. Snyder and the other legislators wanted to extend the managers' power so the managers could suspend local democracy, run all aspects of cities, and break union contracts.

The new legislation passed, and citizens sued, arguing it abridged their right to elect who governed them. Snyder defended the legislation as a tool for helping cities while announcing $92 million in cuts to state aid. Cities might recoup the money if they adopted "best practices." Local activists began gathering signatures to trigger a referendum on the emergency management legislation.

Robin, however, already sensed changes in certain areas of his property portfolio. With the build of a nightclub bouncer, he walked fearlessly through the city's neighborhoods, but he had begun seeing elderly ladies walking dogs and young white girls driving expensive cars in a neighborhood adjacent to downtown called Corktown. He doubled his rents there, charging $950 for three-bedroom houses. Across the city, artists had arrived and private entrepreneurship had started to bloom, and some companies had established downtown headquarters. Midtown's university and hospitals incentivized their employees to move nearby, and Midtown attracted new residents. They supported new stores and restaurants, and a Whole Foods grocery store opened.

People Robin met, though, didn't expect the city to improve. They told him developers had already bought everything valuable.

"Are you out of your mind?" he asked them. When he grew impassioned, his long hair flopped.

"This is just a shit-hard town," the locals said.

People who grew up in Detroit had experienced countless cycles of potential comebacks and failures. Michigan confounded Robin's predictions and initiated a review of Detroit's finances. The city hurtled toward emergency management.

To deter state control the Democratic mayor Dave Bing quickly cut Detroit's budget. "The reality we're facing is simple," he announced. "If we continue down the same path, we will lose the ability to control our own destiny." A Hall of Fame basketball player who later launched a steel-processing factory, Bing sought wage reductions for municipal employees, including police officers and firefighters, increases in employee health care contributions, a higher corporate tax rate, pension cuts, and layoffs. He vowed to recoup money the city lost in a 1998 deal with the state. In exchange for more than $300 million in further state revenue sharing, the city agreed to reduce its income tax rate. Otherwise the Republican-controlled legislature would have cut Detroit's allocation while increasing payments to smaller cities and rural areas. The deal reinstated Detroit's payments in exchange for the tax cut. Ultimately the state did not follow through with the revenue sharing it pledged, and Detroit lost more than $700 million in income taxes.

Detroiters protested the state's expanding review of the city's finances, and the efforts to reverse the emergency management legislation in a popular referendum gained steam. Three times the necessary number of people signed petitions to place the issue on the ballot. Crowds chanted "no takeover" outside review meetings. In Lansing, the state budget had a nearly $460 million surplus after years of spending cuts. In Detroit, Bing scrambled for concessions from unions. Defiant, he announced that he would not support the appointment of an emergency manager. Then he entered the hospital to undergo surgery. The situation reached an uneasy impasse.

From Los Angeles Robin monitored the news from Detroit with the interest of a soap opera devotee. He welcomed emergency management and bankruptcy and predicted it could help him raise more capital to buy more local real estate. He could weave efforts to restructure the city's finances into the narrative of the city's potential he spun for investors.

One hour before Governor Snyder had to decide whether to appoint an emergency manager to Detroit, he pulled back. He seemed hesitant, as a white Republican, to replace the African American, Democratic mayor of a majority African American, Democratic-leaning city. Instead Snyder established an advisory board to oversee the city's financial decisions, budget, and union contracts. The board would hold authority to reverse and reopen the city's choices. To avoid emergency management Bing and the City Council acquiesced. Shouts of "idiots" and "sell-outs" drowned out their announcement. A recalcitrant City Council member implored Detroiters to "stand up and fight," and the city's chief lawyer filed a legal challenge against the board.

Several months later, Michigan voters succeeded in repealing the expanded emergency management legislation, but the victory was short-lived. The state legislature quickly passed a replacement bill, which included protections against its popular repeal. As the threat of emergency management returned, Mayor Bing vowed to improve tax collections, recover unenforced licensing fees and parking fines, and sell a city-owned building. Soon afterward he announced plans to close city parks. By that time the number of city employees had fallen more than 70 percent. Cuts to police and fire personnel coincided with slower services and an increased murder rate.

Despite the efforts of city officials and the anger of protesters, 14 days before the replacement emergency management legislation took effect, in March 2013, Snyder appointed a Washington bankruptcy lawyer called Kevyn Orr emergency manager to Detroit. Orr displaced the mayor and City Council. As resistance to emergency management mounted, Orr wrested control of the city. Robin saw hope for the city in easy reach and, from the comfort of his office in Los Angeles, continued to preach what he called the gospel of Detroit.

* * *

During the emergency management period Charles would press his thin face against his front window and watch as people walked in the middle of his street, rather than on the sidewalks, to avoid walking by vacant houses in the dark. He felt like a nightmare had spread across the city. Nearly half the streetlights had gone dark, including those in his neighborhood. Broken bulbs and stripped copper wiring had become insurmountable obstacles to providing lighting to a city that lacked funds to make repairs.

An alley near Charles's house offered a shortcut to a modest commercial strip. The strip housed a check-cashing counter, a pharmacy, and a lottery-ticket booth all inside one liquor store. Further down, a medical marijuana dispensary, a gas station, a storefront church, and a hair salon operated amid the vestiges of a former clothing boutique, former barbershop, former cabinet maker, and other vacant shops. Charles knew the alley was unsafe, but he walked through it anyway to demonstrate his faith. He tried to puff out his small chest and carry himself in a way that inspired respect.

When he returned home he hunched over the dining room table, reading newspaper articles about the emergency manager's decisions, which made him feel even more alienated. The fact that most Detroit residents voted to repeal the state emergency management legislation and ended up with an emergency manager anyway made his powerlessness clear to him. He concluded that he lived in "capitalism" rather than in a democracy.

Charles vowed never to bother voting again. Voting had revealed itself as merely procedural. Government officials could ignore the results and do what they wanted to do all along. In any case the upcoming election for mayor seemed like a formality; the new mayor would not assume any power to govern the city.

Above all, Charles did not believe that the emergency manager, Kevyn Orr, had come to help people like him. He viewed Orr's task as dissecting the city for the governor who hired him. Then, in an interview, Orr referred to Detroit as "dumb, lazy, happy, and rich." The article touted the resurgence in three Detroit neighborhoods and described the rest of the city, including where Charles lived, as "130 square miles of no man's land." To Charles the comments confirmed the true colors of the emergency manager. Just talking about it made him clench his small fists.

Charles had witnessed the bailouts of both the auto industry and the mortgage industry and experienced the devastating effects of both crises on Detroit. He felt that the crises had wounded the city not just financially but also spiritually. He gave up hope then. Drooped over his breakfast more than three years later, he did not know where he would go when he left his unheated childhood home.

2

Home

S everal years earlier, in late October 2007, Robin boarded
a flight from Detroit to Los Angeles and folded his burly
frame into his seat. On the ground in Detroit his lawyer was
closing on his first investment property. A brick bungalow five
blocks south of Detroit's northern border, the house sold for
$11,000, down from more than $90,000 the same year. The
house had entered mortgage foreclosure.

After attending art school on scholarship Robin had made
two documentary films. Then he had two realizations and
made one decision. First he saw that his upbringing made him
financially illiterate. Second he recognized that his film work
showed people a different way of seeing things. He resolved to
teach himself a different way of seeing money.

He read about wealth, what it was, what it meant, and how
it was built, and he grasped that most of the world's wealth
either had been made or was held in real estate. He sought out
a mentor to help him become a property developer. The

mentor suggested pursuing projects in cities outside Los Angeles. He advised Robin to institute property management systems and hire local staff to apply them, similar to McDonald's franchising methods. Robin approached a venture capitalist who had invested in a film he made about AIDS and asked him to invest in Robin's real estate project. Robin's pitch succeeded, and he secured financial backing for his new métier.

Logging lots of air miles, Robin began to scout undervalued real estate. He studied the markets in Kansas City, Charlotte, Indianapolis, Atlanta, and Detroit. He was looking for houses he could buy in cash and then refinance for new cash, which he would use to buy more houses. He stayed for free on a too-small sofa at a friend's house in Westland, a Detroit suburb named after its shopping mall. In Detroit he found a promising house and launched the business there.

The first house had just one bedroom and one bathroom. It cost $7,000 to renovate, and a working single mother agreed to rent it for $1,000 a month. Robin's lawyer challenged the property tax assessment, and the annual tax bill fell more than $5,000.

Curious about Detroit and Robin's use of his money there, Robin's investor flew in to view the first property and meet the first tenant. By that time Robin had nearly completed a deal to refinance the house and pull $25,000 from it. Impressed with the low cost of the house relative to the income it would generate, the investor offered Robin a further half million dollars to buy more properties. Then the refinancing market froze and the property market crashed.

* * *

On an episode of *I Love Lucy* Ethel and Lucy found jobs at a chocolate factory. Their assignment was to stand at a moving conveyor belt, pick up chocolates, wrap them, and return them to the conveyor belt. The women tied handkerchiefs in their hair and prepared for easy work. Then the conveyor belt started moving faster and faster, sending more and more chocolates down the line. Lucy and Ethel shoved chocolates into their pockets and into their mouths and still the chocolates came. In filmmaker mode, Robin described a similar situation in Detroit with mortgage-foreclosed properties.

Between 2005 and 2015, mortgage foreclosure turned 100,000 Detroit homeowners into renters, eliminating wealth from local families and from the city. Lack of sufficient oversight in the areas of consumer protection, mortgage securitization, and bank capitalization fueled the crisis. Nationwide African Americans received subprime or predatory loans at twice the rate of the rest of the population, and by 2008 more than half of African American mortgage holders held subprime or predatory loans. Detroit had a population that was more than 80 percent African American, and subprime lending proliferated in Detroit more than in most other cities. In 2005 nearly 70 percent of new mortgages in Detroit qualified as subprime, nearly three times the national rate. The loans came with higher interest payments than traditional mortgages and defaulted four times as often.

As the number of foreclosures in Detroit climbed, Robin saw that if he bought the properties that were accumulating on bank balance sheets with low prices, renovated the properties, and rented them out, he could access a growing local rental market. Many of the people losing their homes lacked the resources to leave Detroit, and so they had to rent there. In 2008 banks foreclosed on more than 37,000 local properties; half the properties sold for less than $10,000, and for the next four years Robin bought properties only from banks.

Not only did lenders need to clear foreclosed properties from their balance sheets, they also needed to find cash buyers. Empty properties quickly deteriorated and carried tax liabilities and maintenance costs but no income, and no lenders would write mortgages on foreclosed properties or underwrite loans for their renovation. Robin's ready cash placed him in a powerful bargaining position. One day he identified a house with a $150,000 mortgage in default and offered the lender $7,000 for it. The lender rejected the offer. A month later the lender phoned him to accept it, but Robin said that his offer had dropped to $3,500. The lender agreed to the lower price.

Property represented the largest item in the wealth portfolio of most Americans and a larger proportion of the net worth of African Americans. High rates of high-risk mortgages therefore devastated prosperity in cities with sizeable African American populations like Detroit. In Detroit declining property values eliminated $1.3 billion in personal wealth in 2012 alone. By 2015 African American homeownership rates hit their lowest level since the 1960s, when racial discrimination in lending remained legal. The wealth gap, which measured the difference in total assets, savings, property, and retirement accounts between white and African American families, increased to a factor of six from a factor of four. As African American families had less money to invest in college tuition, entrepreneurship, and down payments on new properties, the wealth gap compounded.

The losses had follow-on effects for cities. Reduced spending translated to slower economic activity in areas such as construction hiring and demand for consumer products, which shrunk income and sales tax revenues. On average banks sold foreclosed Detroit properties for a quarter of their assessed value, and between 2008 and 2011 property tax revenues fell 25 percent. The missing tax revenues in turn reduced cities' abilities to fund public services like libraries and schools and made it more expensive to borrow money to make up the difference. Foreclosure also destroyed neighborhoods.

* * *

Robin pushed the driver's seat back to accommodate his substantial legs and drove a rental car up and down the streets of Detroit, color coding them on his map with green, yellow, and red markers. He marked in green the blocks where families lived to indicate that the blocks seemed like good places to invest. Driving the city, he saw that nice blocks bordered areas where he could pick up houses for $500 that he thought looked completely un-rentable.

As he gained confidence discerning good bets from bad, and the chocolates sped faster down the conveyor belt of foreclosed properties, he developed systems so that his deputies could bid on properties without his input. The systems excluded houses on blocks with more than a threshold number of burned houses and vacant lots, trash, and board-ups. Those blocks looked like war zones to Robin's L.A. eyes, and he assumed no one would rent from him there.

Even on more stable blocks rehabilitating properties tied up cash, and Robin had to keep expenses low to earn a living and satisfy his investor. The best foreclosed properties still generally needed new plumbing, wiring, and ductwork, and new furnaces and water heaters. Even intact windows invariably allowed in drafts, and roofs and basements that did not leak soon would. He carefully tracked how much he could put into the houses and still generate returns and found that he could make the houses "safe, clean and functional," but could not afford to take "beautiful" into consideration. Any improvements he made he had to secure against scrappers, and he masqueraded vacant houses as occupied by scattering toys onto empty porches.

Across the country in areas with weak demand for housing, banks that foreclosed on properties expended few resources to maintain the properties. Lenders neglected foreclosed properties more in minority communities than in others, in documented ways. The properties in minority neighborhoods had higher incidences of unsecured doors, trash, graffiti, broken windows, and unmowed lawns. The blight made it more difficult for those housing markets to recover. To gain access to Detroit houses prior to their foreclosure, before the houses fell apart, Robin began a charm offensive to court local lenders. He drove them around in vans, stopping periodically so that they could explore properties he had bought and renovated. He spun portraits in their minds' eye of what their properties might become in his hands. Some lenders offered him properties for prices below the annual rent existing tenants were paying.

Foreclosing on properties cost roughly $50,000, and when the price exceeded properties' resale values, some lenders initiated foreclosure and evicted residents but did not complete foreclosure proceedings. Lenders seem to have left open proceedings in Detroit more frequently than anywhere else in the country. No law prevented such "zombie foreclosures," and the failure to complete proceedings freed the lenders from paying property taxes on foreclosed properties. The abandoned properties further reduced neighborhood property values and ultimately city property tax revenues. By some calculations, just one abandoned house decreased property values 15 percent through increased fire risk and neighborhood crime. The Michigan legislature eventually responded by revising state law to hold departing families personally responsible for property damage, unless they informed their mortgage lenders they were moving.

As the foreclosure crisis diminished prospects for cities like Detroit, across the country investors like Robin found opportunity but on an even larger scale. Hedge funds and private equity firms bought distressed properties in bulk at deep discounts and rented them out to former homeowners, often in African American communities. In 2012 Invitation Homes, a subsidiary of the private equity firm Blackstone Group, spent $100 million a week on distressed properties, paying cash at a time when few people qualified for mortgages. In Atlanta Invitation Homes bought 1,400 houses in one day. In Oakland, California, investors bought nearly half the properties foreclosed between 2007 and 2011. Renting out previously foreclosed houses had become a financial boon, and the private equity firm Blackstone launched a new bond backed by securitized rental payments.

* * *

In spring 2013 during the emergency management, Reggie eased his roly-poly frame out the driver's-side door of his 12-year-old minivan. He carefully avoided the rust that clung to the outside. On the other side of the van Reggie's longtime fiancée, Tasha, tried to dodge the overgrown grass between the sidewalk and the street, which still bore gray remnants of snow. Similar to Reggie, she had round cheeks and a large build, and in spite of the circumstances, she and Reggie presented a portrait of happy domesticity. Though their city remained in the grip of an uncertain emergency management, today they were searching for a house. Reggie had adopted two adolescent children from his recently deceased mother, who had previously adopted them from a cousin who went to prison. With children a lot of things could happen, Reggie thought, and he wanted his to have "a home they could always come back to."

In the wake of the financial crisis traditional mortgages had become scarce in Detroit. Because new regulations made the mortgages less profitable, mortgage lenders had stopped writing mortgages on houses under $50,000. At other levels of the housing market appraisers often refused to enter Detroit's neighborhoods to conduct inspections, and few area sales provided comparable market prices for them to evaluate. In 2013 when Reggie began looking for a house, mortgages supported the acquisition of only about 530 Detroit properties. Those properties fell primarily within just four of the city's 46 zip codes. The same year banks rejected more than 80 percent of applications for home improvement loans.

Properties in Reggie's price range sold for cash, which he did not have much of, but he had heard about a way to avoid coming up with all the money up front. Land contracts enabled a rent-to-own-style arrangement in which a potential homebuyer made a down payment to a seller, moved in, then paid off the balance of the purchase price in monthly cash installments. The buyer assumed responsibility for all repairs, even during the interim period before the final payment when the buyer did not own the property. If the buyer defaulted on a payment, the seller could terminate the contract without following formal foreclosure or court eviction processes and keep all the payments that the buyer previously made. Land contracts began filling the lending gap at the bottom end of the market, and nonprofits used them in low-income home-ownership programs.

Reggie seemed to care more about becoming a home-owner than about the risks of the arrangement. His cousin introduced him to a woman called Courtney Taylor, who had bought six foreclosed properties at auction, bidding under an alias. An African American woman from the suburbs, she appeared in Reggie's worldview to live comfortably. She acted respectfully, was business-oriented, and joked and laughed "like nothing was an issue." When she offered him one of her houses on a land contract for $18,000, he felt that he could trust her.

The house perched at the head of a row of small, gray, asbestos-shingled houses that stretched down the block. A boxwood shrub nearly swallowed the small front of the house, and the gutter sunk a little toward the middle. Iron latticing crossed the two front windows. A few blocks to the west lay Rouge Park and to the east a public playground, both of them closed because of Mayor Bing's attempt to thwart emergency management.

Reggie had spent all his life in this same corner of Detroit, in the far west of the city, and even without seeing inside the house he knew that he wanted it. He figured the deal offered him his best opportunity to become a homeowner, and he assumed the price of the house was "low" because the house needed a lot of cosmetic work. He knew how to renovate houses and had a large extended family willing to help him. Without negotiating, he signed a contract with Taylor in front of the house.

A few weeks later Reggie received the keys. Impatient to begin working on the house, he drove straight over dressed in work boots and jeans. Turning the key with an ample fist the color of a New York brownstone, he eagerly opened the front door. Then he saw there was nothing there: The house had no pipes, no hot water tank, no furnace, no toilet, and no sinks. Dark paint patched stains and rot from leaks in the roof. He bounded clumsily down to the cellar. With his bare hands, he tore off the plywood that covered the basement walls. Underneath the wood he found rows of staggered bricks that made it look like the whole house had shifted to the left.

* * *

Over the following months as Reggie worked on the house, Courtney Taylor came in person to collect his installment payments. She indicated neither shame nor surprise at the house's condition. Reggie did not know that she had bought it for $2,100. Ever polite, he thanked her and called her "ma'am," his round cheeks dimpling, even as he struggled. He fought to replace all the old carpet because the padding had melted into the floor. He got lucky and found a used furnace. He shorted bills and did without, but he could not afford to fix the cracked foundation or replace the roof. When it rained the basement leaked, and condensation appeared on the walls in several rooms of the house.

Across the country speculators who made bulk purchases of mortgage-foreclosed properties began using land contracts like the one Reggie signed to offload the unprofitable properties from their portfolios onto unsophisticated buyers, often in minority communities. Properties left vacant and scrapped and properties in neighborhoods with low rents or scarce resale prospects did not offer good long-term investments, and the speculators turned to land contracts to liquidate their holdings and avoid the regulations that would have applied to a traditional sale or rental arrangement. Mortgage lenders would have had to disclose the quality of the properties. Landlords would have had to maintain the properties and return deposits when tenants left.

The speculators targeted land contracts to populations similar to those who fell victim to subprime mortgages. Both instruments used the guise of helping low-income families who could not qualify for traditional mortgages attain homeownership. In the case of land contracts, homeownership meant poor-quality houses without traditional consumer protections. The families who bought the properties lacked access to loans to finance the repairs that most of the properties needed, which made it likely for necessary expenditures to lead them to default on the contracts and lose their homes.

Caught up in making the house livable for his newly larger family, Reggie never confirmed that Courtney Taylor was paying the property taxes on the house. Most states, including Michigan, did not require land contracts to be recorded, but few contracts seemed to end in ownership. By February 2016 at least 300 properties of a primary participant in the market for land contracts, a Dallas-based asset management firm, had entered foreclosure in Detroit for nonpayment of property taxes. The firm had purchased more than 6,700 mortgage-foreclosed, single-family properties from the government-sponsored housing lender Fannie Mae at an average price of $8,000 and then resold the properties on land contracts.

By that time Reggie had finished making his house comfortable, and he and his family had grown to love living in it. The living room had neatly painted mauve walls, a brown nubby carpet, lots of framed family photographs, leather sofas with woven pillows, and humming radiators. Reggie prepared giant lasagnas in the kitchen and hosted extended family on the lawn. After he had paid Courtney Taylor in person at the house for months, she suddenly directed him to send money orders to a post office box. He wondered about the changes but decided not to ask questions. He did not want to threaten the homeownership nearly within his reach.

3

Census

SUMMER 2013

Out in Detroit's Brightmoor neighborhood, Cindy rocked in a swing on her front porch surrounded by numerous cats. Summer 2013 brought warmer and warmer weather to Detroit and rumors that the emergency manager would slash public pensions, but Cindy appeared to have had only vague concern for the emergency manager's activities. That evening she could hear a few cicadas buzzing in the brush, but hardly any other noise, until the crack of a car backfiring in the distance broke the silence. As the sun fell below the tree line the worry lines in her face softened in the gentler light. A trickle of neighbors walked by and greeted her by name, interrupting the stillness that had returned. She waved in response, and the motion flicked her long braid across her back. She moved the braid back into place with fingers stacked with metal rings, maneuvering the hair around her long, carefully trimmed fingernails. One neighbor joked that Cindy and her husband, both white, had become honorary African Americans after staying in the neighborhood so long. From her porch she laughed a raspy smoker's laugh. Then she resumed stroking one of the cats amid her hanging plants and tidy litterboxes.

Cindy's grandparents had moved from Arkansas into Detroit's Brightmoor neighborhood in the 1940s for work constructing the bridge to Canada. Brightmoor nestled into the far northwest recess of a city that sprawled across more than 140 square miles. In the 1920s Henry Ford financed inexpensive housing on open land in Brightmoor, and many of his white workers who moved from Appalachia found homes there. The neighborhood became a place for working-class white families to live modestly but comfortably. Growing up a few blocks from her grandparents at her mother's house, Cindy witnessed the effects on the neighborhood of two momentous events: the 1967 riot, called an uprising by those who viewed it as a backlash against racism, and the changes to school busing that occurred in the 1970s.

By the "Long Hot Summer of 1967," racial tensions in Detroit and in other American cities boiled over. In Detroit the African American share of the population had climbed to about 40 percent, yet lower-income African Americans still crowded into subdivided segregated housing, and they found few jobs as manufacturing continued to leave the city. The mostly white police department became notorious for racial profiling and brutality. When the police raided a speakeasy and arrested more than 80 African Americans celebrating the return of their friends from the Vietnam War, rumors spread that the police had used excessive force. As the police loaded the celebrants into paddy wagons an onlooker threw a bottle into the rear window of a police car. Five days of violence ensued. In the time it took for National Guard and federal troops to restore order, more than 7,000 people had been arrested, more than 40 people died, about 1,000 more sustained injuries, and more than 2,000 buildings were destroyed.

To assess the causes of the country's mounting urban riots and possible solutions President Johnson appointed a review board that became known as the Kerner Commission. Seven months after the events in Detroit the commission issued a thick report that stated, "Our nation is moving toward two societies, one black, one white—separate and unequal." It blamed abuses by white police, high unemployment, limited housing, and poor educational opportunities and interpreted the uprisings as an expression of African Americans' desire for "fuller participation in the social order and the material benefits enjoyed by the majority of American citizens." It found the riot participants "anxious to obtain a place for themselves in [the American system]."

Instead of increased integration, however, over the following years white flight from Detroit accelerated sharply, pulling wealth from the city and decimating the population. As fewer and fewer white residents stayed, in 1973 the remaining residents elected the city's first African American mayor, Coleman Young, and the flight then accelerated to an exodus. The city became a majority African American city and acquired a reputation as a dystopia, which left the school system a racial battleground.

While the riots had had a significant impact on the city, Cindy thought that busing had an even larger one. It did on her. In 1970 Michigan's governor signed a bill to block Detroit officials' modest efforts to integrate the local school system, which by then had fewer than 30 percent white students. The state legislation authorized Detroit schoolchildren to transfer at will outside their neighborhood schools, intensifying the segregation of the white students into a handful of white schools. A seeming return to "separate but equal," the situation in the city garnered national attention, and the National Association for the Advancement of Colored People sued. The local branch of the NAACP, the largest branch in the organization, had positioned itself at the front lines of the fight for equal opportunities locally and nationally. Detroit no longer had enough white children to fully integrate its schools, so the court imposed a regional plan for school integration. Busing would transfer city students to the suburbs and vice versa. In protest white families took to the streets, and the Ku Klux Klan torched suburban school buses. The Supreme Court agreed to review the case. The court found that absent evidence of a deliberate action to create the geographic segregation that underlay the regional segregation in the schools, the court had to overturn the plan for regional busing. Because the court could identify deliberate actions by city officials to increase segregation within the city's school system, city officials had to desegregate its schools. The findings prompted many of the last remaining white families to flee the city to insulate their children from busing that ended at the city limits. Prior to the ruling Cindy's school had only three African American children in the whole student body. Overnight her closest friend, Shana Steinman, and all but eight other white children in her class left. Cindy's mother, on welfare, could not afford to move, so she encouraged Cindy to drop out of school. From sixth grade on Cindy stayed inside her house during school hours. She attended roll call every 14 days to thwart truancy officers.

Since then Cindy mostly remained in Brightmoor as a rare white resident of the neighborhood. She left a few times but always came home, drawn back to the neighborhood as if it were a magnet.

* * *

In the decades after busing began, Cindy's front porch provided a front-row seat to Brightmoor's unceasing emptying. Throughout the 1980s and 1990s crime associated with crack cocaine ravaged the neighborhood. One by one robberies caused businesses to close, and in 1999 a bankrupt company abandoned 500 dilapidated neighborhood properties it owned.

At one point over the following years Cindy's block had only one other occupied house. Outside investors bought up large swaths of the neighborhood, mostly empty lots. Raccoons threatened neighborhood children, and Cindy described her environment as "overgrowed."

Smoking cigarettes, her hair getting longer and grayer until it reached her waist and had no more brown left in it, Cindy watched as neighbors lost their homes to mortgage foreclosure and scrappers arrived as soon as the U-Haul trucks left. One scrapper held up everything he took from the house across the street for her to see: a furnace, a hot water tank, metal pipes, ceiling fans, light switches, and electrical outlets. When he saw her phone the police he teased her by moving more slowly as he placed the stolen items in his truck. He rolled down the window of the truck when he left and waved goodbye. Someone else used a hatchet to chop down the back door of the house on the corner, where an older lady had defaulted on a reverse mortgage. Cindy's next-door neighbor woke to find her car on blocks in her driveway. Someone had stolen the tires overnight, and the neighbor immediately decamped to a trailer in the suburbs. The ringleader of a group of scrappers Cindy knew told her that if she did not "get someone" into the now-empty house, the scrappers would "have it that night." So Cindy invited her brother, his girlfriend, and their two children to squat there instead. They had been living in their car. By 2009 she counted 21 vacant houses within a block of her own.

Distant and wholly disconnected from the more central locations of revitalization that had started to emerge in Detroit, the neighborhood continued to revert to a natural landscape. Untamed prairies were taking root where houses had disappeared. The abundant empty space attracted illegal dumping, and people pulled up in vehicles full of garbage.

One evening Cindy's former neighbor who moved to the trailer drove by and stopped in front of Cindy's house. Cindy and some of her 14 cats sat on the porch. Her husband, Dick, was at work, cleaning operating theaters at a Midtown hospital on the night shift.

"What's going on with my house?" the neighbor asked Cindy out the car window.

"I don't know."

"Do they own it?"

"I don't know."

"It breaks my heart every time I drive through here and see the place."

"Then quit driving through. You know what it is."

"Can you at least keep my Japanese maple trimmed?"

Cindy never had her neighbor's choice of an escape from the neighborhood. No one would buy Cindy's house, and even if someone did, the house would not sell for enough to cover the cost of a place to live anywhere else. She did not know which of them had it better, herself in staying to take care of trees or her neighbor in leaving.

* * *

July 4, 2013, dawned in humid drizzle. The fireworks had already happened; the festivities had ended. To save money the city shared the holiday and its costs with Windsor, Canada, and timed the fireworks closer to Canada Day. Soon afterward Governor Snyder ruled out a state bailout of Detroit.

President Obama intimated that a federal bailout would be politically unfeasible. New rumors began to spread about the liquidation of the city's art collection to raise money.

On a Thursday morning so hot the heat shimmered off the pavement, Joe sat at a table at J's Café on Detroit's west side, ensconced in a turquoise pleather booth. Even by Detroit standards J's was a seedy place. A squat, single-story building on a deserted six-lane road, it looked from a distance like a liquor store with a drive-through window.

In his early 50s, with buzz-cut hair and ever-present stubble on his cheeks, Joe bore the rugged look of someone who spent time outdoors. He still had the lean physique and angular jaw of the Marine he once had been. He ordered coffee and poached eggs, which arrived a minute later with grits and toast. As a jukebox in the corner played R&B hits and regulars at the counter joshed each other about their city, Joe settled into his breakfast. He was the only white person in the restaurant.

After a lifetime spent primarily in New Jersey, Joe had grown fed up with living there and visited various cities he thought might have more open space. Detroit felt like the only one he could tolerate. He liked the fact that half the population had abandoned the city, even though the population loss reduced tax revenues and consigned vast areas to derelict housing and emptiness. He appreciated the relative freedom from rules and regulations the city seemed to offer. With two divorces under his belt, he also welcomed the city's affordability. He sold the tree business he owned in New Jersey and moved, bringing with him just one truck and chipper. He felt a sense of possibility that something good might happen for him in Detroit.

Drinking coffee constantly, he spoke at a rapid clip to anyone who would listen. In the interstices he fixed his interlocutors with a piercing blue-eyed stare. He'd developed that expression growing up as the son of a New York City philosophy professor. When he felt passionate, which he generally did, he repeated words and phrases for emphasis in statements like "You're going to hear nothing but community partner over and over and over" and "I don't know what the object is, I have no idea what the object is, I have never heard a stated object," and labeled various people "crooks."

Details of Detroit's finances that the emergency manager, Kevyn Orr, was unearthing evidenced plenty of "crooks" but did not faze Joe. Despite decades of manufacturing decline and population loss, in 2002 Detroit had a balanced budget and its pension funds reported a surplus. Subsequent cuts to state aid and losses in pension investments, however, made it difficult for the city to make its required annual payment to the pension funds. To meet the city's obligations Mayor Kwame Kilpatrick turned to Wall Street. He won awards for the resulting off-balance-sheet deals that generated $1.44 billion for the city. Because the interest rate at which the city would have to pay back the money could fluctuate, he also bought interest rate insurance, known as swaps, to lock in a fixed interest rate. Joe read about it in *The New York Times*.

The financial institutions that sold the insurance may have had legal duties they failed to fulfill to ensure that the city and the public understood the risks of the arrangements. It's possible they should have even refused to enter the transactions. Instead the arrangements seemed to cost the city $14 million more than alternatives. The city ultimately settled with the institutions and did not litigate the issue. In 2008 the stock market crashed, reducing the pension fund balance by about a billion dollars, a loss that continued to compound even after the stock market eventually recovered. Separately, Kilpatrick resigned amid criminal convictions for corruption and went to prison. As the financial crisis proceeded, decimating income and property tax revenues, interest rates fell but the city remained locked into a higher interest rate. While the federal government was bailing out General Motors and Chrysler, Detroit's deteriorating financial position violated the terms of the city's agreements with the financial institutions and triggered penalty payments of several hundred million dollars. To avoid the payments city officials pledged the city's gambling tax revenues as collateral. In the event of another default, the institutions could seize those revenues. Meanwhile cuts to state aid continued. In 2012 a credit rating agency lowered its assessment of municipal debt nationwide. The credit downgrade and Michigan's appointment of the emergency manager eventually triggered a $350 million penalty payment from Detroit to the two financial institutions. In part to renegotiate that and other payments related to the deals, Orr decided to force the city into bankruptcy.

In July 2013, after fewer than four months in emergency management, Orr filed for bankruptcy for Detroit, stating that the city had become unable to pay the money it owed its creditors. Governor Snyder authorized his decision; no mayoral or City Council approval was needed. When Orr announced the bankruptcy he emphasized problems in the city's past governance, alluding to insufficient economic diversification to withstand the contraction of the auto industry, discrimination in the housing market, tensions between the city and the state, and political corruption, among other difficulties. He characterized the bankruptcy as six decades in the making and pointed to the city's failing services. Snyder said the bankruptcy was "about accountable government."

Legal squabbling began immediately. A state court found the bankruptcy unconstitutional because of state pension protections. The protests that began against emergency management resumed, with city workers, retirees, bondholders, and other creditors accusing the emergency manager of failing to negotiate to avert the bankruptcy. Firefighters chanted, "Help us help you," as they marched through the streets of Detroit.

Joe, meanwhile, was enjoying the long history of good things that had developed in the city, including its music and art. As the days grew longer and the nights stayed warm and hazy, he paid $3 covers at local jazz clubs to hear bass players who had played with Aretha Franklin. He sat in the audience among ladies who wore hats and dressed like they were attending church. He did not dress that way and typically kept his wool beanie on at all times. As a one-beer kind of guy, he delighted in service so bad he didn't even have to drink anything. One night at the Detroit Institute of Arts he met a Frenchman who worked as a docent and spoke with him in the fluent French he had learned from his mother in New York. "Detroit will get under your skin," the man told him. The man had visited the city 25 years earlier and never left.

Joe found Detroit physically one of the ugliest places he had ever seen, with highways slicing up the city, but he could also see beauty in it. The problems that plagued the city angered him, but he viewed the breakdown of government services that he perceived as mostly positive. So many people had "dropped away from the process" that he felt he could have an impact and also be left alone. "In the vacuum that developed, you have a chance to make something good happen," he said. He set about trying to buy a house in the city, and he invited his new wife and 20-something daughter to join him there.

* * *

After months phoning brokers in his New Jersey accent and receiving no responses, Joe learned that Detroit's depressed property values made broker commissions so low that few brokers bothered showing houses. He also could not qualify for a mortgage, even though he had strong credit. So he drove the length of the city, his large hands draped lazily around the steering wheel of his truck, scanning for sale signs but finding few of them. Then he heard that most people did not list their properties. Instead they sold them informally, often to people who posted hand-lettered signs that said "We Pay Cash for Houses." Finally he found an online listing for a house in the Bagley neighborhood from someone who bought houses that way, and offered $30,000 in cash. Joe closed on the house knowing that it had major problems, but he felt relieved to have found it.

When Joe moved in he found relatives of the previous owner camped in the house's attic. The two men appeared "zonked on pills," but they struck Joe as nice guys, and he let them stay a few weeks. Then he helped them move to a squat down the street. A few months later he ran into one of them and, chatting at length as he typically did, he asked how they knew each other. The man reminded him that Joe had bought his house.

As the weeks stretched on Joe received collection notices for a $600 electric bill and other delinquent payments. He learned that in the mid-1970s a Jewish family had moved out of the house and an African American family had moved in. After the new owners died, no one maintained it. Over the following decade a leak rotted the back of the house, the kitchen developed black mold, the front steps fell off, and the garage started falling down. Joe estimated the house needed between $30,000 and $50,000 in renovations. But it had electricity and heat of sorts, and all the windows had at least something in them. He approached his time in Detroit as an adventure.

In spite of the condition of houses like his, the Bagley neighborhood was attracting attention from local development agencies and philanthropic institutions. Bagley's Tudor and Colonial houses mimicked the mansions of the nearby University District, with brick constructions and historic details, though in Bagley the houses looked less grand and many suffered neglect. But Bagley still had a high population density, high owner-occupancy rate, and low vacancy rate unusual for Detroit.

Over the previous decade Detroit lost a quarter of its residents. National news headlines like "Detroit Is Basically Broke" and "Detroit Home to Three Most Violent Areas in America," along with the city's place at the top of *Forbes*'s list of "Most Miserable Cities," did not entice many newcomers. Joe was swimming against the tide.

Relatively dense neighborhoods like his showed signs of blight, with some vacant and foreclosed properties. Other neighborhoods, like Cindy's, had lost most of their inhabitants and fallen into desolation. In most neighborhoods telephone wires crossed vacant lots and husks of houses that, like the cast-off clothes of a formerly fat man, had collapsed from neglect or arson. Retail strips hosted a Boost Mobile[†] here or a liquor store there, but mostly the strips had boarded windows. By 2010 the city's population had fallen from nearly 2 million to less than 800,000, and empty space checkered about a quarter of the city. That year Mayor Bing initiated a process to rethink land use in Detroit. To reflect the decreased population densities and to lower costs, he wanted to reduce the area in which the city provided services. "There is just too much land and too many expenses for us to continue to manage the city as we have in the past," he said.

Outside stronger neighborhoods like Joe's, Bing's words sparked rumors of forced relocations that echoed the urban

---

[†] More than 80 percent of customers with Boost Mobile cell phone plans have annual incomes below $75,000.

renewal projects of the 1940s and 1950s. Highway construction had destroyed vibrant African American communities and left residents with no place to live but housing projects. Crowds therefore thronged early community meetings to discuss Bing's land-use plans, outnumbering the available chairs at one meeting by 600 people. Breakout sessions devolved into shouting matches, and rather than discussing long-term goals, people demanded attention to short-term needs like neighborhood safety and the demolition of abandoned houses. Many of the attendees assumed that city officials had already decided how to utilize the city's vacant land and would close down neighborhoods by turning off utilities and bulldozing buildings.

* * *

Joe's African American neighbor insisted Joe must have come from a foreign country. She had never left Detroit, where everyone she knew looked like her and talked like her. A man who lived across the street had to explain that Joe was "American, just pale." The man often dumped the contents of his own garage on the street, the sidewalk, and the front lawn, but Joe could deal with him in the moments when the man was sober. Boys played pickup basketball on the street in front of Joe's house and pointed at Joe, saying, "He white, he white," reminding him that he did not fit in. Another neighbor introduced himself and gave Joe his phone number. A gospel vocalist, he became a close friend.

In the wake of Mayor Bing's planning meetings, charitable foundations provided resources to address residents' immediate demands and also support more ambitious urban planning, beyond what Detroit's planning department could accomplish on its own following budget cuts. Bing's initial effort to deal with abandoned property transformed into a new plan for the city dominated by data-based maps. In December 2012 a new steering committee released a 347-page strategic framework that found solutions to population loss in the city's landscape, with neighborhoods similar to where Joe lived contributing to future economic growth.

In most of the city, including Cindy's Brightmoor neighborhood, the framework offered ideas for repurposing vacant land. Potential uses included reforestation, rainwater retention ponds, solar panels, and food production. Zones the framework classified for "landscape," rather than "industrial" or "neighborhood," could transition into cemeteries and parks, green industry, or "innovation ecological" areas, areas without full services where over time the roads would deteriorate and the land would return to fields. The plan slated Reggie's neighborhood for a park.

American cities generally had between 35 and 75 jobs for every 100 residents; Detroit had just 26. The authors of the framework assumed that boosting employment in concentrated areas would generate living wages for the largest number of residents and increase the city's tax base. The plan therefore prioritized investment in the most stable neighborhoods, like Joe's, and designated a small number of primary and secondary "core investment and employment corridors" for redevelopment, including the commercial area near his house. The area could "become the city's second key district for growth of creative firms," the framework said, by "attract[ing] new businesses or residents that may otherwise choose the suburbs."

The framework envisioned forests, farms, and lakes surrounding a small number of vibrant residential neighborhoods and commercial areas. It spurred a conversation of new ways to think about shrinking cities in the absence of growth over the longer term and the relative roles of under-population and poverty. Yet Detroit's population density, though considerably

lower than in past decades, still surpassed thriving cities like
Phoenix, Houston, and Dallas that seemed easily to fund full
services. Cindy and her neighbors balked at the prospect of
their homes potentially becoming a meadow.

Joe, meanwhile, returned to his truck and steered it through
the broad, flat streets of the city to a meeting about a closed
plant nursery he hoped to buy. *The New York Times* perched on
the front seat. He cruised past the former Jewish Community
Center, now city-owned, and he saw a house that belonged to a
pharmacist who lived on the East Coast. The man bought the
house on the Internet as an investment property and confided
to Joe that he expected Detroit to be an easier place to make
money. Joe seemed to know everyone in the neighborhood. Before long the few businesses that remained on its commercial
street came into view. A few fast-food chains operated amid
defunct family-owned restaurants. Old music venues such as
The Chessmate, where Joni Mitchell and Neil Young played
in the 1960s, had closed long before. Joe wondered why there
weren't more people like him moving to the city, though if it
became less empty, he wouldn't like it as much.

4

Detroit Hustles Harder

FALL 2013

Fifteen miles away in Brightmoor, Cindy's house backed onto so many vacant lots it felt pastoral. She was sitting on a gray couch in the main room of her 700-square-foot house drinking a cup of black coffee and catching up on her laptop computer. The room had sofas against two faraway facing walls and nothing in the middle. She had just returned home from a day spent cleaning houses an hour away in the suburbs and planned to spend the evening shampooing the turf-like maroon carpet tacked throughout the house to get rid of a mess from the cats.

Far from Brightmoor's quietude, at the downtown courthouse that morning eligibility hearings for Detroit's bankruptcy had begun. To enter bankruptcy cities had to have state authorization and fulfill other legal requirements. Immediately before the start of the hearings Detroit residents had three minutes each to air objections to the bankruptcy. Young, old, afraid, and angry, the residents pleaded with the bankruptcy judge to revert to the city's democratically elected leadership and spare municipal retirees from bearing the onus of the city's problems through court-mandated pension cuts.

Ironically, campaigns for a new elected leader were simultaneously underway. A former prosecutor and health care CEO called Mike Duggan was campaigning for mayor as the candidate most likely to earn the trust of state politicians and thereby return Detroit to local governance the fastest. Duggan had moved too late from the suburbs to the city to qualify for the ballot. As a write-in candidate in the Democratic primary he had just beat another write-in candidate called Mike Dugeon, the barber of Duggan's Republican opponent in the general election.

An attorney representing the city closed the session at the bankruptcy court, stating "bankruptcy is never a good thing." Detroit's problems, however, were "enormously complex," he added.

At home on her couch, Cindy tapped her long nails against her computer keyboard to reach Brightmoor's Facebook page. There, people she disdainfully called white flighters, who long ago had moved to the suburbs, posted messages complaining about circumstances in Brightmoor. In response someone else posted about the accomplishments of a neighborhood group called Neighbors Building Brightmoor, which Cindy had not heard of. She immediately navigated to the organization's Facebook page and scrolled through photographs of gardens and art installations that the organization had built. In her free time she did knitting and crafts and appreciated the beauty, rare for the neighborhood, in the photographs. She felt grateful that this small group of committed neighbors were independently trying to find new uses for vacant land. They had claimed 21 blocks of the neighborhood, called them the Brightmoor Farmway, and filled them with garden plots, greenhouses, and pocket parks. Children cultivated vegetables there and sold them at farmers' markets.

Cindy did not have the resources to do much for the neighborhood on her own. She and her husband did not have homeowners' insurance, and they owed money on repairs from a recent house fire. Cindy got only part-time hours cleaning the suburban houses, and every time she paid off her credit card she had to use the card again to buy groceries and gas. She had reached her mid-50s without savings or children to help her out. It struck her that the group's efforts could help make her own bad situation more bearable. She typed a message to the organization's president and bluntly asked for help with her block.

The president, the Dutch wife of a local university professor, responded quickly. She explained that the ample green space and large number of children attracted her and her husband to Brightmoor. She felt she could leverage them to improve life there, in spite of the emptiness and distance from Detroit's remaining jobs. She moved to the neighborhood in 2006 and founded Neighbors Building Brightmoor with a lifelong Brightmoor resident. The president invited Cindy to attend the organization's next monthly meeting.

Cindy attended, and she stood out among the group's members. Mostly white, they had moved to the neighborhood within the last few years from around the country in order to pursue urban farming. None of the Neighbors Building Brightmoor members had met a white Detroiter, like Cindy, who had stayed in the neighborhood through the disruptions of earlier decades. Cindy was also older than the group's members and dressed more conservatively in baggy khakis and a tee shirt, her long hair parted in the middle and tied back in a ponytail. The members told her about the attention the organization was attracting from nearby universities and local philanthropies. University students helped with art projects, a formerly abandoned house had become a community bulletin board, another house had turned into a meeting point for open jam sessions, and empty lots had transitioned into children's play spaces. Glow-in-the-dark cocoon sculptures now illuminated a butterfly garden at night, and a "talking fence" depicted the stories that neighborhood children had gathered from people in their community.

Following the meeting the group's members spent three months helping Cindy clear empty lots near her house and trim back foliage from the surrounding sidewalks. Meanwhile, in November Mike Duggan became the first white mayor of Detroit since the early 1970s. Duggan outraised his opponent, the county sheriff, four to one, through large donations from the business community. The emergency manager nevertheless still held all the power to govern the city. A month after the election the bankruptcy judge found Detroit eligible for bankruptcy and municipal pensions vulnerable to changes. As the bankruptcy commenced in earnest Cindy asked to become the Brightmoor group's volunteer coordinator.

Long ago Cindy had given up faith in any "cavalry coming," and she didn't expect the bankruptcy to do anything helpful for Brightmoor. As the emergency manager, Kevyn Orr, and sitting judges whom the bankruptcy judge appointed as mediators negotiated with financial creditors and pensioners and explored the possibility of regionalizing Detroit's water system, Cindy organized volunteer groups from across the country. Pointing with her nicotine-stained fingers, she directed local college students and suburban church groups to make tires that dumpers left in the street into swings, and swings appeared around the neighborhood. One local boy liked to twist up the swings' ropes and then let go. Another liked to lie spread-eagled while his friends spun him around. Neighbors began hearing laughter from formerly empty spaces. Cindy's volunteers also boarded up vacant houses. She brusquely instructed the volunteers first to gather trash from the streets and neighborhood lots and load it into the houses' back doors, down the stairwells, and up into the kitchens, and then nail the boards across the windows and doors. The trash would block the path of any scrappers who penetrated the barriers. She also recruited neighborhood children to paint art on the boards. Other Neighbors Building Brightmoor members realized that fewer scrappers broke in if they had to ruin someone's kid sister's art. Suns and palm trees and inspirational quotes bloomed throughout the neighborhood on the boards that protected empty houses.

At the bankruptcy court Kevyn Orr spoke of setting aside funds to invest in the city's recovery; Cindy assumed Brightmoor wouldn't qualify. But if the creditors trying to prevent the city from spending money on new streetlights lost their fight, the neighborhood might finally get working streetlights. Orr proposed operationalizing a plan to replace the city streetlights that Mayor Bing had developed prior to the bankruptcy. Bing suggested creating a new public lighting authority, separate from the city, that could issue bonds to finance the project free from the taint of the city's poor credit ratings. Over the following 30 years local utility tax revenues would repay the money that the authority borrowed. The creditors, however, argued that the plan wasted money that the city should be paying them. The city, they argued, should have been lowering costs by reducing services to lower-density neighborhoods.[†]

* * *

[†] The bankruptcy judge sided with the city, and the creditors turned to other battles with the possibility of lessening their losses on the money the city owed them.

On a Monday evening in January 2014, with snow smearing the streets like dirty icing, the St. Christine soup kitchen glowed from within against the early darkness. Inside Cindy sat under fluorescent lights at a circular table. Her sister Suzy sat beside her staring into the middle distance. She had been staying at Cindy's house recovering from something, and together they had come to the soup kitchen for another monthly meeting of Neighbors Building Brightmoor. The soup kitchen was closed, and from the group members' potluck contributions they ate a selection of steamed homegrown kale, takeout pizza, and vegan meatballs. They talked mostly to each other.

After several minutes in which a woman at the same table joked to the woman next to her about her family deeming her a traitor to capitalism, a German PhD student called the meeting to order. Visitors from a series of local food equity organizations introduced themselves, and after every introduction the 30 or so young, mostly white members clapped. To more applause members shared news about the neighborhood farmers' market, a free summer music camp, and free books available at a nearby church. A woman who wore a ring straight through her nose like a bull offered to make soap to raise money to clear tree limbs threatening power lines throughout the neighborhood. A man who arrived late on a bicycle asked if anyone had spare honeybees, and the group prepared to host 1,000 Methodist volunteers. No one talked about the fact that downtown the British auction house Christie's was appraising nearly 3,000 pieces from the collection of the Detroit Institute of Arts, and the fate of Diego Rivera's *Detroit Industry* murals, along with paintings like Van Gogh's *Self-Portrait with Straw Hat* and Rembrandt's *The Visitation*, hung in the balance.

Instead the conversation turned to whether such a thing as a good squatter existed. Cindy could pick a house and find a squatter in it, and she liked having the squatters around. In one house near where she lived a woman squatted with numerous children. Another squatter occupied the house with the barbecue grill. His brother squatted two doors down, and their sister squatted in the house with the wheelchair ramp. They all greeted Cindy when they walked by her house. People commented that the squatters kept the grass cut and their yards neat, unlike some of the investor-owned houses where the investors seemed interested only in collecting insurance checks. When the checks stopped and the houses had given all they could, the investors would leave the properties to foreclosure.

The conversation about good squatters impressed a man attending his first meeting. He worked for a community development organization that operated in the stronger neighborhoods of the city. He had recently moved to Brightmoor in part to avoid running into people he knew through his job. The meeting made him realize how long-term residents of the neighborhood lacked experience advocating for themselves. Grief plagued them, and it was hard for them not to remain fixated on the neighborhood as it used to look, their friends who moved away, and the stores where they used to be able to shop. City officials, meanwhile, left derelict city-owned properties to languish, and the neighborhood grew more verdant and wild.

Unlike those residents, and also unlike the roughly 32,400 city workers and retirees who risked pension cuts in the bankruptcy, newcomers to Brightmoor had their own vision of what the neighborhood could become. They mostly wanted to establish urban farms in the abundant vacant space the neighborhood provided. They were fighting to improve the neighborhood on their own in spite of the structural roots of poverty and disinvestment there. The group members tried to deter drug dealers and prostitutes, but they lacked authority to prevent dumping or deal with burnt-out buildings. They depended on neighbors willing to help maintain the farms and gardens on vacant lots, but the neighborhood had too many vacant lots to manage.

At the meeting a blond woman in her mid-30s called Emma announced that in order to experience Brightmoor's farming community, she wanted to find somewhere to squat. Cindy pounced. Her brother had just qualified for a housing program, and he and his family were moving from the house next door. If Cindy did not find someone else to live there, scrappers would destroy it.

On moving in, Emma immediately installed a wood-burning stove and began ripping out the old carpet, painting the walls, staining the floor, recruiting a roommate, and looping electric cables and hoses out the window to siphon utilities from Cindy's house. It struck Cindy as a lot of effort for a squat.

* * *

As Brightmoor residents considered new ways to convert vacant land into productive uses, Joe grew inspired by the entre-preneurialism bubbling up in more stable neighborhoods like his own. That morning he had done a small tree job in north-west Detroit, then met a local activist at a new combination coffee shop and art gallery. The newspapers scattered around the coffee shop headlined the bankruptcy judge's unexpected rejection of a series of settlements the city reached with the financial institutions involved in Mayor Kilpatrick's pension-funding scheme. The judge emphasized the likely illegality of the underlying transactions and the swaps that froze interest rates on them.

A world away from Wall Street, the coffee shop anchored a

desolate commercial strip on a five-lane road that cut through Grandmont-Rosedale, the neighborhood adjacent to Joe's. The grass grew long beside the road and the road had cracks and few cars, but behind it boulevards with traffic islands sported gracious brick houses where on warm days older ladies rocked on porch swings. The area had the feel of a small town.

In his usual open manner, hyper and chatty, Joe met some small business owners, including the owner of the coffee shop. A younger white woman from the suburbs, she had opened the shop just as Detroit entered bankruptcy. A mentor she found through a local business incubator helped her qualify for a foundation-funded pop-up program that enabled entrepreneurs to test their ideas in space leased for one month. The program launched in the densest neighborhoods outside the city's downtown core, which all lacked stores and restaurants, to show investors and landlords that small businesses could succeed in those neighborhoods. The owner of the coffee shop raised money to buy an espresso machine at an event where people donated $5 to eat soup and hear business presentations. To earn enough money to open the shop more permanently she waited tables. Joe's favorite bakery in his neighborhood, the only bakery, had also opened prior to the bankruptcy using the same pop-up program. During frequent coffee runs he got to know its owner, too. A native Detroiter, she held an MBA from the University of Michigan and won spots in local training programs for aspiring entrepreneurs. Not far away a wealthy 30-something Canadian was trying to manufacture bicycles. While running unsuccessfully for Calgary's City Council, he grew passionate about urban issues and the potential for bikes to contribute to revitalization. Detroit offered cheap real estate, access to manufacturing infrastructure, and abundant attention from the national media. He liquidated property and businesses he owned in Canada to free up cash to start a bike company in Detroit. He had been investing since he was nine years old.

Joe lacked access to comparable resources, but he also harbored dreams of opening his own business. He had a lot of ideas, but in a sea of vacant storefronts he could not find an available commercial space. The owner of the old nursery, long closed, did not want to sell the property. Then one day from his truck Joe spotted an actual for-sale sign. All the commercial spaces within the area sat empty, though the property lay equidistant from a college and a university, just five blocks from each.

A nearby storefront still had a sign for "Christell's Side Door Ladies Fashions" in 60s-style cursive. Another had its brick facade painted to say "Drink Vernon's Ginger Ale, Mellowed 4 Years in Wood." Joe contacted the property management company listed on the sale sign. The staff offered him 22,000 square feet of single-story connected buildings, the color of spoiled milk, spanning the entire block. The management company would finance the sale at an inflated interest rate of more than 7 percent.

As his negotiations for the space progressed it became clear that he had few other options for acquiring the buildings. Despite impeccable credit he could not obtain a standard loan for property that appeared nearly destroyed. He mailed the company his social security number, a copy of his driver's license, and $40,000 in cash. Within 72 hours the staff issued him a land contract similar to the one Reggie used to buy a house. If Joe defaulted on the contract the management company had the right to reclaim the buildings and keep the down payment and all Joe's installment payments. Joe began sending monthly checks to a post office box made out to an LLC.

The terms of the land contract appeared daunting, and Joe never learned the identity of the seller, but he found inspiration in other local entrepreneurs and their new businesses. The arson and scrapping his buildings had suffered did not deter him: Most buildings in the area looked equally torn up. Those that weren't, he couldn't afford. "What can you do, if you can't get a loan?" he said, scratching his stubbly cheek. "It's a catch, but anyway the space costs so much less than back in Jersey." It was not clear, though, how he would bring the buildings up to code or raise money to open a business in them.

* * *

Lola also dreamt of work that amounted to more than just a check. It was evening in spring 2014, and the young single mother was leaving work in the rain. The sky that night, the color of slate, contrasted with the green grass edging the suburban office park. She curved her car past flooded golf courses and soccer fields, and before long the thick trees of the suburbs yielded to the highway. She drove south through snarled traffic, rain pounding against her windshield, then continued east. She glided past suburban ranch houses until finally she crossed Telegraph Road, which marked the western border between the suburbs and Detroit. Abruptly, closed storefronts and vacant land flanked the highway and rendered the landscape of the suburbs a distant memory. She distracted herself chatting with friends through her headset, even as she swerved her car to avoid the biggest puddles. With scant public transportation and far-flung jobs, in the city a car counted as a valuable commodity.

Detroit had spent four months in bankruptcy. The city had just secured settlements on Mayor Kilpatrick's swaps and a multi-million-dollar loan, backed by the city's income tax revenues, to pay for services like police and firemen. By rejecting the first two swaps settlements the emergency manager, Kevyn Orr, presented, the bankruptcy judge saved the city about $200 million. Some observers questioned why the city would pay any settlement money on the swaps, given their potential illegality. The judge maintained that a lawsuit to invalidate the original deals would slow progress in the bankruptcy and risk countersuits.

Lola could spare little energy for these faraway machinations. As usual, she had begun her day early. She awakened her daughter before the sun rose, dropped her off at elementary school, and then drove an hour to her job fielding phone calls about air-conditioning systems. Though formerly she worked as a manager at a different call center, now she worked as an entry-level agent. She missed the old company, which she felt helped her become a leader, and had trouble accepting her lowered status.

Short and busty, she had a wide forehead that made her face look luminous. Most days she wore hoop earrings the diameter of a grapefruit and a heart-shaped rhinestone ring on her pinky finger, a gift from the grandmother of her ex-boyfriend, and she kept her keys on a cord around her neck. She enjoyed the occasional cigar, and she liked her fingernails sparkly. She talked quickly and abundantly to everyone she met, laughing a lot and telling jokes as if she had known them forever. Though she confided sad moments easily and articulately, she rarely seemed to stay unhappy long.

The job, though, made her unhappy every morning when she arrived. "They have managers, they don't even have leaders," she told her friends. To get herself from the parking lot to the office door each day she repeated to herself, "It's a check, it's a check, it's a check."

* * *

Lola's ambition exceeded her job. She wished she could quit to start a restaurant, but she thought starting a business would leave her out on the streets, begging for change. To avoid that she tried to settle for driving 80 miles every weekday between her home on the east side of Detroit and the suburban office park that housed the call center.

On that rainy day, an hour after leaving work she arrived home to collect her daughter from her grandfather. From there the three of them continued to Lola's sister's house, six blocks from where Lola lived, to celebrate the birthday of Lola's younger brother.

As a child Lola lived with her grandparents, parents, and siblings, "like a big old Italian family," at her grandfather's house a few blocks from where she lived now. Her grandfather retired from a grocery store after never missing a day of work in 40 years other than when he had cancer. Her mother owned a hair salon. Lola's mother did the hair of all Lola's school-teachers, and when she turned 11 Lola started washing hair at the salon for tips. She practiced on her dolls and now rarely left the house without her own hair neatly flipped under and her fingernails done.

Her mother never attended college, and she pressured Lola to achieve more. Lola tested into all three magnet high schools in Detroit and chose to attend the one that offered an international business program. She enrolled in three foreign languages and looked up to teachers who, like her mother, pushed her to work hard. Lola liked French, disliked Mandarin, and decided early that she preferred graduating to trying to become popular. In the spring of her senior year, fat envelopes arrived in her grandfather's mailbox accepting her to college at the University of Tennessee and Tennessee State University. Lola's mother, however, discouraged her from leaving Detroit. She told Lola that Tennessee imposed a curfew and jailed people who stayed out too late.

Rather than leave Michigan Lola entered a business management program at a small private college in Flint. Between classes she interned at a faith-based financial services organization. Four years later she received her diploma holding her nine-day-old baby. The baby's father did not want Lola to leave him, but he had not finished college, and Flint seemed to Lola "worse than Detroit." Shortly after she graduated she told him she was going to the store, and her best friend and her friend's godfather bundled her and the baby into their car and drove them to Detroit.

Back in Detroit, Lola and her two-month-old daughter moved in with Lola's mother, and Lola emailed her boss from the Flint internship to ask for help. Lola got a job in the Detroit office of the same organization and dressed for work in bulky pantsuits. Then the organization lost its funding and shut down.

* * *

A cousin who worked at a call center in the suburbs told Lola about a job at the company and encouraged her to apply for it. The company hired her into a contract position selling cell phones, but after a few months the department also closed. She transitioned to another department and quickly blossomed. The job drew on her talents for friendliness and confidence. She became a salaried employee, then got promoted twice and became a team leader in charge of 20 agents. Team leadership, she believed, enabled her to "showcase her talent" in a way that she never previously experienced. Then the company announced that it planned to transfer its operations out of Michigan to save money. Nearly 400 employees at the call center lost their jobs, though the company kept all the workers at its call center in Bangalore, India.

With a child to support and no child support, Lola panicked. Soon after her last day with the company she woke up unable to bear the pain in her side and assumed she suffered from stress. Normally she got tattoos to relieve stress. Inked in various places on her curvy body, she had half a puzzle of a heart, divided between her and her best friend from college; her daughter's name; and the phrase "what the mind can't remember, the heart will never forget," in honor of her grandmother who suffered from Alzheimer's disease. But the pain wasn't stress. She needed an emergency appendectomy and she no longer had health insurance. She went deeper into debt.

As she was recovering from surgery a former coworker from the call center told her about another call center with a job opening. When she felt well enough she interviewed, and the company hired her to work on a campaign for an air-conditioner business. She started again as a temp-to-work hire.

She learned the intricacies of heating and cooling systems and the company eventually made her a permanent employee. The new company still did not offer her health insurance; she understood that she needed to wait until the open enrollment period the following January, though starting a new job generally qualified people to enroll in their employers' insurance plans. Again without insurance, she returned to the hospital in pain. This time she had complications related to an abscess. Her debt mounted.

Lola did not know how she would pay her school loans, car loan, hospital bills, and the cost of a scoliosis brace for her daughter. She considered declaring bankruptcy but then decided against it. When she worked at the first call center she evaluated employment applications and ran credit checks on potential hires, and she knew the company viewed personal bankruptcy as a desperation move. She did not want a potential employer to review her credit and think, "What she do?" Instead she resolved to cut coupons and keep a penny jar as her grandfather taught her. She earned extra money braiding hair on weekends at the hair salon her mother owned 10 blocks from Lola's house. Lola considered moving to Texas, where a friend from the first call center lived, but decided it might be hard to be African American there. Her daughter told her, "You know, Momma, you'll figure it out, you always do."

Meanwhile Lola and her daughter and grandfather arrived at her brother's birthday celebration. Her mother; her mother's second husband, a Jamaican whose accent no one in the family seemed to understand; her sister; her little brother; her nephew; and her brother's girlfriend crowded into the kitchen drinking tequila and eating tacos. Together they sang "Happy Birthday," adding "hey, hey, heys," until the song evolved into a rock song. They improvised and harmonized and eventually joined back together to extend the words "happy birthhhhhhh-hhhhddddddddddddaaaaaaaaaaaaaaaaaayyyyyyyyyy," and then they laughed and laughed.

The birthday made Lola think of her own year ahead. At 26, she wanted so badly to get back to the early promise her life had shown.

5

Bottom Line

SPRING 2014

Miles's house on Rosemary Street, his fourth, was coming along. He had been living in it for about three months and working on it for roughly five, devoting all the time and money he could spare from his paid construction work to fixing it up. After Detroit Progress LLC won the property in the 2012 tax foreclosure auction, the company seemed not to have done anything with the house. That day, the start of the Detroit Tigers' baseball season, a record number of fans flocked to the stadium downtown to watch the game, but Miles stayed home. Instead of sitting and cheering and eating hot dogs, he stretched his long, lean body this way and that to run new pipes from the top of the house down to the basement. Scrappers had stolen every cast iron pipe. Next he would start fixing the upstairs bathroom by first installing a toilet. He kept detailed notes in tall, penciled cursive inside a small notebook. He planned to insulate the entire upstairs, and he hoped that after he had completed all the work, the house might have some value.

Most Detroit neighborhoods did not have the energy, the throngs of people, typically associated with urban neighborhoods. The people who still lived in the city's neighborhoods seemed to keep to themselves. No one sat on stoops, no children played outside, no noises accumulated. Like most people, Miles stayed alert to any unusual activities on his block, and when a lone man approached his house, Miles noticed. Miles straightened his spine and gave the man a hard stare through his aviator-style eyeglasses. The man offered Miles a form for seeking a reassessment of the taxable value of his house. As Detroit's property tax revenues fell, the financial crisis depressed local property values. The city's assessors stopped reassessing properties unless a property owner asked them to. When the emergency manager, Kevyn Orr, evaluated the city's operations and finances, he saw that the city no longer even had any qualified assessors. Rather than complying with the state recommendation of one assessor for every 4,000 properties, the city paid for one outside contractor for every 15,000 properties.

As a consequence, the city taxed overvalued properties. In 2013 evidence of homes selling for less than $100 with assessed values of nearly $46,000 came to light. Michigan law mandated annual property reappraisals. It also required assessments to match market value and required consistent taxation of equivalent properties. Detroit had not complied with state law since the 1950s.

That year, 2014, the state tax commission finally intervened to mandate a citywide reappraisal. Soon afterward the ACLU filed suit, claiming foreclosures that stemmed from illegal tax assessments disproportionately affected African Americans. Detroit's lead attorney called the lawsuit "recklessly irresponsible." Without addressing the effects of the foreclosures on individual city residents and the city, he warned the suit risked ruining the city's ability to gain a stable financial footing, prolonging state oversight of city operations, and further jeopardizing city services.

Miles had not known he could request a reassessment. In careful handwriting he quickly completed the form and soon won a reduction of more than $3,000 from his house's assessed value. The new assessment, however, reflected a market value of more than $27,000, which still seemed higher than the house's actual worth. The new assessment also did not apply retroactively. Miles's property taxes going forward fell by a couple hundred dollars a year, but he still had to pay the full amount of the delinquent tax bills that predated his purchase of the house. City officials insisted that if no one contested a tax bill at the time the taxes fell due, then the tax bill correctly reflected the existing assessment. It did not matter that Miles did not own the house when the city assessed those taxes and that he did not have the ability to contest them.

Miles grew more still as he got angry, and his voice grew deeper and more resonant. The taxes infuriated him. From behind his goatee his expression grew colder and more unsettling, and his cadences rose and fell like those of a preacher. Instead of feeling happy to have secured the reassessment, he understood it to mean his house wasn't worth the money he struggled to pay to keep it. Worse still, he had learned the taxes from before he bought the house were inflated. "Now you're telling us, 'your house ain't worth nothing,' but you've still got to sit up here and pay taxes for value that's not there," he said. "You just got to pick up all these years of back taxes, interest, and all that other stuff that's on there. It was," he said, "the biggest robbery they ever did." He wished his devil would leave him alone.

* * *

Charles had no intention of paying the property tax bill he received. He had just walked in the front door of the old family house in Morningside after visiting his mailbox and finding the official-looking envelope. He wore a baseball cap cocked at an angle evocative of a rapper, a spring substitute for the black fur hat he wore in winter, and bounced a bit as he walked. At the copy shop he frequented in the suburbs he would make copies of the bill, then stash the copies around town with friends. In this way he disbursed several records for safekeeping. He did not know when he would lose his house, but he knew that the property taxes he ignored would eventually catch up with him.

The taxes on his house struck him as way too high, and he seemed to take a measure of pride in his decision to stop paying them. Relinquishing the house felt almost noble, and he flashed a rascal's grin when he discussed his act of defiance, confident that new options would present themselves. As proof of his luckiness, none of his children lived in the house with him any longer. His adolescent daughter Yvonne lived with her mother across town. His oldest son had moved to Florida, where he sold phones and video equipment after dropping out of college there. In a further stroke of luck, Charles appreciated that by leaving Detroit his son gained a better chance of living a longer life. Life expectancy in the city ranked below that of Russia and North Korea.

As Detroit's population dwindled, its property tax rate rose to the maximum level that Michigan law allowed. None of the houses on Charles's block had families in them anymore. In 2014, as the bankruptcy progressed, Detroit had the highest property tax rate of any large American city and more than double the average national rate. If Charles's house could have maintained the same value and moved one block south into the suburb of Grosse Pointe Park, his property taxes would have fallen more than 17 percent. If the house could have moved in the other direction, into the suburb of Royal Oak that bordered Detroit to the north, the taxes would have fallen 33 percent.

In spite of the high tax rate, Detroit's property values had tumbled so far that the city's tax revenues remained low. By 2014 properties there had recovered only a small fraction of their pre-crisis values, and since 2008 property tax revenues had fallen nearly 15 percent. The 50 biggest American cities all had lower property tax rates than Detroit and nevertheless took in substantially higher property tax revenues.

The maxed-out tax rates and insufficient tax revenues made it difficult for the city to function. Adding to the problem, not everyone there paid taxes. The city collected far less than officials projected, and services from garbage collection to infrastructure improvement suffered.

* * *

Charles felt the change in his neighborhood. The situation on his street seemed so terrible that he could no longer even describe it. Only 8 of the 17 houses on the block remained occupied. He had never met worse people than his few neighbors. They rented rather than owned, and he suspected, raising his eyebrows to underscore the seriousness of the affront, that they used Section 8 vouchers for subsidized housing. Investment companies owned several of the houses and did not take care of them. Charles wondered whether the story of his family in Detroit would end with his departure.

Depopulation suppressed not only property tax revenues but also income tax revenues. Between 2000 and 2012 the number of employed Detroiters fell by nearly 55 percent.

Half the decline occurred in 2008 during the financial crisis. Rising unemployment encouraged more people to leave, and tax revenues fell further.

Since 2008 total city revenues had decreased more than 20 percent. Michigan, meanwhile, continued reducing state aid to the city. Over 10 years state aid had fallen more than $730 million. With annual corporate tax subsidies exceeding $20 million, the city also lost revenues to incentives for development downtown.

The subsidies continued even after the city entered emergency management and bankruptcy. Subsidies to incentivize construction of a new hockey stadium overshadowed Mayor Bing's efforts to reduce the city's expenses to fend off emergency management. About three months before the emergency manager, Kevyn Orr, assumed control of the city, the Michigan legislature ratified a stadium deal with the Ilitch family, the owner of a global pizza chain. Five months into the bankruptcy the state legislature approved the deal's financing terms. Detroit would subsidize the project by diverting property tax revenues from the area around the stadium—an area that included the tallest office tower in the city, the Renaissance Center, where General Motors had its headquarters, and the Greektown Casino-Hotel, which had annual revenues of more than $300 million in 2013. The diversion would amount to about $1 billion in lost tax revenues that the Ilitches would use to construct the stadium. The Ilitches would also receive further public money to develop the area around the stadium, an attempt to connect the development taking place downtown with the development in Midtown, the thriving neighborhood near Wayne State University. Though stadiums have offered cities massive building projects and held out promise that fans might spend money on parking and nearby restaurants and that the stadiums might spur new development, most economists have concluded that subsidizing stadiums has cost more than the benefits the stadiums have provided. With season ticket prices starting at nearly $2,000, few residents living nearby could attend hockey games.

Detroit, meanwhile, lacked sufficient revenues to provide adequate services. In the wake of Bing's layoffs the city had a smaller municipal workforce than any similarly sized city. Municipal spending fell 40 percent between 2008 and 2013, and Charles thought back sadly to the time when Detroit had street sweeping, reliable garbage collection, and working streetlights.

Even if Detroit could raise tax rates, higher taxes threatened to drive more people out of the city and off the tax rolls. Perhaps, however, this time the new stadium really would attract suburban residents to hockey games and induce them to spend money in the city.

* * *

Across town on the west side, Reggie felt excited every time he made the monthly installment payment on the land contract for his house. Becoming a homeowner seemed to him the realization of a glamorous dream. He deemed a full four blocks around the house still decent, though beyond them empty lots and decaying properties proliferated. Those properties he assumed belonged to speculators who had rented out the houses without rehabilitating them or later reinvesting any rent. Reggie knew that Detroit had a lot of worse neighborhoods and appreciated that his house had never been broken into and that no one had even confronted him on his street.

Soon the summer would arrive, and Reggie and Tasha were getting ready to drive Reggie's daughter to a summer job fair at her high school. In a few months Kevyn Orr's initial 18-month appointment to run the city would expire. The clock was ticking to finalize settlements with various groups of creditors and avoid more prolonged payments to the lawyers and consultants representing the city in bankruptcy.

Together Reggie, Tasha, and Reggie's daughter walked from the rusty van into his daughter's school, three buoys in an ocean of abandonment. Reggie, dressed in a clean white tee shirt and jeans, said he hoped his daughter would find work for herself. The fact that the neighborhood still had a neighborhood school ranked among the things Reggie liked best about it. The school had falling ceiling tiles and roof leaks molding the carpets, but few neighborhoods had traditional public schools in operation anymore. Detroit's school system also suffered from the city's depleted population and insufficient tax revenues. While Kevyn Orr controlled the city government, the city's school district operated within a separate emergency management that took effect in 2009.

In 1994 the state legislature had instituted a school-choice policy and a generous authorization policy for charter schools. Over the following 20 years, thousands of students and millions of dollars in funding drained from the city's school district, decimating the system. Under the school-choice law, public funding followed students to the schools they chose to attend, and under the charter law, a broader array of institutions than in any other state had authority to establish charter schools. The authorizers earned a percentage of the public funding the charter schools received, and for-profit companies leapt to open schools. The companies and their authorizers aggressively lobbied to advance their own interests, leaving crumbling union-controlled district schools in their wake.

During the 1980s one of President Reagan's economic policy advisors proposed transferring education to the private sector and allowing competition to eliminate low-performing schools. The proposal mimicked the approach of southern states during the 1950s to avoid school desegregation with whites-only vouchers that supported white students in attending white private schools. Although support from teachers' unions provided strength to the Democratic Party, the push for privatization dovetailed neatly with liberal desires to move students into the best schools possible. A series of court decisions made it easier for school districts to resist desegregation, leaving still segregated schools without sufficient funding or support. Monitoring test scores provided a way to demonstrate regard for the resulting achievement differential without venturing deeper into its roots. The first charter school opened in 1992 and within two years, under President Clinton, states gained the ability to spend federal funds to establish charter schools. The George W. Bush administration's No Child Left Behind policy permitted students in poorly performing district schools to transfer to charter schools. During Obama's tenure, states received greater freedom to carry out school reforms that encouraged the growth of charter schools. By the time Reggie and his family escorted his daughter to the job fair, charter schools could use public funds to pay for facilities, and increasing amounts of public money flowed from traditional school districts into privately managed charter schools.

In Detroit as the authorizers approached caps on the number of charters they could issue, the Michigan legislature approved new rules that lifted the caps. The new rules removed a separate requirement for the state Department of Education to monitor charter schools' performance and issue annual reports on the schools. Charter schools, even for-profit ones, no longer had to pay property taxes on their school buildings. The state also asserted control over the Detroit school district's board, and observers expected the takeover to facilitate the opening of more local charter schools.

During the six years that the state controlled Detroit's school board, the school district's $100 million surplus dissipated into a $200 million deficit. Thousands of students left the school district, triggering a $225 million loss in state funding as money followed the students to their new schools. Reggie's daughter stayed, though. She had a learning disability, and charter schools did not offer programs for learning disabled students.

* * *

In 2006 Reggie welcomed the news that Detroit's elected school board would regain control of the local school district. It seemed to him that local board members could see firsthand the system's problems; lawmakers more than 90 miles away in Lansing only thought they knew what needed to be done. The board, however, could not plug the holes that had developed in the district's finances during the period of state control. In 2009 Governor Jennifer Granholm appointed an emergency financial manager over the city's school district. The new manager held a master's degree in business studies and spent most of his career as a professional city manager before becoming president of Washington, D.C.'s Board of Education.

The emergency financial manager closed numerous Detroit schools, slashed the school district's workforce, and instituted auditing controls. The deficit continued to increase, however, with students leaving the system at a faster rate than the city lost population. By 2011, when Snyder assumed the state governorship, more than half the city's schoolchildren attended charter schools, the second-highest number of students in the country. Even as the city's population continued to fall, the number of charter schools kept growing. Though test scores revealed mixed results, philanthropists including Betsy DeVos, who later became President Trump's secretary of education, backed politicians who supported charter schools. Faced with the state's school-choice policy and charter-authorization law, the school district's emergency manager had few alternatives to further cost-cutting measures and school closures.

In Snyder's first year as governor he established a new state-run school district in Detroit that consisted of new charters. He transferred 15 poorly performing schools from the city's main school district into the new district, called the Education Achievement Authority, or EAA. The middle school Reggie's daughter attended became part of the new district. Without other options nearby, she stayed at her school. Schools in the EAA operated under state control in every area, including areas beyond fiscal management. By then the deficit in the city's main school district had climbed to nearly $690 million. Now the system lost further students to the EAA. Over the same period the number of charter schools in the city increased by more than 100 percent. Since 1995 an average of seven new charter schools had opened every year in the city, nearly all run by for-profit companies. Reggie found his daughter's new school ill-equipped to help her.

Under Snyder's expanded emergency manager law, the same law under which Detroit itself operated, the power of the traditional school system's emergency manager expanded to encompass even academic issues. Over the following years a series of emergency managers inflicted further spending cuts on the city's school district, which continued to encourage more students to leave its schools. In 2012 alone the system lost more than 20 percent of its students. Each student who left carried more than $6,000 in state funding with him. Budgets planned for a specific number of students had to be hastily revised. Fixed overhead costs like heating a school building remained the same no matter how many students left. As students departed, the emergency manager had to force further financial cutbacks. The system needed to retain students to retain its funding, but the loss of students necessitated cost-cutting measures that drove more students away. Enrollments hovered around 50,000 students, down from a peak of nearly 300,000.

In 2012 more than 30 schools in Detroit's school district closed, and the closures caused additional drags on the system's finances. Onetime costs to secure buildings reached $100,000, and maintaining closed buildings cost $50,000 a year. Neglected water pipes froze and flooded; police had to respond to intruders. Faced with the high costs of maintaining closed schools, the district's first emergency manager considered abandoning closed school buildings to save money. By 2012 the district was instead trying to sell more than 120 vacant buildings and related land. Robin, by then deeply enmeshed in local property investment, made an offer on one of the buildings, excited by its stately architecture and central location, but the school district switched off the building's security system before the ownership transferred, and scrappers immediately destroyed the building. A plan to convert a vacant school in Cindy's neighborhood into a nonprofit tire-recycling facility collapsed when someone firebombed the building.

Local students had gained more choice through charters, but data indicated the charters did not improve students' learning outcomes. Reggie's daughter left the Education Achievement Authority for a high school in Detroit's school district. More than half the city's charter schools performed no better than the district's schools in math and reading, and many performed worse. At the state level 84 percent of charter-school students performed below Michigan's average in math, and 80 percent performed below Michigan's average in reading. Between 2010 and 2014 the number of Michigan charter schools that ranked within the lowest 5 percent doubled. Detroit's charter schools spent less money per student than the city's traditional public schools and more money on administration. For-profit companies ran nearly 80 percent of the state's charter schools, the highest proportion in the country. Institutions hundreds of miles from Detroit, in the far reaches of the state, authorized local charters. Only the authorizers had the authority to shut down failing charter schools, but the authorizers received money for every operating school that they chartered. The state's roughly 40 authorizers included not only conventional school districts but also community colleges and public universities. Few reduced their profits by revoking their authorization for poorly performing schools. Even when one did, a new authorizer could grant a new charter and assume the financial reward. The schools insinuated themselves into the local education landscape like weeds.

By the time of the bankruptcy Detroit's school system lay in disarray, and Reggie remembered his education in the district's public schools he and Tasha attended together as having a far higher quality. He seemed helpless in the face of his daughter's poor education. Even after enduring three separate emergency managers, the school district's debt had grown exponentially, and the student population had continued to shrink. At least Reggie's daughter no longer languished in the state-run Education Achievement Authority. EAA schools performed no better than when they operated within the local system. Once the state took over, school enrollments dropped and test scores fell. It seemed that the problems in Detroit's school district resulted from inadequate funding, rather than maladministration. Meanwhile as the bankruptcy sped toward its conclusion, media reports suggested that the city's revival might depend not on balancing the city's budget but on improving its schools.

6

Exit from Bankruptcy

FALL 2014

Miles woke early on a Saturday morning in November 2014 to continue renovating his house on Rosemary Street. He did not know how many more days remained that autumn warm enough to work on it. Already leaves had started blanketing his lawn, and the nights ushered a chill through his broken windows.

He had parked his truck in his grass-covered driveway, and he walked outside to retrieve some tools from it. As he returned to the house with long strides, he spotted something stapled to the front door. A plastic bag encased a yellow paper. The paper, a notice from the Wayne County treasurer, said Miles's house would enter foreclosure and public auction unless he immediately paid outstanding property taxes from 2012. The paper also instructed him to attend a hearing downtown about the house. Looking over his slim shoulder he noticed yellow bags on doors all down his street.

In 2014, while Detroit remained in bankruptcy, one in

every five local properties entered foreclosure, not because the homeowner owed money to a mortgage lender, but because of unpaid property taxes. In 1999 Michigan enacted a new law drafted by the national free market think tank the Hudson Institute to streamline and accelerate tax foreclosure. Legislators wanted to facilitate transferring properties into new private ownership where the properties would resume generating tax revenues. Under the new law the county treasurer took immediate ownership of properties with two and a half years of unpaid taxes, and then sold the properties in a series of public auctions. The state-mandated process stood out for its strictness. It took place out of court, while many states handled tax foreclosure through court processes that offered protections to the occupants of the houses. Interest rates on delinquent property taxes in Michigan started at 18 percent, among the highest rates in any state. Florida, by comparison, levied a 3 percent interest rate.

Because Michigan properties entered tax foreclosure after two and a half years of nonpayment of taxes, foreclosure statistics lagged economic conditions, and a couple years after the financial crisis of the late 2000s, tax foreclosures began to sweep Detroit. Miles joined 115,000 local residents, living in 85,000 properties, who risked losing their homes in 2014.

"How does a bill [from 2012] have anything to do with me?" he asked out loud, his devil lurking. The tax records he reviewed downtown before buying the house indicated unpaid property taxes from 2013 but none from 2012. Why did the yellow notice find him responsible for $3,600 in outstanding 2012 taxes, now more than two years overdue, plus 18 percent interest?

Miles felt the ground dropping from under him just as Detroit's fortunes might rise. In September Mayor Duggan and the City Council regained the power to govern the city.

A few days later city officials finalized a multi-million-dollar loan backed by the city's income tax and casino revenues. The loan would provide money to cover the city's operations after bankruptcy, pay creditors what the bankruptcy awarded them, retire the loan that supported some of the bankruptcy's expenses, and leave anything left over to invest in recovery. Once the bankruptcy ended, the city had to sell the new loan in the bond market. The sale would reveal the extent investors penalized the city for bankruptcy.

* * *

Miles followed the instructions on his yellow notice and attended a hearing downtown. Winter had descended on Detroit, and he turned his beaten-down truck off a slushy, potholed street to park, his movements graceful. The lot seemed unusually expensive, $9 an hour instead of $5, and he did not know how much time he would need. He sighed and paid, then walked over to the Cobo Center, the hulking concrete and glass convention center that every January hosted the city's auto show. Inside he found himself in a roiling mass of hundreds of other people, all clutching yellow notices.

During these, the waning days of Detroit's bankruptcy in late 2014, various groups of creditors were also fighting the city, trying to recoup more money the city owed them. The city, meanwhile, fought the suburbs for permission to lease the city's water system and use the payments for system improvements.

As those battles raged, Miles sat straight-backed inside a vast hall within the Cobo Center, waiting for his chance to fight to save his home. He had not expected to be among the people at the convention center trying to keep hold of their houses. When he drove downtown in the snow the previous winter, records of back taxes from 2012 would have kept him from buying the house because they would have spelled near-automatic foreclosure.

Earlier, officials let occupied properties slide, but this year every tax-delinquent property received a foreclosure notice. If the officials expected the hearings and possible home forfeitures to recoup tax revenues for the city, however, they were wrong. Delinquent taxes far exceeded auction sales. A property in the Morningside neighborhood that entered foreclosure for about $12,000 in outstanding taxes, for example, brought in $1,600 at auction. Most properties that sold in the auction sold for less than the amount of taxes owed, many for the minimum bid of $500. Numerous properties did not sell at all, and those properties stayed in public ownership where their maintenance acted as a drag on the municipal budget. In the 2014 auction a mix of corporate and individual bidders, mostly from outside the city, won about 2,300 properties for $500. No one even bid for nearly 8,500 properties. Between 2012 and 2014 the tax foreclosure auction generated only about $110 million in tax collections out of about $700 million owed.

Speculators bought properties at auction, then stopped paying taxes on them. In subsequent tax foreclosure auctions they bought back the properties after the properties reentered tax foreclosure, scrubbed of the taxes the speculators originally owed. Eventually the city tried to block this abuse by allowing only bids from entities with no delinquent taxes, but speculators simply incorporated new companies to bid. Close to 80 percent of properties that sold in the auction between 2011 and 2014 became delinquent on their taxes again, and the challenges that foreclosure presented continued even after the bankruptcy. Only about 8,000 of the nearly 46,000 properties that sold at auction between 2011 and 2015 remained current on their taxes, and more than 6,000 reentered tax foreclosure. Houses that entered tax foreclosure more than once generally degenerated until they could no longer sell.

Community advocates emphasized that if the auction displaced the occupants of even one house, that vacant house would cause the city further revenue losses. In 2014 more than 7,000 of the nearly 17,200 properties that sold at auction appeared to be occupied. Once the houses deteriorated the properties would spread blight throughout their blocks, depressing property values and increasing the probability of further abandonment and tax loss. One-sixth of the homes auctioned in Detroit's 2014 tax foreclosure auction eventually ended up vacant. Instead of recouping tax revenues, the state foreclosure process left the city to devote resources to demolishing deteriorated houses and finding uses for empty space.

* * *

Miles risked losing his house, but the size of the Cobo Center and the sheer number of people there for the hearings contributed a festive feel. Staff in yellow vests pointed people toward large signs that designated sections of the hall for various groups such as "homeowner occupants" and "non-deed holders including renters." Police clutched the guns in their holsters and paced. News reporters posed with microphones and recorders.

Though descriptions of Detroit often focused on disinvestment, the state tax foreclosure process catapulted the city to the attention of property speculators. Some bought properties at auction to resell to unsophisticated investors, misrepresenting the properties' potential to generate rental income. In 2017 the owner of a bulk acquirer of tax-foreclosed houses pled guilty to wire fraud for intentionally misleading foreign investors. His company bought several thousand Detroit houses at auction, many for $500, then resold them to overseas investors for 10,000 percent more by marketing the houses as refurbished and rented, even when the houses had been scrapped or left vacant.

Other speculators bid on properties to hold, either because low prices justified bets on a resurgence in the Detroit property market or because they learned that the properties lay in the path of planned public projects. Seventy percent of the more than 2,000 properties held by one pair of speculators bordered properties owned by the city or local nonprofits.

Amid the crowds and noise at the Cobo Center, as people scrambled to find where they were supposed to wait, Miles sat quietly and overheard people describing how they had rented from companies that apparently did not pay property taxes. Many of those tenants did not understand what was happening to them or whether they would get to stay in their homes. Some speculators had no experience managing local properties and simply abandoned even occupied properties to foreclosure when the properties became expensive to manage or maintain. At auction other speculators deliberately acquired occupied properties, intending to flip the properties to existing tenants or owners for a profit.

Few people bid on Detroit properties at auction to live in the houses themselves: By the 2016 auction, 20 bidders were buying more than a quarter of the properties that sold. Through the auction, the largest Detroit property owners came to include an investment firm run by an Irish television host who promoted himself as a consumer advocate though the firm had lost 90 percent of its investors' money; another firm registered to a suburban real estate agent who bought about 430 properties in the 2013 tax foreclosure auction but did not maintain or pay taxes on many of them, causing the city to spend nearly $230,000 to demolish her houses; and the local family that owned the Ambassador Bridge, which provided the family with a monopoly over trade across the Detroit River to Canada. The family strategically bought properties to block projects that could compete with the bridge and to facilitate the family's construction of a second bridge to Canada.

"It was a whole bunch of us little guys there downtown," Miles said later. "The big investors got away with whatever they wanted, and the little guys there like me were the ones who were suffering."

* * *

Miles waited for three hours among crying babies and elderly ladies a fraction of his height. It emerged that a portion of his tax bill stemmed from an old water bill that a previous owner of the house had not paid. Under state law the city had the right to transfer unpaid water bills to delinquent property tax bills, and water bills became a driver of tax foreclosure. Once foreclosure occurred the foreclosure process should have expunged the existing water debt, but the county treasurer did not always communicate well with the city water department. Even when the information transferred, city clerks did not always follow through and remove old water bills.[†]

Such attempts to boost revenues, rather than help people survive, made Miles feel sick to his stomach. Water bills in Detroit had grown increasingly expensive. Between 2006 and 2016 rates increased nearly 200 percent. As the population of the city got smaller the vast infrastructure supporting the water system remained in place. Water rates rose to the highest level in the country in spite of the city's poverty incidence, more than double the national poverty rate. The city water department cut maintenance efforts, eliminated staff, and often

---

[†] In 2015 the city changed its policy and stopped tacking unpaid water bills onto property taxes.

looked the other way when people failed to pay their bills or made only partial payments on the bills. The bankruptcy, however, ended the leniency.

The bankruptcy treated the water system as a valuable city asset. As the Detroit metro area grew and sprawled the city had retained control of the water system's infrastructure, and surrounding counties had to pay to use it. Kevyn Orr included the water department's assets and debts as assets and debts of the city in the city's bankruptcy filing. During the bankruptcy he explored monetizing the system, and shutoffs of customers with delinquent accounts surged. Miles kept his water even as he risked his house. He paid his water bill but not the property taxes from 2012 he knew nothing about.

In February 2014 the water department announced plans to shut off all customer accounts delinquent by 60 days, roughly half the accounts in Detroit. In May the department circulated 46,000 notices of imminent terminations and carried out 4,500 shutoffs. A tweet from the department stated, "If you're stealing water, we're coming after you." Before long the department was turning off water at 900 properties a day. Investigative reporters discovered the department did not target commercial customers even though more than half the city's commercial and industrial users fell behind on their bills and collectively owed $30 million. Among the overdue commercial accounts, Ford Field, where the National Football League's Detroit Lions played home games, owed more than $11,000, a sum far higher than the $3,600 debt that triggered the foreclosure of Miles's house. The department's records listed the bill to Ford Field as undeliverable and associated the address with J.L. Hudson, a department store that the city demolished in 1998.

As the number of terminations reached 150,000, service disruptions appeared to present an imminent public health crisis. By some estimates the shutoffs threatened 300,000 people, a large proportion of the city's remaining 700,000 residents. Experts from the United Nations visited the city and declared a violation of the human right to drinking water and to nondiscrimination because of the disproportionate effect of the terminations on African Americans. One week later water rates increased nearly 9 percent. The city scrambled to design payment plans. Within six months fewer than 300 of the 24,000 people who enrolled in the plans remained current on them. Parents lived in fear that the shutoffs would cause Child Protective Services to take their children away. In Miles's view the parents should have worried more about the safety of the water itself. After the news broke of lead in the water in Flint, he stopped drinking city water.

Old infrastructure led to frequent water main breaks, and many Detroit properties had leaking pipes. Even as customers lost access to water, it sprayed from broken pipes in abandoned buildings. A city councilwoman complained that the department should have addressed its own inefficiencies prior to the terminations. She cited bills sent to the wrong addresses and water shut off at the wrong properties. Scrappers scavenging copper frequently broke water pipes, leaving water running and basements flooded for months, driving up costs for no benefit. The city did not know whether the houses where the department shut off water had occupants.

Not long before Miles sat fearing the loss of his home at the Cobo Center, which itself had no water fountains, residents began fighting back and activists joined them. Detroiters snaked water hoses between houses and parked their cars over water valves to prevent further terminations. Former department employees used metal rods to restore service. Churches established emergency water hotlines, and volunteers delivered donated water to families and staffed water hubs. Spray-painted messages proclaiming "The Water Belongs to the People" began cropping up on the walls of vacant buildings. When a group of Canadians drove 750 gallons of water to the city in a seven-vehicle caravan, headlines screamed, "CANADIANS FIGHT TO KEEP WATER ON FOR 79,000 IN DETROIT." Local schools opened locker rooms to students for showering, and parents washed children's clothes in school machines. The national nurses' union organized more than a thousand protesters to march in downtown Detroit. The bankruptcy judge ruled that he lacked jurisdiction over city services and warned that "Detroit cannot afford any revenue slippages."† The shutoffs continued.

* * *

Finally Miles heard his number called and had the opportunity to make a case for keeping his house. Pushing his eyeglasses up his nose with well-groomed hands, he detailed one by one what he viewed as Detroit Progress LLC's transgressions. He spoke as if delivering a sermon, stirringly and with simmering rage. He demanded to know why the taxes from the years between 2012, when the company won the house in the tax foreclosure auction, and 2014, when the company sold him the house, did not remain the company's responsibility.

As Miles spoke to his hearing officer, Detroit was moving through the final phases of its own court process after only about 17 months in bankruptcy. Eventually most creditors would agree to settlements, so the bankruptcy would generate few precedents beyond the bankruptcy judge's early finding that bankruptcy could modify municipal pensions. At the

---

† The bankruptcy process concluded in a plan that entailed transferring water and sewage operations to a regional entity that made annual payments to the city to lease the system. The arrangement would generate new money that the city could use to improve its local water infrastructure. The suburban politicians whose support became necessary for the deal to move forward, however, barred the city from using the payments for further local investments or providing further local services.

Cobo Center, meanwhile, the hearing officer told Miles that he assumed the property from the company at his own risk and city records had no guarantee of accuracy. Miles persisted.

"If you could show me a bill from 2013 in 2014, why couldn't you show me a bill from 2012 in 2014 before I spent my money?" he asked, stepping forward.

"The 2012 bill must have come out at an in-between time and then posted to the records after a delay. That's why you didn't see it then."

"But if I was sold the house without being told about a whole year of taxes, then the whole thing was basically a fraud."

"You'll have to get a lawyer. This isn't for that type of argument."

Miles's only option to forestall foreclosure was to enroll in a payment plan. He couldn't afford the plan, so while he would struggle to keep current on the charges, he would continue to risk his house. No one at the convention center told him about the state poverty tax exemption for people below the federal poverty line. He likely qualified, and the exemption would have relieved him from paying any property taxes at all. In 2016 the American Civil Liberties Union and NAACP argued that thousands of Detroit residents who should not have had to pay taxes on their homes lost them to tax foreclosure, causing the city unnecessary vacancy, speculation, and blight.

The city did better in bankruptcy than Miles at his hearing. With few prior municipal bankruptcies to guide them, the participants in Detroit's bankruptcy crafted new approaches that shortened the process and improved its outcomes. The Michigan legislature agreed to expand Medicaid, enabling the city to transfer some municipal health care costs to the federal government under the federal Affordable Care Act. The bankruptcy judge empowered other sitting judges to mediate privately among the city and its creditors to reach settlements that averted prolonged litigation. Foundations and other contributors softened the consequences of the bankruptcy for the city and its pensioners.

It appeared that the collection of the Detroit Institute of Arts could legally qualify as an asset of the city that could be sold for cash to repay creditor claims; the potential for pension cuts among vulnerable citizens also loomed over the bankruptcy. At a deli near the courthouse three months into the proceedings, the president of a foundation ran into one of the mediators in the bankruptcy. The chance meeting became the genesis of a plan to solicit donations from philanthropic organizations and other entities to reduce cuts to pensions, contingent on ownership of the art collection transferring to a charitable public trust insulated from creditor claims. This Grand Bargain, as it became known, acknowledged the precarious position of the pensioners, most of whom already received just $19,000 per year, and the potential strain they posed to local social services, as well as the importance of the art for generating revenue for the city and maintaining locals' access to culture.

The contributions raised more than $800 million in new money in a bankruptcy that otherwise would have included few assets. Japanese firms, for example, contributed more than $2 million, and Michigan, whose declining revenue sharing with the city had contributed to the city's difficulties, committed $350 million. Most pensioners agreed to 4.5 percent cuts, the elimination of cost-of-living increases, and reductions in post-retirement health benefits. Financial creditors that may have had entitlements to proceeds from the sale of the art eventually agreed to smaller settlements that also awarded them property development rights that could gain value. Few other distressed cities, however, would have had the same access to so many major donors.

* * *

It occurred to Miles that people from the suburbs who drove through his neighborhood probably felt that people like him didn't care about where they lived. Those people had no understanding of the kind of hurdles that people like him faced. "What can we do," he asked, "when we do so damn bad?"

For about $180 million in costs the bankruptcy plan eliminated $7 billion in debt and balanced the municipal budget. The city agreed to pay in full the creditors that had arranged for collateral to back their loans, but it renegotiated the amounts it would pay to creditors that had not done so. In addition to the settlements, the bankruptcy plan identified possible new efficiencies, cuts, and fees that could increase revenues. The plan predicted such changes could generate more than a billion dollars in savings that the city could eventually invest in infrastructure and other service improvements while still maintaining a balanced budget. Several analysts interpreted the bankruptcy as providing more than $1 billion for services. Not all the money, however, was guaranteed.

Over the long term officials would have to realize efficiencies to generate surpluses. The bankruptcy plan contemplated new sources of revenue from raising bus fares and expanding bus routes, to quadrupling the cost of parking tickets, to more quickly collecting taxes and fines, to training the fire department to provide billable emergency medical services. Higher costs seemed difficult for people like Miles to afford. Accomplishing the changes would entail hiring 700 further city employees, but the city would still have about 20 percent fewer employees than it averaged between 2008 and 2012.

For Detroit to exit bankruptcy, the bankruptcy judge had to determine that the city could make the payments it offered in the settlements while still meeting its responsibilities to its citizens. Many potential sources of new funds to support services depended on improvements to city record keeping and other technology. In testimony to the bankruptcy court an outside analyst noted that unless the city quickly and effectively managed new investments into record keeping and information technology, persistent inefficiencies could undermine the rest of the bankruptcy plan. Even though dozens of tech startups opened in the city, attracted to cheap rent, low salary expectations, and easy media attention, the city itself lacked sufficient access to technology.

The emergency manager, Kevyn Orr, had documented a series of problems with the city's payroll, financial, budget development, property information, property assessment, income tax, and police department operating arrangements. The financial systems of city departments could not communicate with each other, and police precincts also could not share information. Officials could not view financial results in real time, and employees manually booked most accounting entries. Cutting a single check in the city cost four times the national average.

It therefore should have come as no surprise that the property records that Miles had reviewed did not reveal the outstanding 2012 taxes on his house. All the city's systems seemed to bear the effects of depressed tax revenues, the distressed local economy, and the workforce reductions in the lead-up to emergency management. Between 2011 and 2013 the city ombudsman received 3,600 complaints from residents who failed to receive tax bills or received tax bills for the wrong property.

On December 10, 2014, Detroit officially exited bankruptcy. Over the following years the new mayor, Mike Duggan, would have responsibility for carrying out most of the restructuring of the city's operations to find money for further improvements. Even as power returned to elected officials, for the next 13 years the state would continue its oversight of the city, a condition of the state financial contribution to the Grand Bargain that protected the art and assisted pensioners. No one could predict how future revenues and expenses might vary from the figures the bankruptcy plan projected. Numerous unforeseen events could transpire to knock the city off course, among them a major recession and significant cuts to federal and state support. Alternatively the city could attract a surge in private investment. Even if it did, however, it remained unclear what the future held for the struggling, striving people of Detroit.

Part Two

Emergence

7

A Decent Home[†]

SEPTEMBER 2016

In October 2016, nearly two years after Detroit exited bankruptcy, Indian summer lingered in the city. Where one might have expected children squealing and parents and grandparents chatting across lawns, though, the neighborhoods still felt empty. The parks, shuttered to forestall emergency management, had reopened, but prostitution and illegal dumping made them unsafe. In Reggie's neighborhood on the west side of the city, only the sporadic buzz of a distant lawn mower disturbed the silence.

There Reggie's rusty van sat parked in the driveway, an oil spot spreading beneath it. Inside the house he and Tasha were gathered in their usual spots, one on each leather sofa in the living room, dressed in tee shirts and jeans and drinking coffee, while home renovation shows blared in the background. Their

---

[†] A stated objective of the Federal Housing Act of 1949 that facilitated homeownership outside of redlined neighborhoods in which banks refused to extend home loans to African American borrowers.

two Yorkshire terriers, spotless from frequent baths, romped at their feet and hid underneath the glass coffee table, but Reggie no longer smiled his chubby-cheeked smile.

"Hush your mouth," Reggie or Tasha said softly each time the dogs grew too rambunctious. Because of their grandchildren, they had chosen gentle dogs, but the dog called Tuxedo still caused trouble. "I'm not the only person who ever tried to do everything right," Reggie said to Tasha, as he tenderly shooed Tuxedo away from his shins and observed the dog with soft brown eyes. "It backfires, I understand that. You take your chances going through a land contract instead of actually getting a loan and buying a home."

Their house no longer belonged to them, or even to Courtney Taylor, who wrote the land contract for it, though Reggie completed his final payment to her several months earlier, and she agreed to transfer the deed. Then she stopped answering his phone calls, and he began to see strange people in the neighborhood looking at the property. Early one morning a young Asian man drove a small car down the block, stopping to take pictures and write notes. He photographed the front and the side of Reggie's house, and Reggie assumed the man was a real estate investor. Reggie stayed inside, biting his tongue because the man did not set foot on the lawn.

By winter Reggie did not know where his family would be living. His blood pressure was climbing, and Tasha was coming down with the flu. From the sofa he drummed his thick fingers against the glass coffee table and jiggled his legs, waiting.

* * *

But back before that, a month earlier, a smile spread across Reggie's gentle face and dimples appeared as he greeted two white women who surprised him by approaching his front door. The women volunteered for a local nonprofit focused on housing issues. They were canvassing as many houses in tax foreclosure as they could, hoping to reach people before the annual county auction of tax-foreclosed properties began. That year the county entered 23,000 properties into payment plans and slated about 20,000 properties for bidding.

The volunteers' records variously listed the house as owned by a Charles Plant or a Courtney Taylor. The volunteers told Reggie that by negotiating a payment plan at 6 percent interest, whichever one of them owned the house could have kept the property out of foreclosure. Charles Plant and Courtney Taylor, however, had disappeared with eight other houses in their names also scheduled for auction. By paying down more of the outstanding taxes at 18 percent interest, non-owners could also postpone foreclosure, but the short deadline for making the arrangements had passed without Reggie knowing about the impending foreclosure, and he spent his money instead on making the house livable for his family.

The volunteers described scenarios that might now transpire. Someone could win the house at auction, in which case the new owner might evict Reggie and his family. Alternatively, no one could bid on the house at auction, in which case the house would enter the land bank, the quasi-governmental entity responsible for managing city-owned properties and returning them to productive uses. The previous year the land bank absorbed nearly 15,500 tax-foreclosed properties that did not sell at auction. During the bankruptcy it had assumed control of city-owned land previously held by nine separate local agencies. It now managed around 100,000 properties, around a quarter of the land in the city. The land bank's size overshadowed the next largest land bank in the country, near Flint in Genesee County, Michigan, which owned only about 11,000 properties. The inventory of the land bank in Detroit exceeded the ability of its staff to deal with individual properties, and the staff had to run computer algorithms to triage properties in bulk into different categories and programs. Along with vacant houses and empty lots, the land bank controlled 4,000 occupied houses, and it struggled to function as a landlord.

Reggie told the volunteers that he wanted to do whatever he could to keep the house. He called them ma'am and told them how important it felt to stay in the first house he'd ever bought, in the neighborhood in which he was born and raised, even though the house leaked and the foundation crumbled.

The volunteers presented a third scenario: Reggie could win the house at auction himself. They offered to bid on it for him using his money. The auction would take place online, and their involvement would spare him the $2,500 deposit to participate and the need for access to a computer. The previous year 28,000 properties entered foreclosure. With money provided by the tenants, the agency had won about 190 of the 9,500 properties that sold in the auction.

Reggie, his concern reflected in his broad face, asked for assurances that participating in the auction would not displace other families like his from their houses. He would only bid for his own house. Neither he nor Tasha had money to spare, but he said they would scrounge what they could to bid. He played drums at his church and did informal house painting, and he was searching for more work. Tasha earned money caring for elderly people. Maintaining the house consumed a lot of their time.

By paying bills in partial amounts, they scared up $1,400. Then they struggled to pay off the rest of the bills to keep their utilities on. Relatives gave them $50 here and there, which Reggie and Tasha would return when they could, but Reggie refused to ask people from his church for help. He worried that other members of the congregation faced similar problems. In the rattletrap van, he brought all the money he and Tasha gathered over to the agency, aware that the man who photographed their house would have more money to bid. The auction would take place sequentially by zip code, and no one knew when bidding for Reggie's house would begin.

* * *

Robin had a bad back. He lay across the sofa in the big yellow house in Detroit's West Village neighborhood with his hair cascading across a pillow and his beard intertwining with a fluffy blanket. He tried to persuade one of his small dogs to join him there. His wife, a social worker from the Detroit suburbs whom he had met in Detroit, had cancelled his walk and made him lie down. She wanted him to work less and start taking better care of himself, and maybe lose some weight.

A month earlier Robin and his wife packed a car full of belongings and drove from Los Angeles to Detroit. They had decided to spend more time there so that Robin could continue to build his reputation in real estate and expand his Detroit projects. He loved Los Angeles, its creativity and energy, but he also felt drawn to Detroit.

Today, though, his back made him cynical. From the sofa he surveyed the living room, kitchen, and bathroom of the yellow house with his lips turned down in a frown beneath his long mustache. The living room floorboards looked uneven, the kitchen windows had plastic to block out drafts, and a vise grip hooked to the shower to keep the spigot from leaking. The 103-year-old house seemed a microcosm of the rest of Detroit. He saw enormous potential, but he could only invest what he might recoup in rent, and rents in the city remained low. Recently the aggregate value of real estate in Ann Arbor surpassed Detroit, despite Ann Arbor's small fraction of Detroit's size. Robin constantly ran projections and jotted down math, and he already knew the difficulty of making his costs balance returns in Detroit. Periodically he put the yellow house on the market for $275,000 to see what offers it attracted. No one would pay much for a house in such a bad school district.

Generally Robin didn't buy property in the tax foreclosure auction, and he told people that in a proud tone of voice. Auction bidders could not view the houses in person, so he could not apply the systems he developed, which required calculations of the likely price of renovations. He had seen a listing, however, for a property in a promising location and waived his rules. After consulting three websites that showed pictures of an intact house, he bid on it. He thought with $60,000 of repairs he could rent it for $1,200 a month.

Robin won the house, closed, and arranged a crew to start working on it. Then he looked inside and immediately realized his mistake. The house had deteriorated beyond renovation. He made a series of phone calls, cancelling his crew and donating the property to an urban farming organization. The organization resold the house to a member for a few thousand dollars. Robin knew the buyer. She had already invested $400,000 trying to restore it, but she had not yet walked away.

* * *

Robin's friends approached him about jointly developing two gothic houses the land bank owned into Airbnb vacation rentals and hostel beds. His friends met him for drinks, then drove him by the properties. "Like everything in Detroit, by moonlight you look at these things and they're amazing," he said, pushing back his hair from his face. He and his friends started imagining what they could create with a few renovations.

With the pipeline of bank-foreclosed properties slowing

and the uncertain profits in the tax foreclosure auction, Robin and many of his friends had grown curious about the land bank. Each day in an online auction the land bank offered three of its roughly 30,000 houses for sale. It also sold some houses directly to the public, uncleaned and with no guarantee of clear title.

The next day Robin hoisted himself into his truck and drove by the land bank houses that his friends showed him the previous evening. The houses had turrets and spires, but in the daylight it seemed obvious to him that every detail of the properties would have to be restored. The land bank's auctions and direct sales depended on the ability of potential buyers like him and his friends to access capital to buy and rehabilitate neglected houses, both obstacles in a city where lending had collapsed. The land bank had to put houses up for auction multiple times to win sales.

For this reason the land bank was developing a new program in which it would auction renovated houses, and a local mortgage lender would extend financing to qualified buyers. The land bank intended the program not only to move properties more quickly from its inventory, but also to achieve higher-value sales in the neighborhoods that might support them. Higher sales prices would contribute to higher assessments for nearby houses, which in turn could spur increased mortgage lending and also make property rehabilitation loans more available. The first house in the program, however, sold for the minimum bid. Within two years the land bank sold 44 renovated houses at an average loss of $21,000 per house.

Still considering the two gothic houses, wedged into the sofa with his dogs, Robin did not know if he could even navigate the land bank's acquisition process, let alone fund the repairs. Three of his broker friends bet him that he couldn't.

* * *

Reggie and Tasha stared at the television, still in disbelief that they no longer owned their house. Reggie looked uncharacteristically close to anger. He imagined the auction winner, who bid under the name Wilburn Small, as an actual person, and most likely the young Asian man he saw photographing the house. In fact Wilburn served as an alias for a real estate investment company with operations across the country. The company won the house for $3,800 along with several houses in the neighborhood. Reggie could not understand why Detroit officials were welcoming outside speculators at the expense of people like him who had lived in the city all their lives.

Reggie's cousin William joined them in the living room, speaking loudly to be heard above the din of HGTV and barking. A bearded man with a hard-boiled look and a flirty swagger, he bore little resemblance to huggable Reggie.

William recently got out of prison, and he referred to his time away as vacation. He owned a house nearby, but while he served out his sentence the house had become uninhabitable. It no longer had windows or pipes, and roof leaks had damaged the inside. If he could afford to fix up the house, Reggie and Tasha and Reggie's children could live with him there, but with a prison stay on his record William was having trouble finding a job. Until he found one he couldn't even afford boards to secure the house or a tarp to shield the roof. In the past he had worked at a General Motors foundry until it closed, then driven large trucks. After that he entered the local real estate frenzy, flipping houses for a professional boxer until the real estate market crashed.

While William waited for his son to pick him up to drive him to a temp agency, he tried to make Reggie feel better about losing the house. William tried to convince him that he did not want it.

"You do a good job of making sure you can do the upkeep as far as repairing the sore eye view of the house and stuff, but I'm not trying to cut through the chase or anything, it does have issues."

"When it rains, you will *get wet*, for sure," Reggie agreed, nodding.

"The cracked foundation causes shifting of the whole structure itself. Without repairs being done it can even—the whole structure itself can cave inward. Like a earthquake happened. It's basically a premature earthquake has taken place. As long as the damage is worsening and not stable, eventually you'll have an implosion. Everything will collapse to the inside."

"And that's only a small portion of the damage. The leak that's going on back there, it's the worst."

When he failed to convince Reggie it would be good to leave the house, William turned to speculating about what it would take for the owner to back out of buying it.

"Some of them are being bought by outsiders, outside the state of Michigan, for investment purposes, and they hoping they can get in and do as little work as possible and rent 'em out right away and make money. If they see the kind of damage been done to the structure, a lot of them will take their losses and run."

"Once he takes a look at it and finds it not worth it, maybe I could offer what he paid for it, or something like that. I'm sure if the city did an inspection, they probably wouldn't even let anyone stay here."

William began calculating how much money "Wilburn Small" could "gross" on the house a month, given what Wilburn could probably sell or rent it for, the cost of the necessary repairs, and maintenance. He decided Wilburn would have to tie $30,000 into the property for five years before he could make a profit. But again the conversation led away from the conclusion William wanted for Reggie.

"Don't get me wrong, if you had a hundred houses or you a millionaire, it will be worth it 'cause you'll get it back eventually," William said. "That's what they do. They come up here and buy 'em out of bulk. If you a Rockefeller $30,000 is nothing to you, let alone five years."

That year, 2016, investment companies bought 88 percent of the homes sold in Detroit, up from 35 percent in 2010. And though Reggie got his money back from the housing agency, he thought that he'd best hold on to it until he heard from Wilburn Small.

8

The Architectural Imagination†

OCTOBER 2016

Dressed for outdoor work in a football team sweatshirt and sneakers, Joe arrived unshaven at his friend Anthea's house, not far from his own in Bagley. One of Anthea's sons was eating a clementine and drinking bottled water, another was playing the piano, and her daughter was examining a stink bug. The family was saving the bug for a local college that solicited specimens. Anthea sat beatifically in the middle of the floor, her long hair streaming down her back, making medals out of clay. As Joe sat down in an armchair, tucking his lanky legs beneath him, the boy playing the piano abruptly stopped and danced across the room carrying a cowbell.

The house looked like someone had staged it professionally. Anthea's family recently moved from about nine streets away. She and her husband found hardwood floors underneath

---

† The name of the U.S. Pavilion Exhibition in the 2016 Venice Architectural Biennale, which modeled designs for speculative projects for specific sites in Detroit.

the old carpet in the living room, sanded them and stained them charcoal, and painted the walls dove gray.

A young mother of Jamaican origin and a lifelong Detroiter, Anthea, Joe told her with characteristic warmth, was his "black kid sister." Her husband drove asphalt trucks and in the winter hauled rocks, and she homeschooled their three young children. To help children in the neighborhood blow off steam and learn healthy habits, she also organized a children's running club. She hoped the medals she was making would help the participants feel a sense of belonging. She also planned to sew the children tee shirts.

Bagley had both beautiful houses like Anthea's and blighted houses like Reggie's would become if he no longer maintained it. City officials understood that, in addition to depressing neighboring home values, blight correlated with higher crime rates, more prevalent disease, and more frequent fires. As Detroit lost revenue from property taxes due to foreclosure and population loss, the city also lost money dealing with blight. Boarding up and securing vacant houses cost a few hundred dollars each. Tearing them down cost more than $10,000.

In the wake of the bankruptcy city officials piloted an anti-blight program in five "tipping-point" neighborhoods where they hoped to make a visible impact. Cracking down on landlords who failed to maintain their properties, the city hired seven new inspectors for two neighborhoods, including Joe's. As budget problems reduced the number of inspectors, the landlords profited as the city lost money: Detroit ranked in the country's top five counties with the highest annual gross rents and in the top five zip codes with the highest potential single-family rental returns. Relatively high rents overshadowed landlords' insufficient investment in maintenance and improvements. In the "tipping-point" neighborhoods the land bank had recently started seizing dilapidated houses unless the owners agreed to rehabilitate them quickly. In the first year and a half of the program the land bank gained title to 1,000 properties. Even the man who oversaw the program owned a house that qualified for seizure; he won it in the tax foreclosure auction.

Without much paid tree work going and plans for his commercial space stalled until he had money to rehabilitate the buildings, Joe started spending time clearing overgrown alleys behind abandoned houses in Bagley and picking up trash on land where houses used to stand. It seemed to him that "every time a tree fell down the lights went out," and in his New Jersey accent he told people that where he came from no one would tolerate that. He met an ex-convict and on an impulse offered him a few dollars an hour to help with the work. The man agreed but told him robbing houses and selling drugs paid better. Soon an older man saw them working and joined them. Joe found it peaceful working outdoors on sunny fall afternoons and felt a sense of possibility and energy in the neighborhood.

* * *

As Joe worked, with his sweatshirts and wool beanie standing in for a winter coat, people from the neighborhood stopped and chatted with him. Joe could talk and talk. He met an elderly grandmother with no home who moved from squat to squat. He got to know a lady on crack whom he later drove to work a few times, and he met a coke dealer turned pastor, "the Preacher of Prairie Street." He became close to a woman who ran a hair salon and a white man from the suburbs called Mike who until the 1980s ran a neighborhood linen service. Mike remembered all the businesses that closed in the area: a tuxedo shop, upscale restaurants, Brickley Dairy.

Observing the neighborhood through his piercing blue

eyes, Joe noticed that it did not have any playgrounds. He decided to build one on a lot where a house had burned down, which turned out to be located around the corner from Anthea's place. The empty lot sat next to a burnt-out house on one of the roughest blocks in the neighborhood, a block that had eight more empty houses and few homeowners. After he finished clearing garbage, couches, and weeds from the lot, police data indicated that crime on the block fell. He loudly told a city official he knew to tell the mayor, "There's a new neighborhood strategy, and it's called giving a fuck."

Through his work on the playground Joe and Anthea became friends. When she attended her first community meeting in Bagley, someone told her about Joe and his playground. She introduced herself to him, the tall white man in the corner, and explained that she graduated from college in eastern Michigan with a degree in elementary education and teaching. She had been active in her old neighborhood and served on the board of a nearby community center. She wanted to help. "I love this neighborhood," she told her husband when she got home, radiant. "We have a neighborhood association, and somebody is putting in a pocket park, and it's going to be great." She felt hopeful the playground could bring at least one of the city's vacant lots back into use.

Prior to the bankruptcy Mayor Bing planned to demolish 10,000 blighted properties; during the bankruptcy the Obama administration assembled a task force that identified 78,000 blighted properties that needed to be razed. Administration officials extended permission to Michigan officials to spend federal money intended for mortgage relief to underwater homeowners on demolitions within the state. The state denied mortgage relief to more than half those who applied for it, the highest percentage in any state, but officials expected the elimination of abandoned properties to buoy the value of surrounding houses and prioritized those homeowners. The emergency manager, Kevyn Orr, streamlined procedures for hiring demolition contractors and paid the contractors with federal funds.

The contractors tore down 300 houses a week. They started in the most stable neighborhoods and moved through subsequent neighborhoods in descending order by population density. The uptick in demolitions triggered a spike in the cost of infill dirt. In 2015 reports emerged of contractors inflating demolition costs and mishandling asbestos. In 2016 federal authorities suspended funding of the demolitions amid indications that the city did not hire the lowest bidders for the work and did not properly bill costs to the state.

The demolitions resumed at a slower rate. New blight continued to develop, and tax foreclosure contributed more. No matter the speed at which the city tore down houses, blight continued to propagate. Even in the nicest neighborhoods vacancies increased nearly 65 percent over four years. Meanwhile demolitions were littering the city with vacant lots, but federal funding ended at the demolitions and did not cover efforts to repurpose the lots. The land bank owned more lots than it had resources to maintain, and the private market did not function to bring them into private ownership. The city needed a plan for what to do with them. Joe's neighborhood provided the canvas for the city's first experiment with new land uses.

* * *

Still wearing his beanie and looking the ruddy outdoorsman, Joe updated Anthea on his progress helping her mother buy a vacant lot from the land bank. Before it entered tax foreclosure the property belonged to an Australian investor who thought he had bought a house, though the property had long before transitioned from a drug squat, to ashes, to an empty lot. Anthea's mother, a nurse, had fought for demolition of the burnt remains of the house, and now she tended a garden there, wheelbarrowing in fertilizer to improve the clay the demolition contractors used to fill the hole from the house's foundation. During the bankruptcy the emergency manager, Kevyn Orr, eased a city requirement to fill such holes entirely with soil. When it rained the clay ran off the lot and clogged the drain in the middle of the street. The lot sat next door to Anthea's mother's house and across the street from Anthea's, and Anthea's mother was trying to participate in a land bank program in which next-door neighbors and community groups could buy vacant properties for $100. Joe was also finding the process difficult to navigate. It seemed to him that the land bank had conflicting mandates, and sometimes tried to return land to productivity by simply gambling on reserving land for possible future private development.

Joe spoke quickly, and before long he drifted from the subject of the land bank lot into an extended complaint about Detroit's lack of ice cream. "There's no ice cream down here, just junk," he told Anthea. The only ice cream parlor near Bagley occupied a single-story brown commercial strip between empty lots and shuttered stores and across the street from a car repair shop and an abandoned school building. Inside, employees scooped ice cream from behind bulletproof glass. "It's so depressing to go in there," he said. "I'm totally against bulletproof glass." Between the glass and his New Jersey accent, none of the employees could understand his order, and he couldn't understand them, and then they handed him his ice cream cone though the glass. "You don't get an ice cream cone handed through bulletproof glass, you know what I'm saying. You want the whole experience."

Anthea had never visited the ice cream parlor but thought it looked nice. Unlike everyone in her husband's family, who left Detroit as soon as they got the chance, moving to the suburbs as proof of success, Anthea embraced her neighborhood. Most African Americans in Detroit's suburbs lived in census tracts more than 80 percent African American, and she loved the relative openness of Bagley and its old houses. She felt connected to the city and to the challenge of contributing to it.

In addition to homeschooling her three children Anthea took a community class on entrepreneurship, which gave her an idea for the burnt house next to Joe's playground site. She thought the house could offer a hub for increasing neighborhood literacy rates. Only 14 percent of Detroit's third graders read at grade level, and about half the city's adults could not read, trapping families in poverty. Anthea imagined hosting programs at the house that included entire families in the learning process. The retired schoolteachers and principals who lived in the neighborhood could first teach parents how to read, then show them how to teach their children how to read. The retirees would get to spend more time around younger people. Everyone would benefit from the presence of a safe, well-resourced, available space.

Like the playground, the abandoned house probably would not cost a lot, and Anthea, shaking out her long hair with both hands, believed that she could establish her programs for not much more money. Together with the playground, she and Joe might cheaply transform their immediate area more effectively than the outside consultants now descending on the neighborhood to figure out what to do with its vacant lots. The consultants' plans for the area seemed a centerpiece in Mayor Duggan's bid for reelection to a second term. Duggan needed to demonstrate his administration could improve neighborhoods beyond downtown and Midtown, parts of the city Detroiters referred to as "the neighborhoods."

Anthea wanted a say in the plans. She worried that outsiders would beat out the people who had been living and investing in Bagley and its surroundings for so long. If she were in charge she would offer commercial space to neighbors who could not access it on their own. She felt strongly that they deserved the opportunity to establish themselves in their own community. She and Joe waited anxiously to find out more about what might transpire.

* * *

After leaving Anthea's Joe drove over to see Mike, the man who used to run the old linen service in the neighborhood. Mike also wanted to chat about the city's plans for the area. On the drive over to Mike's old building Joe slouched in his seat and tried to ignore the strip malls out the truck's window. It annoyed him that the businesses open amid the shuttered storefronts and abandoned land repeated themselves every few blocks. He complained about feeling stuck inside a hamster wheel of hair places, check-cashing places, chicken or fish places, and out-of-business places. Liquor stores bracketed more liquor stores, up to the maximum density of liquor stores the law allowed. There weren't even Chinese restaurants.

Soon he pulled up in front of a warehouse that looked vacant. Bricks filled the windows and doors, and the short driveway sat empty. After hesitating briefly, he located a corrugated metal door at the end of the driveway. He knocked and the door immediately swung open. Inside he found Mike, Mike's car, and the various keys Mike used to lock himself inside the building as a further safety precaution. Though Mike no longer lived in the neighborhood, and, unable to compete, sold his customer list to a national chain, he held on to the building with the old laundry equipment inside. A pale, older man who chatted away amiably in an even, at times sardonic, tone, he still felt nostalgia for the good times he experienced there. Joe thought Mike should open a linen-machinery museum. He treated Mike with the reverence he seemed to pay every long-time inhabitant of the neighborhood.

"But what are they actually going to do?" Mike asked Joe. Mike had accompanied him to meetings the city held about the neighborhood plans, looking suburban and relaxed compared to more anxious neighbors. But even after listening to discussions about bike paths and traffic patterns, Mike still did not entirely understand what would happen.

"Is it going to be like by Wayne State [University]?" Consultants had leveraged the university and nearby hospitals to anchor redevelopment in the surrounding area.

The staff at the city planning department, which had gained more talent and diversity in expertise since the bankruptcy, had adapted the Detroit Future City strategy from the Mayor Bing era with advice from the outside consultants. The staff planned to target three strong neighborhoods, including Bagley, along with three adjacent weaker areas. Fitzgerald, where the old laundry and Joe's commercial buildings were located, offered Bagley's weaker adjunct. Fitzgerald had numerous blighted, fire-damaged, and abandoned wood-frame houses.

The planning staff then carved out a quarter square mile of Fitzgerald between a small local college and small university as a pilot development area. In that quarter square mile the land bank owned 40 percent of the land, largely through tax foreclosure, an average amount relative to the city's other neighborhoods. In some parts of town the land bank owned nearly 80 percent of the land.

Directing a combination of local, federal, and philanthropic resources into just one quarter square mile would enable preservation of 100 land bank–owned houses there. A development company would renovate the houses into a mixture of rental and sale properties, reserving 20 percent of them for affordable housing. Some land bank–owned houses in the area appeared too blighted to save, and the developers would demolish those. On those lots and numerous existing vacant lots the market could not support construction of new housing, but the planners assumed that the better-looking the neighborhood became, the better the investment into rehabilitating the first set of houses would perform. A separate set of developers would therefore convert the lots into more attractive, lower-maintenance landscapes. From contiguous vacant lots the developers would construct a park, a quarter-mile greenway, and a bike path. Nearly 200 remaining scattered empty lots would become wildflower gardens and meadows. If the neighborhood eventually stabilized to a point where those lots gained value, another developer could buy them from the city and build new housing on them.

Joe balked at outside consultants coming into the area and imposing their vision on it. "They might make it work here because it's sandwiched between two universities and close to still well-to-do areas," Joe told Mike, pulling on a pair of work gloves against the chill of the warehouse. "I don't see it working anywhere else, if it even works up here."

* * *

His high cheekbones coloring in passion, Joe worried that outside developers would "blow up the neighborhood," put in safe national chains, then proclaim Fitzgerald a newly thriving neighborhood. "That's not a neighborhood, it's an artificial creation that's been shoved on top of literally the houses and the graves of a real neighborhood."

"Is it even what people want up here, the Shinola and the Pumpkin, like near Wayne State?"

Mike was referring to a street in Midtown a few blocks

from Wayne State University with newly constructed condos and storefronts. Shops and restaurants there included the luxury watch store Shinola, which leveraged images of Detroit's struggles in national advertising, and a chain restaurant that served truffle fries and Korean short rib pizza to Wayne State students. To Mike it seemed the city was copying for Fitzgerald the same development playbook it had used downtown and in Midtown before the bankruptcy.

The next phase of the project in Joe and Mike's neighborhood would entail improving the commercial street that separated Fitzgerald from Bagley. If people moved into the newly rehabilitated houses in Fitzgerald, density would increase to support more local retail. To attract small businesses the planning staff wanted to communicate a sense of investment. The land bank owned few of the properties along the commercial corridor, so the consultants suggested narrowing streets and adding bike lanes to make the corridor appear more welcoming to pedestrians.

Along those streets, if all went well, new businesses would reduce other developers' perceptions of the risk of investing in the area. The planning department would encourage developers to convert the existing one-story commercial buildings into mixed-use properties that would blend residential and commercial activities. Above the storefronts new housing for students at the college and university would further increase neighborhood density to support additional businesses and perhaps even improved transportation. Detroit had mostly single-family detached housing, which fared poorly in competition with the suburbs, where people could find similar houses in better school districts and with better services. If Detroit offered a more urban lifestyle, perhaps it would appeal to seniors unable to maintain large yards and young professionals who preferred apartment living.

Joe thought the plan might succeed in increasing property tax revenues but felt that there had to be broader gauges of success.

"No one's clamoring for mixed-use housing and a fucking Starbucks on Six Mile," he told Mike, his speech accelerating and volume rising. "What people are clamoring for is a place to eat apart from the McDonald's that's here and a place to shop other than the liquor store or the CVS."

Joe's voice softened as he told Mike that he had noticed a stooped older woman hobbling down the street and had offered her his arm. When he asked where she was going, she answered, "shopping." By "shopping" she meant a CVS drugstore and a liquor store down the block. There was no place else for her to go. In Joe's view, the consultants picked the neighborhood and asked themselves, "How can we gentrify it?" instead of trying to provide what people there actually needed.

City officials eventually planned to adapt the Fitzgerald strategy in further neighborhoods. Detroit had more than 20 square miles of vacant land, and in neighborhoods with less density than Fitzgerald the private market seemed unlikely to return. Planning department staff were exploring new relationships with various federal agencies that could contribute alternative approaches to developing sparser neighborhoods. The National Parks Service considered supporting new greenways, and the Department of Agriculture considered a potential role for federal farm loans.

When Mayor Duggan visited Fitzgerald to drum up community support for the plan, the older man who helped Joe and the ex-convict clean up the alleys left the mayor's speech dazzled. The man's wife also said she felt excited about the changes. Joe dutifully acknowledged their perspectives. "It's not like I've been here that long," he told Mike, "but don't they get it? Haven't they been hustled before?"

9

If You Build It

As autumn turned into winter and the snow began, Miles
stood on top of a ladder, painting the ceiling of a north-
east Detroit barbershop. His height made the ladder almost
unnecessary, and he looked very thin, almost wiry.

Miles felt grateful to have the painting job. He knew a
dwindling number of people who still sometimes called him
with work. He hoped that by working that day, a Saturday,
and finishing early, he might convince the owner of the barbershop to offer him more to do. Miles's grip on his house remained weak and uncertain, and he needed to make as much
money as he could. His devil still hung around.

Two billionaires seemed to be developing most of downtown. Desperate city officials appeared to consider the fate of
the city in their hands. Though unlike Fitzgerald and other
neighborhoods, downtown had a functioning private real estate
market. The officials nevertheless offered the developers seemingly limitless subsidies, hoping the developers would create

jobs and lure new residents to revitalize the tax base. The sub-sidies so far had not led to more work for Miles.

Traditionally the city relied on tax increment financ-ing to spur development. The approach, which underlay the construction of the new downtown hockey arena, where the Detroit Pistons had just agreed to play, enabled the city to sell bonds based on the amount that property tax revenues within a defined area might increase because of the develop-ment project. Like mortgage securitization, in which finan-cial institutions sliced up the future payments on mortgages and sold the slices to downstream investors, the city projected the property tax revenues that might flow from a new project, sliced those future revenues into pieces, and sold the pieces to outside investors. The investors' money paid a private devel-oper to construct the new project.

If the project did not produce the full increase in property tax revenues that the city sold rights to, the city took the loss. If the project increased property tax revenues in the expected amount, the money paid the investors and did not directly boost city tax rolls. Even successful projects therefore pro-vided the city more buzz than actual bucks, unless the projects spurred subsequent, unsubsidized development. This rarely happened, and limited evidence indicated that such financing helped the cities that used it.

But Daniel Gilbert, the owner of the mortgage lender Quicken Loans, demanded more in return for revitalizing vacant sites. As Miles scrounged small home repairs Gilbert began lobbying for state legislation that, along with provid-ing developers with projected increases in property taxes, also diverted increases in income and sales taxes to the developers.

In a city in need of jobs and investment, and a state loath to contribute to the city, government officials would eventu-ally agree to the subsidies Gilbert demanded. In his own small corner of the city, Miles understood that "God's not just gonna hand you everything"; he had to work for it. Long-term city residents like him, as well as small-bore entrepreneurs, however, lacked access to public spoils that made success easier to find.

* * *

Miles never seemed prouder than when he talked about the heyday of his work before Detroit's property market crashed. People came from everywhere—New York, California, Washington, D.C.—to buy houses. Once he built rapport with them and showed good results, the money flowed. Back then he "believed in his career."

As a teenager he chose construction as a way to fend for himself. He never met his father, and his mother stopped working when his brother's father died. Miles introduced himself to men he saw working outside and earned money doing small jobs for them. When he finished high school he took a six-month evening class in building trades. Computers could not do the work, and he thought it would provide him a sustainable living. Since the financial crisis, as he suffered year after lean year, he doubted his choice.

Lately he heard that new construction projects were finally returning to Detroit. To survive he desperately tried to meet the people buying and selling properties. He spent the morning networking by handing out business cards at his local laundromat.

Neither Dan Gilbert nor his deputies did their laundry there. In 2011 Gilbert relocated his mortgage lending company Quicken Loans from the suburbs to downtown Detroit with $50 million in incentives from the state. In the following years Gilbert's holding company, Rock Ventures, bought more than 85 Detroit buildings. As Gilbert shifted 15,000 employees into the city, many of them found housing in the residential towers he bought and renovated downtown. Businesses catering to his employees sprang up in other buildings he owned. The increased density and new restaurants and stores contributed vibrancy to downtown, and he helped brand the city a place of rebirth and opportunity. He donated widely to philanthropic causes, co-chaired the local blight task force, and urged his employees to perform volunteer work for the city. Quicken Loans, however, faced federal scrutiny for its potential role in the subprime mortgage crisis. Though company spokespeople maintained the firm neither wrote nor originated subprime mortgages, a lawsuit filed by the Justice Department suggested that over five years the company falsely represented that it underwrote mortgages with due diligence in order to qualify for Federal Housing Administration insurance. The federal insurance protected lenders against homeowners' mortgage defaults. When homeowners could not pay, taxpayers, not Quicken, absorbed the losses. Gilbert now stood to reap enormous personal rewards as the value of his downtown real estate holdings rose.

He planned to build out more than 3 million further square feet of downtown real estate, including a new skyscraper and 900 apartments, which he predicted would generate 15,000 construction jobs and 9,000 permanent jobs for Detroit. Within a few years the new subsidies for redeveloping abandoned properties that his lobbying secured would pay all the state sales and income taxes generated during qualifying projects', including his own, construction and half the state income and withholding taxes owed by people who later lived and worked at the properties. The developers would also claim any increases in local property tax revenues their projects generated.

Critics charged that the new subsidies would prevent new

developments from contributing to the city's revitalization. All
the revenues from the projects, even indirect revenues, would
flow to developers like Gilbert. Michigan already offered more
tax breaks and incentives to businesses and developers than
other states, but the state had not experienced corresponding
job growth. Miles sensed that money traveled from downtown
to the suburbs and beyond, keeping neighborhoods like his "a
blender full of junk."

* * *

Miles returned home from hustling for work at the laundromat to his empty living room, where the ceiling still stood
open to the elements. Construction felt like a dying field, and
he wished he could retrain to become a physical therapist.
People always got injured. He could not, however, keep his
house and also spare time without income. Even his plan to
watch online courses in advanced construction techniques on
his phone had recently ended in him defaulting on the loans
the institution offered him to cover the small tuition.

In spite of his bleak fortunes, he projected dignity and
elegance. Standing to his full height, he recounted how activists
in Detroit were fighting to make companies that profited from
public subsidies contribute more to the city and its residents
in return. The activists noted a $175 million tax break the
city extended to a gas company expanding a refinery. The expansion created only 15 jobs for local residents. The Ilitch
family developing the new hockey arena, who reported a net
worth of $3.2 billion, promised to hire Detroit residents into
more than half the 5,500 positions the family expected the
project to create. Though the Ilitches received $440 million in
state and local subsidies, they did not meet the hiring target.
They maintained the city did not have enough skilled workers.
Miles wondered what that meant for people like him and his

friend Charles, who knew construction and could not make a living.

The activists lobbied for a referendum on a new rule to require developers of projects above a threshold cost, with public subsidies above a set amount, to meet with local community members. At the meetings the developers and community members would have to devise a benefits agreement, in which the developers pledged corollary community aid like jobs for local residents, neighborhood environmental protections, or neighborhood beautification efforts.

In Lansing state officials tried unsuccessfully to block progress on the ballot initiative with a bill that would ban such requirements on developers and also prevent cities from raising the minimum wage; in Detroit city officials worried the activists' demands would impede the city's ability to compete for development projects. Local officials devised a rival proposal that would compete with the activists' in the referendum. The government's proposal increased the threshold investment and public subsidy that triggered a benefits requirement and made potential benefits agreements practically unenforceable. Developers of qualifying projects would only have to meet with a neighborhood advisory council, made up of members mostly handpicked by city officials, that would interact with developers in a purely advisory way. The council would have the opportunity to present concerns before the developers negotiated actual agreements with the city planning director. Any concessions developers offered to the council would have no binding legal force.

In Detroit both proposals—the one that activists put forward and the more conservative response—reached the ballot in November 2016. The head of the city's economic development team mailed a protest letter to the City Council. The letter suggested that the city should be lowering barriers to

development, not raising them. Because of its high taxes, reputation, and crime rate, the city already did not compete well.
On Election Day the more conservative proposal prevailed.

Neither proposal addressed a more primary barrier Miles
now faced. When large companies hired local workers onto
construction projects, they requested copies of contractors'
occupational licenses and documentation of occupational insurance. Miles did not have either one. The license would have
cost more than $300 and required a 60-hour course, and the
insurance would have necessitated further payments. Previously in his construction career none of the people he worked
for asked for proof of them. He knew he did good work, and
people could see that he did. Even the lowest-level construction tasks for the companies now coming to Detroit required
valid driver's licenses and transportation. Miles currently had
both, but he could lose them at any time. If he ever missed
a payment on his auto insurance, he would jeopardize his license and his truck. Without further work he risked his right
to drive and his house.

* * *

In late fall 2016 Robin updated his systems to require the
contractors he hired to have professional licenses and insurance. Their subcontractors would have to have their own tools
and their own transportation. He would start taking copies
of driver's licenses, and he would no longer pay contractors
in advance. Contractors would have to complete the first third
of a job and then he would inspect their work and pay them
for it. He had suffered through too many contractors who
disappeared, subcontractors who turned up late to jobs, and
contractors who cashed his checks and then denied receiving
them.

As Robin saw it, the only way for him to squeeze value

from a vacant building nobody wanted was through his management skills. Even in relatively strong neighborhoods close to downtown his tenants could not consistently pay, and his rentals had high turnover. The cleanup costs after a tenant left dragged down his bottom line. Recently a tenant lugged an old sofa in from the sidewalk, contaminating a whole building with bedbugs. To stanch his losses he was growing increasingly strict with evictions, though hiring the bailiffs and the dumpsters also cost him money. He stayed afloat by winning property tax reductions on his properties.

Working in the city's inner neighborhoods near downtown, smoking as he went, Robin still bought properties in cash and rehabilitated them in cash. He depended on cheap acquisition prices to front renovation costs for degraded properties that did not offer a clear path to revenues, but he no longer accessed a supply of inexpensive mortgage-foreclosed properties from banks. Now he searched for motivated sellers who mismanaged their properties into losses, sellers like landlords whose furnaces got stolen three times in a month or who over-rehabilitated properties in areas that did not support sufficient returns.

Most properties Robin put under contract he eventually decided not to buy. Even at low prices he risked acquiring properties and making improvements, then finding himself unable to rent the properties or sell them.

Ten years on from the financial crisis, the mortgage market in Detroit still did not function normally. In 2016 only 710 homes sold in Detroit with conventional mortgage financing, a fifth the number of mortgages in cities with similarly sized populations. About 30 of the mortgages came through Detroit's new Home Mortgage Program, in which philanthropic donations backed loans to people with higher credit scores than conventional mortgages required. Qualifying buyers received two loans: one for the value of the house and a second loan of up to $75,000 that represented the value the house would have if fewer local sales were occurring in cash for reduced prices. Buyers could use the second loan to cover renovations. Most people continued to pay cash even for expensive properties, including the $1.6 million Fisher Mansion, which had 15 bedrooms, 17 bathrooms, a pub, a private chapel, and an indoor pool.

Robin saw few options beyond investor contributions for financing his work. Allowing more people beyond his original investor a say in how he spent his money repelled him and undermined his idea of himself as an independent *macher*, a person who got things done, yet he had already accepted funding from the chief technology officer of a startup in San Francisco who gushed about how much he loved Detroit. To Robin the real estate markets in Detroit and San Francisco seemed worlds apart. "Nothing pops here," he said. "Everything takes 20 years of hard work. It's not like this town is filthy rich, looking for space to pay a lot of money for, like in San Francisco or some of the other hyper markets in the country."

* * *

Robin kept waking from a dream in which he walked into properties and announced, "I will restore this house, but I have to work alone and in total secrecy." In the dream he had special powers that enabled him to wave his hands to make improvements. He could emerge after a week with a renovated property.

He still found Detroit real estate incredible, but the difficulty of restoring it increasingly weighed on him. It was proving hard to become wealthy in the local real estate business. All around he saw properties that people acquired a few years earlier that still had boards on the windows. The real estate had fallen into such poor repair that the price of restoration seemed almost limitless. A renovation that he expected to cost $20,000 could easily balloon to $150,000. When most developers decided they could not recoup the cost of rehabbing a building in rent and could not find a buyer, they simply walked away.

As he drove through the streets of Detroit, crunched behind the steering wheel of his truck, Robin saw buildings he knew would take a million dollars and nine months of hard labor to repair. He could point to few properties that inspired confidence that they would look better in a few years. Most people would not undertake the investment in turning them around unless they could see a clear path to revenues, and he could hardly call Detroit a boomtown.

Robin's own neighborhood seemed somewhat less edgy than it did in 2009, when he bought the yellow house, and he chuckled when he saw "blond girls holding hands with dudes" entering and exiting the apartment building across the street. When he bought the house, the West Village ranked as one of the most stable neighborhoods in the city, with a 75 percent occupancy rate, historic buildings, and proximity to the Detroit River and the wealthy suburbs of Grosse Pointe. It hadn't, however, had a restaurant since 2004. During the bankruptcy a man who owned several shops in the suburbs opened a new restaurant in the neighborhood without bank loans. It took two years.

Another restaurant followed, and now the West Village had a coffee shop and a bakery too, but even the relative stability of his neighborhood did little to shield Robin and his wife from Detroit's developmental gaps. When a water main broke, he noticed low pressure in his faucet and assumed the house's deteriorating pipes had calcified. Then he learned that his house sat within an area under a mandatory boil-water advisory that affected broad swaths of the city. He still did not understand exactly what had happened, but he knew he would feel "horrified to find out." Meanwhile that year water shutoffs spiked, though when they originally increased, officials said the shutoffs would quickly reverse "a culture of delinquency." In 2017, 27,000 households, one in six residential accounts in the city, had their water turned off.

The modest development taking place in the West Village seemed to Robin unlikely to reach less central neighborhoods of Detroit for decades. Ever the artist, he coveted a vacant gothic church that still had intact pews, stained glass windows, and a full organ. Someone had bought the building for $5,000 with big ideas but insufficient capital and now wanted to offload it for a small profit. Robin made an offer. He toured the church three times, circling the main chapel with heavy-booted footsteps that echoed through the enormous space. He loved it, but he decided to walk away. Just running the church's boiler would cost thousands of dollars a month, he knew. Even if he could afford to renovate the church to rent out, only low-paying artists would want to live there. He phoned the seller's broker and told him to withdraw the offer. Robin wondered how long it would actually take for development to spread to the rest of Detroit.

10

Having Trouble Getting to a Job? Start Your Own!

DECEMBER 2016

E arly December 2016, with Christmas approaching. The temperature climbed into the 30s, then plummeted back down to 19 as the weather shifted between rain and snow. Detroit officials had lit a 60-foot spruce downtown as Aaron Neville sang blues carols, and the skating rink opened. Finally home from the call center where she worked, Lola was standing in her kitchen, chopping potatoes with a giant chef's knife. "Go put your stuff back up and put out clothes for tomorrow," she yelled to her daughter, Delilah, now seven years old. "Take pony and I don't know what the dog's name is and give me a kiss." The width of Lola's knife nearly exceeded the diameter of her hoop earrings, and between the knife and her nail extensions she had to take care.

Though cooking remained her favorite thing to do, it had taken so long for Lola to drive home from work that she was having a difficult time mustering the energy to prepare dinner. Delilah could barely wait to eat.

Since the bankruptcy, Mayor Duggan had appointed a new director of workforce development and revamped the existing oversight board that set workforce development policies, but the jobs landscape remained dismal, the city's heyday as "America's Arsenal" long past. Lola's mother often said that her children should find work they would do for free, and Lola still wished she could start a restaurant. As she drove to the suburbs and back every day for work, she dreamed about rotating her menu among foods like Italian, vegetarian, or even vegan and serving soul food every weekend. She would buy fresh ingredients daily and never take shortcuts. Instead she spent her days answering questions to her call center about air-conditioning systems.

In the living room, all Lola and Delilah's belongings sat on the floor in piles. Lola had toyed with the idea of moving and started gathering up their things in preparation for leaving. A gang operated in her neighborhood, and recently she had received a letter slipped under the front door from the president of a company telling her that the company had won the house in the tax foreclosure auction. The letter instructed her to check a box on an enclosed form to indicate whether she wanted to continue renting the house at a market price, buy it from the company, or enter a land contract. The company paid $5,100 for the house in the auction but would charge four times as much for a sale and about six times as much for a land contract. Though the company's president appeared to work as a CrossFit instructor in Florida, he owned more than 30 properties in Detroit in his company's name. Lola tossed the form in her trash can but soon retrieved it. She realized she did not have a choice. She did not have money to spare for a move, and once tax refunds began arriving landlords would raise rents. She was still fighting to gain ground on the bills that piled up after she had surgery without insurance, and she needed to focus on Delilah. The fight seemed to dim her characteristic sparkle.

Ensuring a good Christmas for Delilah now became Lola's priority. She planned to buy her three different sets of pink shoes, a coat and clothes, a dollhouse and more toys, two video games, and a video game control. She also planned to redecorate Delilah's bedroom with purple and pink walls and a glitter ceiling. The whole family had already agreed to help with the painting. In return Lola would cook Christmas dinner, so she needed to be able to afford the groceries. She was planning a menu of chicken leg quarters, a ham, dressing, macaroni, roasted potatoes with carrots, shrimp Caesar salad, string beans, strawberry and caramel Oreo cheesecakes, and a pineapple-upside-down cake. She promised herself she would work and save and try to eliminate distractions.

The following morning the alarm rang early. Delilah's elementary school started at seven. Wearing her keys around her neck as usual, Lola walked out the front door ready to start the car, drop Delilah at school, then drive the hour to the call center. But her driveway was empty. Her square-shaped frame seemed to crumple as she realized someone had stolen her car.

From her purse she dug out a sparkle-covered cell phone with a broken screen. A few minutes later her 83-year-old grandfather arrived. To get Lola to work and back he would spend four additional hours driving, on top of his routine afternoon school run to collect Delilah.

A few hours after he left Lola at her call center, a man from her car financing company phoned to tell her that the company had repossessed her car. Tears rolled down her cheeks as she fought to catch her breath and keep her sturdy legs from shaking. She had not made a payment due two days earlier. Though he offered the car back for $840, more than three times what the company charged her each month to pay back her car loan, she did not have the money. She also did not know how long she could manage her commute without the car.

* * *

On a frigid January morning, Lola and her grandfather drove to the call center while Delilah stayed in bed with a stomach virus. Lola's grandfather had been driving Lola to work every day for a month. By now everyone at the call center knew him, and when his car turned into the parking lot they stopped to talk with him. Lola, though, chafed at having to rely on him. She knew that to drive her he missed watching his football games, and the snow and ice made the ride even longer. That morning she convinced him to let her drive him in his car, but she worried about him driving himself home in the bad weather.

She wanted a job that she could get to and that paid enough for a car. Economic shifts had cannibalized good jobs from Detroit, leaving it with five times fewer jobs than its suburbs. Nearly two-thirds of employed Detroiters commuted to the suburbs for work. About 40 percent of the commuters had positions that paid less than $15,000 a year. The daily outmigration of city residents for low-skilled work persisted even as corporations moved high-skilled jobs back to Detroit to attract young professionals. Only a little over 10 percent of adult city residents had college educations and more than half lacked high school degrees. As downtown shined with new corporate towers, sports venues, and restaurants, residents held few of the jobs.[†]

Working so far away from a sick daughter felt even worse to Lola than burdening her grandfather. That morning,

---

[†] In 2015 Detroit residents held 28 percent of the jobs in the city, and since then the number had fallen.

without other options, she had left out chicken soup and saltine crackers as she rushed out the door on her grandfather's honk, with her straightened hair moving in one sheet across her face. At the call center she sneaked her cell phone into her cubicle and texted Delilah a lot. The call center felt too far away should something happen. She joked that stress from the car and her daughter was making her lose weight as her penny jar also grew skinnier. She knew that she had lost her appetite.

A New York investment bank pledged funding to train Detroit leaders in workforce development skills. Workforce development would play an important role not just in individual residents' lives but in the city's future. As city residents like Lola drove to jobs in the suburbs the city lost income tax revenues. No law required suburban employers to withhold city taxes, and Detroit had to rely on the employees to volunteer the tax payments. In 2009, as the city suffered the effects of the financial crisis, the arrangement cost the city over $140 million. In 2012, when Governor Snyder brokered the consent agreement that briefly averted emergency management, the state promised to pursue a mandate for suburban employers to withhold city taxes. Several bills to compel the withholding failed in the state legislature. Business lobbyists maintained that a requirement would impose unfair administrative burdens on suburban businesses that received no services from Detroit in return.

In Detroit, meanwhile, suburban residents with jobs in the city paid a lower rate of city income taxes than Detroit residents, and not all Detroit residents paid. Prior to the bankruptcy the city's efforts to pursue delinquent taxpayers waned under financial pressures. Now a prominent downtown law firm allegedly owed nearly $1 million in unpaid taxes for income it earned from suburban clients. It emerged that fewer than 15 percent of tenants paid income taxes in 33 high-end apartment buildings in the city's central core, buildings populated by young white professionals. To boost collection rates, after the bankruptcy the state agreed to collect Detroit's taxes. The staff remaining at the city tax office had insufficient manpower even to process returns.

The state legislature, however, began its January session with a proposal to eliminate state income taxes. In 2011 Governor Snyder rewrote the tax law to shift the state's tax burden from companies to individuals in order to attract jobs to the state. The new law reduced corporate income taxes, increased sales and personal income taxes, including income taxes on pensions and other retirement income, and reduced the earned income tax credit for low-wage earners. In 2016 existing tax credits absolved companies of more than a billion dollars in taxes, while the new corporate income tax brought in less. Personal income taxes represented the state's largest source of revenue. To fulfill the commitments Detroit made in the bankruptcy plan, the city needed to find money somewhere.

* * *

Lola liked chatting with people who phoned the call center. On a routine Tuesday morning one of her callers gave her an idea for a new job. He suggested that instead of offering support on the phone for air-conditioning equipment, she should sell the equipment at a store. His buddy worked for a home improvement chain and earned plenty of money.

Excited at the prospect of spending more time with her daughter and being able to address her delinquent bills, Lola asked her grandfather to stop at Detroit's branch of the same chain on the way home from work. The store sat next to the old Eastland shopping mall, about a mile from her house. Lola had opinions about the best way to drive anywhere, and the routes she suggested generally started with avoiding traffic lights by driving through the mall's mostly empty parking lot. Now in bank ownership, the mall suffered repeated shoot-ups.

Much as she wanted to work closer to home, under no circumstances would Lola actually take a job at that urban outpost of the home improvement company, she explained, her hoop earrings swinging. Instead she would rather drive nearly an hour to a suburban store, where she could earn higher commissions. She needed to be where the money was, and the money was in the suburbs.

As long as that remained the case Detroit's tax base remained in peril, and the city had few resources to attract companies with jobs for local residents. Since the mid-1980s companies enlisted cities in a national sweepstakes in which local governments competed to offer inducements to attract and retain companies, even as the cities struggled to fund schools, libraries, police, fire protection, bridges, and parks. Corporations hired outside consultants to negotiate gifts from cities, playing on politicians' desires to burnish their job-creating bona fides. By 2012 states, counties, and cities were giving up more than $80 billion each year in corporate incentives. Cities were competing with suburbs, and states were competing with states. Yet local economic development officials operated in a vacuum, with little advance knowledge of the efficacy of the subsidies they offered to businesses or whether businesses would live up to their promises of the jobs that they would create.

Economists cited several examples as evidence for the misguided nature of the subsidies. In 2009 Michigan gave General Motors $779 million in tax credits at roughly the same time the company received a $50 billion federal bailout and closed seven Michigan plants. The plants' host locations had met all the company's demands, and along with the tax breaks the state had made free buildings, worker training, grants, and further incentives to the company.

Inside Detroit's home improvement store, Lola gathered herself up to her fullest height, which was not very tall, and delivered her best pitch. She announced she had a college degree. Though people did not expect her to know about air conditioners, she knew all about models and makes, and she could help people with any questions about the devices.

But the company had no openings at any of its regional locations. Its only available position was a job watering plants.

Detroit's economic development team, meanwhile, marketed the city as a place with affordable real estate, proximity to Canada, and a legacy of art, music, and culture. Beating out Ohio, the city won a Chinese automotive fuel tank manufacturer in exchange for several million dollars in state incentives and city property tax abatements.[†] The company created 50 positions at the new plant. Perhaps, company executives suggested, they could employ more people there in the future. A few years later Amazon would bring the stakes of the competition for new jobs into stark relief when it announced a national search for a second headquarters location. Company representatives openly solicited as many incentives and tax breaks as they could in return for the new headquarters. A city in Georgia offered to change its name to Amazon and gift the company 345 acres of land.

In the communities where business leaders considered relocating, infrastructure seemed their top priority. Corporate executives favored places with young, educated, white-collar workers and access to clients. Detroit could offer few of those attributes and ultimately failed even to make Amazon's short

---

[†] Detroit lost out to southeastern Wisconsin on FoxConn, the Taiwanese company that manufactures products for Apple and Amazon. Wisconsin offered the company $3 billion in subsidies, more than $230,700 a job.

list of host cities. Detroit had insufficient mass transit and a low likelihood of attracting talent over the long term, Amazon spokespeople said, though the city's proposal offered the company $4 billion in subsidies. Detroit's position in the national jobs contest appeared a chicken-or-egg situation. The city failed to attract companies because of its decaying infrastructure and failing schools, and reluctance to invest in Detroit and cities like it further produced decaying infrastructure and failing schools. Eventually the company would select New York City and a suburb of Washington, D.C., for the new headquarters, then abandon its New York plans when local residents protested the subsidies.

Lola left the home improvement store deflated. Her usually abundant energy seemed dulled. No way would she, a college-educated woman, stoop to watering plants. She needed another idea.

* * *

A thin layer of snow iced the median on Livernois Avenue and snarled traffic. A February storm had arrived, alternating flurries and freezing drizzle. Wind-chill temperatures plunged below zero, and the sky turned the color of industrial steel. Joe sat drinking a coffee—black—and gabbing with the woman working the cash register at the organic bakery that opened in his neighborhood nearly four years earlier, just a few months after Detroit entered bankruptcy in 2013. On the ride to the shop he had driven past his daughter as she struggled to walk her new pit bull on the uneven sidewalk, now made slippery in the snow. She moved to the city a few months earlier, following a stint in the Netherlands as an au pair, and she easily found work as a bartender at one of the numerous new downtown restaurants popular among politicians and businesspeople. The restaurant where she worked opened during the bankruptcy in a building owned by Dan Gilbert of Quicken Loans. She was making hundreds of dollars in tips a night, more than she made as a bartender in Manhattan, but Joe disdained the restaurant as over-priced, over-crowded, and over-trendy.

The bakery where Joe sat, with its amateur pastel murals on the walls, mismatched throw pillows, and whimsical lamps, offered a different landscape from the sleek restaurant where his daughter worked. Most people in the shop knew each other. Currently they were discussing the news that city inspectors raided an old auto body factory and closed it down, sending artists renting studio space there scurrying. The seven buildings in the complex had provided the largest art and small business haven in the Midwest, but code violations like illegal plumbing and flammable walls now displaced glassblowers, furniture makers, and others. The buildings, meanwhile, served as a backdrop in previews of a Batman film screening throughout the country because of the menacing atmosphere they imparted.

At the bakery everyone commiserated with the buildings' former tenants over the difficulty of starting businesses in Detroit. Since opening in 2013 the owner of the bakery fought and struggled to acquire the permits and approvals necessary to convert her space from "pop-up" to permanent use. She still had to bake in a communal kitchen about 12 miles away, rather than in the bakery's kitchen. She fretted about finding enough customers in the city able to afford organic, homemade baked goods.

The owner of Joe's favorite coffee shop had announced that she was shuttering her shop. She had just won $45,000 from Motor City Match, a local program that matched funding from federal block grants and philanthropic contributions to money small businesses raised on their own. Her customers lent her the money to qualify for the match. But even with the grant she could not afford to hire any employees, and she still had to waitress to support herself and the business. The value of federal block grants had fallen 80 percent from its peak in the 1970s. By February 2016 Donald Trump had emerged as the Republican front-runner in the presidential election, and from office he would later propose a budget that eliminated the grants altogether.

Detroit, meanwhile, was trying to champion small businesses as a means for fueling neighborhood recovery. The Canadian who started the bicycle-manufacturing company prior to the bankruptcy had also not achieved profitability yet. Initially he had trouble finding an adequate manufacturing space. Most that he visited appeared so beat-up that they would cost too much to renovate. Eventually he bought a building from friends of friends in cash. He could not obtain a mortgage. The property taxes on the building, about 10 percent of the space's value, threatened to sink the business. Between the taxes and the cost of raw materials, the price he had to charge for his bicycles made them unaffordable for most city residents and more expensive than bicycles constructed in overseas factories. Unable to sell many bicycles, he kept the company afloat by assembling branded bikes for businesses outside the city, including a Colorado brewery and a New York bike-share operator. He had hired as many Detroit residents as he could, and the responsibility of paying them on time, when he knew that most of them lived paycheck to paycheck, weighed on him. After he lost his contract with the New York bike-sharing company, he had to lay off 80 percent of his workers.

In five years he had invested $2.5 million of his own money into his bicycle company, as his efforts to attract outside financing largely failed. Though city officials seemed to make every effort to support entrepreneurship, reducing red tape and providing mentors, they could not address factors outside local control or offer much money to startups. State policies impacted local property taxes. No federal incentives supported American-made bicycles, even though the federal government spent taxpayer money to buy police bikes, park bikes, and military bikes. Bank loans depended on proof of three years of profitability, a difficult achievement for any startup. Private investors favored high-tech companies that could quickly achieve scale, not manufacturing companies with high infrastructure costs and incremental potential growth. To launch the Shinola watch company its founder invested profits from his other global company, the fashion design company Fossil. Joe's friends' experiences angered him, his feelings always just below the surface, and he wondered whether he could navigate Detroit's entrepreneurial landscape any better and find success.

* * *

Still wearing his wool beanie, Joe sipped his coffee and worked on plans for his commercial space. He had installed electricity and Wi-Fi there while he continued to make the monthly payments to acquire the property. He wanted to open a community gathering place that would serve coffee and food, but reality continued to dash his dreams. Sitting languidly in his chair, like a bearskin rug that had been tossed there, he simply could not make the numbers for a community space add up.

Even though the demand for urban services in more stable neighborhoods like Joe's had increased, not much private lending existed to enable small businesspeople to fix up local properties. The properties did not offer enough value. Even the larger businesses opening downtown generally could not raise enough money from banks or by selling equity. Financing neighborhood-based projects was even more challenging because the projects had smaller reach, higher risks, and lower potential yields.

Joe doggedly tried to find funding anywhere he could. The city's primary small business program, the program that provided matching funds to his friend who closed her coffee shop, only matched funds for business owners who had already secured loans and also put up some of their own capital. The banker who once underwrote Joe's home mortgage in New Jersey confirmed Joe could not get a loan for renovating his buildings; the money Joe spent to buy the space did not count as capital for the matching grant.

Mission investors, investors who sought social improvements alongside financial returns, meanwhile scrambled to fill the space that the private lending market and public programs could not satisfy. Mission investors operated in Detroit more actively than anywhere else in the country, and community development financial institutions, or CDFIs, played a particularly large role there. CDFIs, independent community development agencies, offered credit in underserved markets from federal contributions. Several charitable foundations also pledged funding to Detroit's CDFIs. Mainstream financial institutions provided further capital to meet their obligations under the Community Reinvestment Act, a 1970s law that addressed the history of discriminatory practices in lending by encouraging financial institutions to serve low-income neighborhoods within the institutions' existing risk tolerance. One financial institution that sold subprime mortgages prior to the financial crisis had also begun lending money to CDFIs active in the city. Several states had sued such lenders for settlements, but Michigan's attorney general declined to pursue similar actions, ignoring Detroit activists who urged him to reconsider. The head of Michigan's Foreclosure Task Force attributed the decision not to sue to the influence of bankers who participated in state anti-foreclosure groups. Others described concerns that pursuing the banks would have further limited local mortgage underwriting. Mayor Bing pointed to the chaos of the time just before the bankruptcy and the incapacity of understaffed, underfunded city agencies to bring lawsuits.

Joe met with a staff member from one of the CDFIs, exchanging his outdoors ensemble for more corporate clothes. The agencies used the same loan-evaluation process banks followed but had greater flexibility. CDFIs could offer longer loan terms and lower interest rates and accept slightly higher risk in their lending. They could also take junior lending positions to banks, reducing risks for the banks, which enabled the banks to lend when they otherwise would not. The CDFIs still, however, needed to manage their losses, and Detroit residents had the lowest credit scores of any city's residents in the country.

Joe and the CDFI staff member he spoke with did not see eye to eye, and nothing came of the meeting. Nevertheless Joe completed the final installment payment for his commercial space. After he mailed his last check, a representative of the management company that oversaw the sale took him out to lunch to celebrate. They went to a restaurant in Joe's neighborhood that specialized in chicken and waffles and Kool-Aid and was owned by a former NFL player. The restaurant earned several million dollars in sales a year, and Joe and the manager stood in line for a table, waiting among people from the wealthier neighborhoods in the city.

The interior of Joe's space, however, still had "Jesus save me" graffitied across a wall, and the roof still leaked. Staying current on property taxes would be difficult. Prostitutes gathered in the inset doorway, and Joe worried about the buildings burning down. He joked about it, but his wry humor did not fully mask his concern. He would have to sit on the still empty space until he could save enough money to bring it up to code, and doing so could take years, if ever. Underlining the precariousness of Joe's situation, a few months later President Trump would propose eliminating federal funding of CDFIs.

Urban residents had limited political power to assert their interests at either the federal or state levels. In the 2016 presidential election a meager 35 percent of urban voters supported Trump. The Senate, with two senators per state, underrepresented the most populous states. Tight urban clustering, perhaps exacerbated by partisan gerrymandering, also left House districts less representative of urban residents than the residents' share of states' populations. State-level legislative districts also suppressed urban representation.

The Trump administration extolled local capacity as a justification for further cuts to federal support. The 2019 budget recognized a greater role for state and local governments and the private sector in addressing "community and economic development needs." Trump claimed to be "spending a lot of money on the urban cities" while advocating cuts to established housing, economic development, and after-school programs, as well as the Department of Housing and Urban Development. The department's secretary, who grew up in Detroit, criticized social programs as encouraging "dependency."

By the time a medical marijuana company offered to buy Joe's space, Joe knew several people in the neighborhood who got by selling marijuana on the street. He felt medical marijuana would not satisfy any unmet need the community had. What people in the neighborhood wanted, he believed, were affordable places to gather and to eat. His space remained shuttered, locked, and empty as he lost money keeping up with the expenses.

II

The Motor City

FEBRUARY 2017

I n the gold 2005 Cadillac DeVille he borrowed from a friend years earlier, Charles went for a drive with some friends. As he approached the railroad crossing near the Chrysler plant not far from his house, the sound of a horn interrupted his banter. Just as the railroad gate came down he slammed on his brakes. The van behind him kept going. The thump thrust Charles against his seat belt and nearly out of the driver's seat.

The van backed up, but Charles and his friends stayed in the car. Suddenly less jaunty, Charles waited to see if the van's driver would call the police. Someone with valid auto insurance would do that.

The van's driver also remained in the van. Time passed, and Charles's breathing slowed. Then he and the other driver got out of their vehicles. They nodded at each other, acknowledging their understanding that neither of them had insurance. They hugged briefly, then returned to their cars.

Forty-four years earlier Michigan implemented no-fault

auto insurance to lower the cost of insurance; instead the cost rose. Rather than suing drivers for medical expenses, under the no-fault regime drivers could claim directly against their own insurance companies, regardless of fault. The state made no-fault insurance mandatory so that every resident's insurance company could reimburse its own policyholders out of court.

Michigan's Supreme Court held that mandatory insurance necessitated rate-setting procedures to ensure fair and equitable rates. The ruling made insurers equalize the rates they charged across the state. The insurers maintained they could raise suburban rates to levels high enough to cover their costs in urban areas, or they could keep suburban rates low and stop offering insurance in cities.

Nationally, urban residents commonly paid more for auto insurance, perhaps because of higher traffic densities and crime incidence in cities, or perhaps because of redlining. Insurers charged more for insurance in minority neighborhoods than in white neighborhoods with similar levels of risk. In Michigan all but four insurance companies stopped doing business in Detroit. Eventually, in 1996, the governor pushed the state legislature to overturn the rate-equalizing requirement. The controls on auto insurance fell away just as health care costs increased dramatically.

* * *

"We cool," the van's driver said out his window as he drove off. Charles rode a few blocks further, then pulled into the parking lot of a small liquor and grocery store to wait for his heart rate to return to normal. A bricked-up building without windows that also cashed checks, the store where he parked sat on a half-empty, weed-covered block.

Charles started to laugh, and the noise reverberated through the deserted parking lot. How wonderful that two people without insurance had hit each other. Nobody got hurt, and neither did his friend's car. Everything would be fine.

After the governor removed the constraints on auto insurance companies, the companies set rates based on zip codes, with further consideration of driving records, age, gender, car value, and educational level. Rates in Detroit skyrocketed. Insurance there cost more than anywhere else in the country, upwards of $6,200 a year, compared to the national average of $815. Some surveys revealed costs of nearly $10,000 a year in Detroit, more than the price of housing in many of the city's neighborhoods. The majority of residents stopped paying for coverage. Nearly 60 percent of drivers did not have insurance and drove illegally. If they got caught they faced significant consequences: up to a year in jail, monetary penalties and fees, and suspension of their driver's licenses.

Just beyond the city limits insurance rates fell by about half. In parts of Grand Rapids auto insurance cost just $370 a year. Not surprisingly, therefore, numerous attempts to change the system failed at the state level. Mike Duggan nevertheless campaigned for mayor on reducing costs for Detroit residents, though the issue did not fall under the city's control.

Having regained his composure, Charles continued on his way. He and his friends were meeting another friend who previously worked for the city and now had difficulty affording insurance as he adapted to changes to his pension and health care benefits forged in the bankruptcy.

When he assumed office, Mayor Duggan followed through on fighting for cheaper auto insurance. With most jobs so far outside the city, he called affordable insurance a matter of civil rights. He sought state authorization for a separate insurance regime, just for Detroit, that would reduce costs by capping unlimited coverage there. The proposal failed. Subsequent proposals for the whole state failed too. A suburban politician, L.

Brooks Patterson, compared capping coverage to a nineteenth-century train heist. Later proposals limited the amounts auto insurers paid to medical providers to Medicare's set fee schedule, and the state senate majority leader called the limits price fixing. Detroit's representatives, meanwhile, complained the proposals did not go far enough to end redlining, because insurers could still base rates on zip codes and credit scores.

Abuses of the system continued. No-fault benefits included rides to medical providers from designated transportation companies. The companies billed insurance more than $100 dollars each way, generally to stand-alone clinics. The clinics' providers charged higher rates than hospitals, which had negotiated network benefits with health insurance companies. MRI scans at the stand-alone clinics, for example, cost no-fault insurers more than $5,000. Hospitals billed Medicare about $500 for the same procedures.

* * *

Unlike Charles, Miles could never outrun his mistakes. A couple years earlier he had tried to save money on his auto insurance. Someone he met claimed to be able to find him cheaper insurance than other companies offered, and Miles took out a policy with an entity doing business as GEICO of Southfield. Police caught him in a rolling stop at a stop sign, determined his insurance was fraudulent, and called in a tow truck. "GEICO of Southfield" had no connection to the national company GEICO Insurance owned by Berkshire Hathaway. As soon as the police left, the tow-truck driver told Miles that if he paid twice the towing cost, the driver would give him back his truck instead of towing it. Miles agreed to pay the driver. In order to collect the truck from the tow lot and avoid storage fees, he would have had to show proof of valid insurance, which he could not afford.

For driving without insurance, the police filed misdemeanor charges against Miles. On top of the misdemeanor
penalties of several hundred dollars, he would also have to pay
$1,000 in driver's responsibility fees over two years and $125
in driver's reinstatement fees. In 2003 the state legislature
sought to balance the state budget in part by imposing further
charges on drivers ticketed for specific offenses. Since then the
responsibility fees raised more than $100 million for the state.
When drivers completed their responsibility payments, they
had to pay the reinstatement fee to drive again.

In court Miles struggled to suppress his emotions. He
explained to the judge that he worked as a contractor and
needed his truck to get to job sites. Public transportation in
Detroit entailed buses. The bus system, unlike other municipal transit systems, did not receive financial help from the
state. In the lead-up to the city's bankruptcy, the city saved
money by privatizing the system's management; continued
financial shortfalls prompted service cuts. Since the bankruptcy, city officials touted increased on-time bus departures,
improved maintenance, and better police patrols. A onetime
federal grant helped the system purchase some new buses, and
state matching funds enabled some expanded routes and more
frequent service. The system's budget, however, was smaller
than before the bankruptcy. Service remained limited, and
safety concerns persisted. By 2016 the entire system had lower
weekday ridership than the two busiest bus lines in New York
City. A Detroit factory worker made the national news for the
21-mile walk he took to work every day to avoid the local bus
system.

Prior to the bankruptcy, in 2007, a group of local business
leaders, hospitals, and philanthropic organizations initiated a
plan for a three-and-a-half-mile, privately funded light rail line
that would connect downtown Detroit to Midtown. Mayor

Kilpatrick advocated a more ambitious plan that extended the tracks to the city's northern border. Though initially supportive of the longer line, the federal government eventually withdrew its financial backing due to concerns over the city's ability to fund its share of the project. Instead the federal government advocated new bus rapid transit service along the same route, which would cost less. The consortium of private investors, meanwhile, continued to push for the shorter rail line they originally proposed. The federal government agreed to contribute to the shorter line if the state passed legislation to authorize a regional transit authority that could initiate referenda for investment in a better regional transit system.

Over the previous 45 years, the state legislature had tried and failed 24 times to institute similar legislation. Historically, white suburban leaders feared regional transit would carry undesirables into the suburbs and reduce suburban housing prices, while Detroit leaders feared regional transit would cede local control to regional agencies dominated by suburban politicians who would work against the city's interests. In the 1970s southeast Michigan forfeited federal money for regional transit because city and suburban leaders disagreed about how to spend it.

In the courtroom Miles told the judge that in addition to driving to work he needed to take his daughter to school. She did not live with him, but she was about to graduate from high school. Talking about her, his voice grew more plaintive. The judge took pity on him and entered a judgment of "No fines, no fees." Miles considered the problem resolved, but it wasn't.

* * *

A few weeks later a bill for drivers' responsibility and drivers' reinstatement fees arrived in the mail for Miles. To waive the fees, the judge would have had to change the fraudulent insurance charges to charges that did not carry fees, and the judge had not done that. Now until Miles paid the fees or entered a payment plan with the state, he could not drive. He could no longer get to suburban jobs. The city bus system and the suburban system operated independently, with four separate transit agencies. City bus routes terminated at the city limits. The few suburban buses that crossed the border between the suburbs and the city did not pick up passengers within the city on the way in or drop off passengers inside the city on the way out. In the aggregate the region spent less than $70 per person on public transportation, compared to more than $230 in similar parts of the country. For Miles to get to a job in the Detroit suburb of Rochester Hills, where about 370 new houses had been built the previous year, a 35-minute drive straight north would, on public transportation, become a five-hour odyssey involving four buses and a five-mile walk.

Meanwhile private efforts to realize the light rail line within Detroit continued. Though the light rail could not improve regional transit, a new regional authority could. With unified support from Mayor Bing, Governor Snyder, and the Obama administration, the legislation for the regional authority passed. The authority then placed an initiative onto the November 2016 ballot to levy a small property tax increase, $120 a year on a $200,000 property, to fund a variety of new regional links. Eight-five percent of the money raised within a county had to be spent in that county. In the 2016 election the measure would pass in the counties that included Detroit and Ann Arbor but fall well short of majorities in the other two suburban counties affected.

As county leaders bickered over regional transportation, Miles did his best to follow a payment plan with the state for his responsibility fees. He kept the correspondence and bills for the plan in neat piles on his glass coffee table and took notes on salient points in careful cursive. He posted a $50 down payment and then a $50 payment for the first month of the plan. The following month he posted a second payment. If he ever failed to make a payment he would lose the right to drive again. Nothing about his future felt certain.

A few months later the light rail would open to the public. By then called the QLine for one of its benefactors, Quicken Loans, the tracks traversed the sections of the city experiencing the most investment and economic development, where many of the rail line's financial backers owned real estate. People with the highest incomes lived in that portion of the city, which represented 2 percent of its total land mass. The route duplicated an existing bus line. Critics charged the $140 million investment in light rail could have instead helped poorer Detroiters in dire need of greater mobility; more than a quarter of the city's households did not have access to cars. The QLine's advocates maintained that the short rail line would connect cultural, medical, educational, and commercial institutions scattered along the line, spur nearby economic development, encourage more dense patterns of land use, and provide an initial leg in an eventual regional transit system.

Before the QLine opened, as Miles drove himself and a friend to work, the police ran Miles's license plate number through a plate reader. The police determined he did not have valid auto insurance. They ordered both men out of Miles's truck and took the plates. In fact, Miles had bought valid insurance a few weeks earlier. It seemed the police had made a mistake.

* * *

Reggie had auto insurance, but he still needed more money to finance a move. He had received a letter purporting to come from the new owner of his house, but Reggie knew that anyone could have found out that the house entered tax foreclosure and the tax foreclosure auction. Until he saw a copy of the deed, he refused even to meet the letter writer face-to-face. Reggie's family continued to live in the house.

There, Reggie was lumbering back and forth in the snug kitchen he had renovated himself. His cousin William crowded in with him and reminisced about a dinner Reggie prepared the previous Tuesday, with turkey and Italian sausage. He could "cook his behind off," William said and squeezed him as if he were a teddy bear.

While Reggie and William palled around, in the living room Tasha lay on the sofa with the television tuned to a home improvement channel, fielding phone calls on a pink cell phone. She had recovered from the flu but then kept falling ill again. Extended family phoned to ask about her asthma, and Reggie brought a steady stream of soup and other snacks over to the sofa for her. Then he decided to take her to the doctor for stronger medication.

When they arrived at the hospital, a minibus was idling in front of the entrance. Reggie tapped a large finger on the driver-side window of the vehicle. "What are the requirements for a job like driving this?" he asked the bus driver. With the phone number of the company that owned the minibus tucked in his jeans' pocket, he and Tasha entered the hospital. When they returned home, he phoned the number and talked his way into a job driving for the company.

The new position entailed dropping people injured in car accidents at doctor's appointments across the state and billing their auto insurance companies for the service. Generally Reggie would work between six and six, though his schedule would vary with demand. The company paid no benefits, but the hourly rate, which added up to about $85 a day, would help when his family had to move. He expected to keep the job until something better came along with benefits, perhaps in 5 or 10 years.

12

City on the Move[†]

FEBRUARY 2017

Reggie's new job provided him with only a modest career transition in a local economy still dominated by cars. Earlier he managed a tire, wheel, and automotive service in the suburbs. He worked for the company for 10 years and planned to keep working there until he retired. When his mother received a breast cancer diagnosis, however, he took a leave from his job to take care of her. His large brown eyes watered when he talked about his grief over her death and the events that followed. When he tried to return to his position, the company told him he could not come back.

Since then Reggie and his family stayed afloat on the $1,000 in state and federal funds he received each month to support his adopted children. He also found painting jobs through word of mouth and short-term positions through temp agencies. In the course of his temp work he learned to

[†] The title of the promotional film Detroit submitted in its unsuccessful bid to host the 1968 Olympics.

operate machines to make nuts and bolts and screws, but in all the short-term jobs he took, he never saw anyone hired full-time. In hindsight he knew he had let his emotions get the better of him when he left his position as a manager. His fortunes had never recovered. He hoped that driving the mini-bus might offer him a new start and help him in finding a new home for his family.

His cousin William was also doing temp work while he lived with Reggie's family, but William had not yet found his way to a stable income. He was growing increasingly disillusioned with his prospects. Companies "are belly-over real easy now to where it's no real secure jobs anymore," he told Reggie as they sat with the dogs in the living room.

William began reminiscing about the heyday of the Big Three auto companies and regained some of his usual bluster. "I hate to say it, but our economy, because of a lot of out-sourced work that was done with our businesses, you can't say that because you work at a particular company that you'll be able to see yourself retiring at that company."

"With the help of God we make it through."

"These are the breaks."

Until Reggie knew his own options and could make concrete plans for his family, he decided to consider his house just a bad business deal and focus on driving and saving money to move. He had never invested in anything before, though, and never experienced anything similar to losing a house he paid for and brought up to basic living standards.

"We don't cry, we just move on," William said.

"That's all we do."

* * *

Charles cruised the east side of Detroit in his borrowed Ca-dillac with his daughter Yvonne next to him in the front seat.

It was not so much snowing as spitting February dampness. He had picked up Yvonne from her high school, and they were talking about strategies for memorizing text. Charles was bundled into a pretty green-gray sweater with a horizontal weave, under a three-button waffle shirt, under a thick hooded sweatshirt. He also wore a cap with furry earflaps. Because of pain in his mouth from his old oral cancer, he was speaking through the side of his mouth, which gave him a bunnyish look.

That day, known as spring count day, school attendance determined how much funding every public school in Michigan would receive from the state. Chronic absenteeism remained so high in Detroit that on count day local schools tried to lure students to show up with free meals, prizes, and parties. The funding available from the state, however, amounted to only half the amount per student in New York City or Boston.

Charles was driving his daughter to her after-school program, where she acted in plays. Soon she would have to recite a pledge in front of the other program participants, and he was helping her prepare. He hoped she would have the skills to carry on his family's legacy. She was becoming a good actress, and he wondered if he could find her a movie to audition for, if anyone made movies in Detroit anymore. "We striving to be all she can be," he told his friends.

Mid-soliloquy, lights flashed in Charles's rearview mirror as a police car drove up behind him. He pulled over and the police confiscated the borrowed car. The license plate reader had alerted the police to his lack of auto insurance. They left him and his daughter, carless, by the soggy side of the road.

Slowly Charles and his daughter trudged to the nearest open business, a fast-food taco place. Charles moved with less spunk and sass than before. Once safely inside the restaurant he pulled his cell phone from his pocket and phoned a friend to pick them up. A former semi-truck driver now on disability, the friend arrived in a 2004 Ford Escort that once belonged to Charles's mother.

To collect the car Charles had been driving, Charles's friend who owned it would have to miss work to go to the tow lot. He had a job at a suburban yacht club. Retrieving the car would also necessitate Charles paying the cost of the tow truck, the daily parking fee at the tow lot, and drivers' responsibility fees. Without a way to get around and earn the money to cover those costs, Charles's debt at the tow lot mounted.

* * *

"Don't you ever let anyone convince you that your education is not important," Charles said to Yvonne in the living room of the old family house. He could not contain his frustration. Still without access to a car, he had offered to pay someone to drive her to school. Her mother, a custodian at another school, told her she could stay home instead, and he had just found out. He planned never to speak to his daughter's mother again.

If Charles could not drive Yvonne to school and her mother did not approve of him paying someone else to drive her, then she would have to take the public bus to get there. High schools in the local school district did not provide transportation to students. Lower and middle schools offered school buses to those students who lived more than three-quarters of a mile from the closest school in the district. Most charter schools did not assist their students in getting to school.

Prior to enrolling in high school Yvonne had attended a charter school. She did not, however, choose the charter school in the sense school-choice advocates seemed to champion. Her district elementary school closed, and she received an assignment to attend a nearby charter school instead. The charter school described itself as a "preparatory school," and Charles thought it could award college credits. For that reason he liked the school, though in lower and middle school his daughter remained too young for college credits.

The high school Yvonne attended within Detroit's public-school district felt more familiar to him. His sister, his nephew, and several of his friends all graduated from it. In the 1970s another of his sisters got a job there as the school's first African American bookkeeper. Charles assessed the school as similar to others in the city: Students who came to learn, could learn, and those who didn't, wouldn't. He tried to push his daughter to take her education seriously. The school's metal detectors and armed police jarred him, though, and the students' uniforms made it hard for him to identify his daughter when he could still pick her up from school.

Regaining his composure, he told Yvonne that in the short term he would send her to school on the city bus with a pair of scissors in her pocket, which she could use to defend herself on the bus and at the bus stop. In the meantime he would try to borrow another car, but he still could not afford to insure it. He would have to choose between buying fraudulent insurance on the street or paying for legitimate insurance for a week while he registered new plates. Either way, he would risk losing his car again. As much as he missed his mother, he felt grateful she did not know about their circumstances.

Near his and Yvonne's feet sat an old family television, encased in a four-legged mahogany box with the word "color" embossed in cursive toward the top. Had it worked, and had he turned it on, the local news would have mentioned a proposal in the state legislature to eliminate $270 million from public programs in order to facilitate cuts to income taxes. If the proposal succeeded, the Department of Health and Human Services would undergo the largest reductions, along with the Department for Talent and Economic Development and a program that helped at-risk communities with redevelopment. In 2011 when Governor Snyder slashed business taxes, he predicted that companies would use the additional money to invest in the state and hire more people. The cuts, however, had not increased state revenues, and the general fund remained about 25 percent lower than in 2000.

Without yet knowing about the potential cuts, Charles set off for his barber on foot. "I can't run that good, but I can walk," he said over his shoulder.

* * *

In early June 2017 as she took the outdoor stage downtown for her final performance, Aretha Franklin greeted the crowd. "I knew you were waiting," she started to sing. On the east side Lola and her daughter, Delilah, were engaged in a heated tic-tac-toe match. "You're cheating," Lola said, her glitter nails scraping across the paper.

Like Charles, Lola wanted what was best for her daughter, and like Charles, she still waited for the day when she could deliver it. In May, just as the state senate debated raiding money earmarked for schools to facilitate the proposed income tax cuts, a new school superintendent started work in Detroit. Words like "hope" and "transformation" infused his speeches, but Lola remained skeptical of a fresh start. She worried about the ability of the city's schools to develop Delilah's talents. She wanted to send her daughter outside the city for school, but for that she would need to buy a car or burden her grandfather still further.

The superintendent assumed power because the state legislature pulled the plug on emergency management of Detroit's school system. The crisis in Flint brought new scrutiny of emergency managers. During state oversight of Flint, lead leached into the city's water supply, sickening children. The scandal offered evidence that state-appointed managers did not always deal optimally with local challenges.

Instead of continuing with emergency management, Governor Snyder proposed bailing out the school district using the same approach the federal government used to rescue General Motors during the recent financial crisis. Snyder's plans entailed splitting the school district in two, leaving debt in the old system and transferring responsibility for educating students to a new system. The strategy depended on state financial support, and the bill to carry out the plans included provisions to appeal to right-wing legislators. For example, the new school system would no longer have to hire certified teachers, and teachers who staged sick-outs would face new penalties. Earlier the teachers protested conditions in the schools and the lack of state concern by calling in sick in spiraling numbers, effectively shutting down nearly all the district's schools. Teachers protested again when the most recent emergency manager, the judge who presided over the city's bankruptcy, announced the school system could not pay teachers through the summer. The judge replaced an emergency manager for the schools who had earlier served as an emergency manager in Flint during the onset of the water crisis there.

Governor Snyder's proposal to bail out the school district passed by one-vote margins in both houses of the state legislature. Democrats wanted the plan to include stricter regulation of the city's charter schools. Several Republicans balked at lending further public money to a mismanaged school system. Filing for bankruptcy over Detroit's school district, however, did not offer an appealing alternative. The district raised money through bond financings backed by state credit. If the district defaulted on the bonds, the state would lose money, and the state's future ability to raise funding would suffer. The city's bankruptcy did not threaten such bad consequences for the state. The school district, moreover, had languished in emergency management for seven years, amassing further debt, whereas the city operated under emergency management for just four months prior to entering bankruptcy.

Late at night, home from the call center, Lola's worries centered on the fact that Delilah did not feel challenged at school. She scored 100 percent on every spelling test and earned straight A's in every subject. When Delilah asked for harder work, her teacher told Lola that either Delilah had completed first grade before or she needed a higher-level class. Lola wished she could find a school along her commute to the call center that would do a better job teaching Delilah, whom Lola considered "a freaking genius," how to transform into a leader. She reminded Lola of herself, only nicer and with better manners.

By bailing out Detroit's school district the state enabled it to spend more money on educating students rather than paying down debt, but the bailout did not resolve underlying structural challenges. Abandoned by middle-class families, the district still educated a costly, high-risk population and gained no new tools to compete with charters. The state did not provide the new system with much money to repair facilities, leaving the schools without funds for needed upgrades.

* * *

Delilah's school operated within the Education Achievement Authority, or EAA, the state-run school district Governor Snyder established within Detroit in 2011. Ninety-nine percent of the students at the school identified as economically disadvantaged. Fewer than 4 percent of the fourth graders tested proficient in English; none of them tested proficient in science.

Lola didn't know "what the hell" EAA meant, other than that the summer vacation seemed shorter than in the traditional school system.[†] The state-run district had not improved student performance, enrollment had plummeted, and an EAA school principal had gone to prison for taking kickbacks, following a federal corruption probe of the system. At the end of the school year, all the EAA schools would return to Detroit's city-run school district, but Lola didn't seem aware that the final days of her daughter's whole school system approached.

Lola did, however, know that a school closure list compiled by the state's school reform office included her neighborhood's only traditional public elementary school and also the upper school Delilah's lower school fed into. The school reform office, which had responsibility for turning around the state's worst-performing schools, planned to close every school that for three consecutive years scored in the bottom 5 percent of state rankings. Twenty-five Detroit schools qualified, including half the EAA schools.

Lola was not the only person concerned. A political maelstrom developed over the proposed school closures and their consequences. One school slated for closure had just received financial support from the Ford Motor Company to convert unused classroom space into a community center. Another had just moved into a new building, funded by a $50 million voter-approved bond offering, and people had bought homes near the new location. The mayor argued that the clo-

---

[†] Teachers in EAA schools did not belong to unions and earned higher salaries that reflected their longer school days and longer school years, and they did not pay into the retirement system. The principals also had more authority over their budgets and hiring.

sures would force students without access to transportation to attend nearby schools that also risked closing in subsequent years.[†]

Rather than wait for the fallout, Lola wanted to find a new elementary school with homework Delilah could not finish in two minutes. When she talked about Delilah, her eyes shone more brightly and she could barely suppress a smile. The neighborhood offered plenty of charter schools, but Delilah had not taken any tests for charter school admission, and Lola did not know how to sign her up for them. Lola also seemed confused about which schools qualified as charters, mentioning Detroit Country Day, a $25,000-a-year private school in the suburbs that did not participate in the charter system. She thought some charters charged tuition.

Eighty percent of district and charter schools in Detroit had opened or closed during the time since the state's emergency management of the school system started, and one in three elementary school students changed schools every year, often during the school year. Parents reported moving their children in search of better schools, though poverty and housing instability also combined with Michigan's liberal school-choice policies to result in further school transfers. The previous academic year 900 students changed schools four times, and only a small minority did so because they moved house. The constant student churn weakened relationships among students, parents, and teachers and made it difficult to evaluate teacher performance. Enrollment instability correlated with poor learning outcomes for all students, even those who did not switch schools, and increased dropout rates.

The new superintendent and new school board running

[†] Ultimately, the closures did not take place. Instead the schools entered into agreements with the state that required them to improve. The schools had a deadline for setting goals and a deadline for holding conversations about the goals.

Detroit's new school system initially balanced the system's budget in part by leaving 300 teaching positions vacant. Fewer teachers translated into larger class sizes. The state did not cap the number of students per class, and some schools had classes of more than 50 students, though the average class size hovered around 22. Lack of individual attention seemed likely to drive more students from the district. Fewer students would reduce state payments and ultimately bring about further teacher vacancies, in a seemingly unstoppable downward spiral. Facing this terrain, Lola decided to send Delilah to the school her sister's children attended. A suburban charter school just beyond the city limits, it had a student body nearly 100 percent African American, and 80 percent of its students qualified for free lunch. The school ranked even lower in test scores than the schools in Detroit's system, but Lola liked that the suburban charter offered accelerated programs and parents could check their children's grades online. Her sister could help drive Delilah. Lola submitted an application and waited. If Delilah enrolled, Detroit's school district would lose funding from yet another departing student.

13

The Campaign

JUNE 2017

Cindy thought that her neighbor the squatter, Emma, needed to hurry up and find herself. Emma was nearly 40 years old. An Asian man had showed up at the squat in Brightmoor carrying a clipboard loaded with addresses. Cindy planted herself squarely in front of him, her round chin pitched forward, and demanded to know who owned the house. Initially he pantomimed that he did not speak English, but she bulldozed on, making him look at the house's worn-out roof and burst pipes. Only afterward did she tell him that she knew someone who wanted to buy the house, meaning Emma. The man gave her a business card for a property management company in the suburbs, which was surprising given that no company had ever done anything to maintain the property. Emma phoned and wrangled the name and address in China of the house's owner. Through her network of organic farmers, Emma found someone who spoke Chinese and mailed a translated letter to the owner. After hearing no response, Emma quit the squat for seasonal work in Alaska, leaving a neighborhood garden half-planted and the house next door to Cindy empty and exposed.

On the other side of Cindy's house a series of related companies were trading a house in and out of tax foreclosure. Tenants came and went, people squatted, and recently a young African American family moved in. Cindy hoped the family would be able to stay. With her gray hair gathered in a ponytail, she knocked on their door and gave them a Neighbors Building Brightmoor newsletter. She told them their "landlords" did not own the house and advised them to keep an eye out for signs of foreclosure.

Over the following months, during the summer of 2017, Mayor Duggan's reelection campaign reached full swing. In August he prevailed in the Democratic primary over State Senator Coleman Young II. Young, originally called Joel Loving, changed his name to highlight his relationship with his biological father, Coleman Young, the city's mayor from 1974 to 1994 and its first African American mayor. His long tenure represented the apex of African American political power in the city. In the general election in November Duggan and the younger Young would face each other again. The election seemed a referendum on the progress the city made during Duggan's first term. On the stump Duggan highlighted the return of routine trash pickup and street sweeping to Detroit and new streetlights. Young countered with criticism of the lack of change in "the neighborhoods," the term locals used for areas of the city beyond downtown and Midtown. Duggan adopted the slogan "One Detroit" to signify his concern for the whole city.

Combatting crime was another area of contention. During the bankruptcy, police response was so bad that the new police chief, hired by the emergency manager, called on "good"

and "law-abiding" Detroiters to arm themselves against crimi-
nals. In the wake of the bankruptcy officers continued to leave
the city for positions that paid more and had not just under-
gone benefit cuts, as Detroit's had in the bankruptcy. By 2015
fewer police officers patrolled the city than at any time since
the 1920s. The officers patrolled a smaller population, but
they struggled to cover the same 143-square-mile land mass.
City officials spoke of plans to hire new officers from inside
and outside the city, but due to criminal records, unpaid traffic
tickets, and other problems, most applicants did not qualify
for the jobs. Officials also had trouble recruiting officers who
reflected the city's demographics.

Cindy tried her best to continue helping her neighborhood.
For her birthday her husband Dick bought her a lawn mower.
Now she mowed three days a week, covering nine separate vacant lots, her long braid trailing down to her waist as she went.
"Anyone don't like it, they can kiss my lily-white ass," she said.
The city only had the resources to mow land bank–owned
lots in the neighborhood twice a year, and the mowers only
had time to cut the few inches directly adjacent to the street
and the sidewalk. For safety reasons Cindy only mowed when
Dick was at home. She worried about muggings, shootings,
and other violence.

Meanwhile the president of Neighbors Building Brightmoor was pushing her to enroll in a series of gardening
classes. Cindy attended an urban farm management program,
then won a grant that paid for raised gardening beds. In her
new beds she grew potatoes and kale, tomatoes, onions, and
lettuce. A woman down the street stole all the tomatoes.

* * *

Freckles spread across Cindy's nose and cheeks from the time
she spent outdoors. "Why is this even here?" she asked aloud

as she drove past a burnt-out house on her way to a planning meeting. A heap of clothes, cleaning supplies, and Neighbors Building Brightmoor newsletters protruded from the back seat of her rattling Ford Escort, and she wore the clothes she dressed in to clean houses in the suburbs. "Son of a gun," she said as she passed another house that had burned. She and other members of the group had been chasing scrappers away from it.

As Cindy drove through Brightmoor, downtown 300 wealthy former Detroit residents mingled over drinks and canapes. The event, intended to pique the guests' interest in investing in the city, took place under the high arched ceiling of the city's vacant train station. An 18-story Beaux-Arts building that opened for train travel in 1914, at one time the station provided an elegant launching pad for inter-city travelers and soldiers in both world wars. But the building had not seen a train for decades, and its marble floors, carriage entrances, and mahogany-paneled smoking room decayed over years. Now with graffitied walls and floors spattered by bursts of color from rogue late-night paintball players who braved scrappers and a razor-wire fence, the empty husk of the station loomed over the city. After the bankruptcy the billionaire owner of the station installed windows in exchange for public parkland he coveted for private development.

Cindy did not have money to invest and did not receive an invitation to the festivities, but through her volunteer work she was meeting powerful people in the city. She had already mentioned one of the burnt-out houses to her city councilman. She knew him from serving on his blighted properties and vacant lots committee. When the county commissioner offered her free tickets to a baseball game, she rushed to tell her husband. When University of Michigan students chose the overgrown lot across the street from her house for a new park, she wept. And in pictures from her swearing-in ceremony for the board of a neighborhood organization she grinned from ear to ear, the hardness that she often affected entirely absent. Mayor Duggan officiated the ceremony, and even Cindy's stepdaughter came to celebrate her, in spite of their history of "knock-down, drag-out fights."

Now Cindy parked in front of a storefront painted with multicolored farmyard scenes, which sat in a single-story strip mall next to a boarded-up liquor store missing half its roof. She had arrived at her planning meeting for the Brightmoor Artisans Collective. Grabbing her maroon purse, she walked briskly from the car to the front door, glancing over her shoulder. The city's police chief claimed an 11 percent reduction in violent crime since the start of the bankruptcy, but FBI data indicated that over the previous year violent crime surged nearly 16 percent. The agency ranked Detroit the most violent big city in the country. When the police chief disputed the agency's data, a local newspaper columnist quipped: "A magical post-bankruptcy elixir of less cops, making less money, making fewer arrests [led] to less crime." In 2017 the city still had fewer officers than before the bankruptcy.

Detroit officials' primary response to crime entailed a program in which business owners voluntarily installed video surveillance systems. A green light marked the systems, alerting people that cameras were recording them. The city provided extra patrols to businesses that paid to install the video systems and to store the digital files the systems produced, but many of the patrols were virtual and took place from a central video monitoring station.

The Brightmoor Artisans Collective tried for a more bottom-up approach. During the bankruptcy it spun off from Neighbors Building Brightmoor to create a new community space where people could learn how to make, market, and eat affordable, healthy food. The group bought a building out of tax foreclosure and launched a weekly farmers' market in the parking lot, then opened a commercial kitchen in which people prepared pickles and jams from their unsold produce. At Cindy's meeting a couple dialed in on their Apple laptop. Someone else arrived late dressed in cycling gear. That night's agenda covered plans to add a nonprofit café and a store where people could sell the food that they made. The kitchen and community spaces could host nutrition and cooking classes and other community events. Numerous outside benefactors, including state and federal agencies, were funding the group's programs. Could one vibrant space catalyze safety and stability in the area?

* * *

A couple weeks later, dressed in baggy jeans with her hair down, Cindy baked a sheet cake for a retirement party for the president of Neighbors Building Brightmoor. After no one volunteered to replace the president, she had nominated Cindy for the position. For decades Cindy considered herself the neighborhood's "token honky," and since finding the group she had tried hard to find a place for herself in it. Now she felt like she had finally found one, and she embraced her new identity.

Running late, she left the cake to cool and grabbed her maroon purse. Heading out the door, she nearly collided with her sister Suzy. Cindy had offered to help hang blinds for a new member of Neighbors Building Brightmoor, a woman called Breonna who had recently arrived from the West Coast. On the drive over to her house Cindy passed three burnt houses in a row and more clustered across the street. Most had no roofs and about half of each building remained. "That pisses me off," she muttered. "You've got all these people here trying to maintain, but that one should be torn down, and that one."

The houses stood open, without even boards to prevent children from wandering in.

On the campaign trail, meanwhile, Mayor Duggan said, "I don't need any statistics to know that this city isn't as safe as it needs to be." Rather than boost resources for Detroit's police, however, Michigan legislators introduced a bill to extend to private security guards the authority of public police. The legislators described the proposed legislation as a way to supplement safety efforts in cash-strapped Michigan municipalities. The proposal, though, raised questions of accountability: The private guards would neither purport to represent the public interest nor answer to the public.

Nevertheless residents of wealthy Detroit neighborhoods like Palmer Woods, Sherwood Forest, and Boston Edison had started paying monthly assessments for enhanced private security. City officials made it easier for neighborhood associations to impose the charges, and if a resident missed a payment, that could count toward tax foreclosure. Brightmoor's residents did not have the money for such protections.

Cindy turned onto the rutted driveway of Breonna's one-bedroom bungalow, which had potted plants filling the front walk. Californian, with blond hair and rosy cheeks, Breonna had an open, bubbly way of speaking. To join the tight-knit community she believed Detroit's urban agriculture movement provided, she had packed all her belongings into her small Volkswagen and driven east from San Francisco to Detroit. As she drove up the driveway of the urban farm where she had arranged a room to live in, a farm that specialized in burying dead trees to fertilize the soil as they decayed, she thought everything about the place looked dead, too. She saw pillows stuffed into broken windows and drooping plants and immediately turned her car around. She found a rental house that bordered a different farm, then suffered two break-ins there.

The private security in wealthier neighborhoods freed the police to focus resources on less-well-off areas, while organizations like Neighbors Building Brightmoor worked to improve those areas from within. Those who received services like private security on the basis of their wealth, however, inevitably became less willing to support and pay for stronger public services that benefited everyone. Communities that paid their own way detached themselves economically, racially, and socially from the rest of the city, which caused greater inequality.

A man Breonna met introduced her to his neighbor, who offered her his foreclosed house for free; later she could try to buy it in the tax foreclosure auction. The house had mold-covered walls and cigarette-butt floors. Nevertheless she volunteered to pay the owner's delinquent utility bills and, to guarantee her ownership rather than risk the auction, take responsibility over his back taxes. She worked freelance technology jobs and had enough money. Neighborhood children began showing up at the house, and she took them in, tutoring them in mathematics and keeping a stock of board games for them to play with. Her seemingly steady presence, big-boned and open, offered a sort of port in the storm that was the neighborhood. But the kids argued and hit each other hard, and she could see that it hurt and could say only "no hitting." She felt ill-suited to a lot of the things that she had dived into. When she gave a salesman her new address to deliver a bed, he asked her if she knew she lived in a rough part of town. Since then she'd bought a baseball bat and slept with her lights on.

Back at Breonna's house Cindy tried to be helpful and started to advise Breonna on how to hang the set of blinds she was struggling with.

"You know if you..."

"No talking, I'm trying to think."

Unaccustomed to being dismissed that way, Cindy nearly punched her.

"No use throwing salt in my wounds," Breonna added. Breonna felt insecure about her ability to fix up her house herself, in a neighborhood where people did not hire people for renovations. The suggestion from Cindy seemed to hit a nerve.

And so Cindy drove home. She smoked loose cigarettes she kept in a Ziploc baggie in her purse.

"You didn't deck her?" Cindy's sister Suzy asked her, surprised Cindy simply left. Suzy had come to stay with her after serving time in prison on a drug charge, and Cindy had just started telling people about Suzy's criminal record and struggles with addiction.

* * *

Mayor Duggan put out a new campaign ad. It featured the skyline of Detroit, with a voice-over intoning, "What is at the heart of this city?" The answer: "The heartbeat of our neighborhoods." Robin had met Duggan at a ribbon-cutting ceremony for a Midtown apartment building he rehabilitated. Prior to the renovation Robin's son produced a zombie movie there.

Robin also still devoted time to filmmaking even after moving to Detroit, and a script he co-wrote was gaining traction in Los Angeles. He described the plot as a tale of adventure in a dangerous place, where structural forces that should have been caring for children had broken down. The story would resolve in the healing of relationships and systems that at first appeared too damaged to fix.

With cinematic settings in mind, Robin awoke to a flickering orange glow outside his window and decided to find the source. He grabbed his coat and thumped down the steps from the second floor of his yellow house to the sidewalk. A crowd of neighbors had formed, all looking in the same direction toward the light.

He joined them. Catching the rhythms of the crowd, he slowly walked a couple blocks from his house. When they reached a burning apartment building, all of them abruptly stopped. They watched as the fire tore through the structure.

Robin struck up a conversation with a fireman. He told the man he might buy the building. It seemed like a good investment, and he had restored fire-damaged buildings before.

A few days later he learned about the events that led up to the fire. A friend who worked with the police described to him how a murderer had set it to cover a gruesome, drug-related killing. Robin felt horrified he had gone outside thinking, "Hey, let's go look at the fire trucks," not knowing something so terrible had taken place.

The fact was that a lot about Detroit struck him as no more than an illusion. If he peeled back a beautiful orange vision, crime festered underneath. Prior to the bankruptcy the garbage didn't get picked up, and it still kind of didn't. The American mind-set of growth and expansion, he found, had failed the city. He envied people who did not need to worry about whether they made a profit and could focus on fixing up local buildings in ways that actually made a difference. He keenly felt his limited understanding of Detroit. He wished he had the luxury of patience for the city to improve.

* * *

A few days before the mayoral election, Miles received a bill for additional drivers' responsibility fees and drivers' reinstatement fees in the mail. He had orderly files of all his paperwork, and he had faxed a state office copies of the valid insurance and registration he had when the police took his license plates. Then a letter had arrived confirming that the traffic stop occurred in error, and he got new plates. With his eyeglasses slipping down his slender face, he wanted to know why the state had still levied fees on erroneous charges.

He was trying to be "a legitimate person, handling legitimate business." Now if the police caught him driving with unpaid fees, they could arrest him. To explain the situation he walked five blocks to the police station in his neighborhood. None of the officers there could help him: The fees had already entered the system. To remove them he would need a judicial order following a court proceeding. Until he could drive, he could not work, and until he could work, he could not drive. "How you supposed to be a contractor if you can't carry materials?" he wondered. Even if he could get to a job site, he would not have a valid license to show his employer. With simmering anger, he used his cell phone to read about debtors' prisons.

The mayoral contest, meanwhile, grew increasingly racially charged. Young aired an ad arguing that federal investigations into Detroit's demolition program indicated corruption equivalent to former mayor Kilpatrick's. "Why does Duggan get a pass, while Kwame Kilpatrick goes to jail for 28 years?" the ad asked. "It's as simple as black and white."

As Young continued to direct his underdog campaign against Detroit's "uneven" recovery, the next payment fell due on Miles's original payment plan from the fraudulent insurance he once used. He only had $40, so the state kicked him off the payment plan. His truck continued to sit in the driveway. Before long the air ran out of one of the tires.

Unable to find anyone to give him a ride to a gas station, he put his tire in a wheelbarrow and wheeled it nine blocks. He clutched his coat around his long neck tightly against a sudden autumn chill. The wheelbarrow bounced and swayed, especially where dead grass poked between the sidewalk's concrete blocks.

Finally he reached a seven-lane road and then a gas station, one of the few open businesses for miles. He swapped his tire for a new one and began his walk back home. "How is this the Motor City and nobody can afford to drive?" he wanted to know.

* * *

Given the overburdened court system, it took Miles three months to get a court date to dispute the second set of fines and fees, the ones imposed on the unfounded, mistaken charges. The day before the court date, he risked arrest by driving his daughter to the suburbs. She had a job interview at a taco chain, and he wanted to help her on a path to a more stable future. When he arrived at the court the next day, eager to argue his case, he learned he had missed the hearing. It had been scheduled for the previous day. Following instructions to reserve a new court date, he rode an escalator upstairs. It was there that a clerk flagged him. "We've got three felony counts on the computer showing up for you," the clerk said, and Miles's slim jaw dropped. "We wouldn't recommend you walking any further without a lawyer. You could be arrested."

Part Three

Prospects

14

Report Cards

NOVEMBER 2017

At home in his empty living room, with the ceiling still gashed open until he found time to repair the pipes and insulation underneath, Miles hunched over meticulous files of old court records. The criminal charges that prevented him from entering the courtroom had arisen 14 and a half years earlier. Back then, when he handled money for work or inspected vacant properties for people who wanted to buy them, he carried a gun. He ran a gauntlet of drug dealers, angry tenants of deadbeat landlords, and neighbors who thought he was stealing. With his lanky appearance he wanted extra protection, but he never bought a license for the gun. In 2003 he was arraigned on criminal charges. At the preliminary hearing the prosecuting officers never showed up, so the judge dismissed the case.

In the years since then Miles heard no more about the case, and he left any interest in guns behind. After his near miss from prison he decided to face his problems in the way he imagined people did in the suburbs, where he did not see liquor stores on every corner. He gave up fighting and gave up drinking, and he put his faith in God instead.

Miles could not understand why the old gun charges had reappeared. The lawyer who represented him back then had retired. Unable to afford a new lawyer, he had been repeatedly phoning the court's main number and taking the bus to the courthouse downtown asking for help, but no help came. Using his cell phone he had just found a record of the warrant against him online, which he strained to read through his glasses on the small screen. He wished he had a computer, though he thought it would get stolen as soon as he took it out of the box. He bent his lean frame over the coffee table to write a long letter by hand to the chief judge. He titled it "Civil Rights Violation Complaint" and sought at least a court date to resolve the old charges against him. He wrote that he did not understand what had happened and that he needed someone to help him handle it. He needed to regain his license; he needed someone to pay attention.

As Miles's past threatened to catch up to him, Mayor Duggan won a new start. Duggan had asked to be judged on whether the city's population increased under his leadership, and it hadn't. Nevertheless in November 2017 Duggan beat Coleman Young II in a landslide, having outraised him 56:1. Voter turnout did not break 20 percent. In the 2018 midterm elections more than twice as many Detroit voters participated. Racial animosity had continued to sully the campaign as Young drew contrasts between the young professionals arriving in the city and the older residents who left seeking better schools and more opportunities. Long an epicenter of racial activism, in the city new advocacy organizations had sprung up since the bankruptcy in response to perceived attempts to marginalize African American Detroiters in favor of young, white newcomers. The night before the election, Young held a rally with the theme Take Back the Motherland.

"There are haves and have-nots in every city in America," Duggan said after the election. "We're building a city here that it doesn't matter where you start, you have the opportunity to be successful." Miles meanwhile had not received any response from his letter to the chief judge. With the fear of arrest still looming over him, he took the bus to the courthouse again. "I'm just trying to get a court date," he told anyone who would listen. A clerk told him that judges never read letters like his, but she said he could deal with his auto insurance problem by waiting in line for the walk-in traffic court.

On the day of the next walk-in session, Miles took another bus to the courthouse, paid a bond to protect himself from arrest, and met the lawyer the court assigned to him. Miles's devil sat beside him, waiting for him to mess up. In court, the judge agreed the second traffic stop occurred in error: Miles had valid insurance. He should not have had to pay fines and fees on that erroneous charge. He still, however, had to pay fines and fees on the earlier charge of driving with fraudulent insurance. Interrupting the court-appointed lawyer, Miles asked the judge for help with the warrant for the old gun charges. As a traffic judge, she could do nothing. Miles left the courtroom partially vindicated but still in trouble. Then he noticed the judge had not struck from his record the fines and fees for the mistaken no-insurance charge. The lawyer had already moved on to the next defendant.

Local governments found a steady revenue source in fines and fees. The fees ensnared offenders like Miles in the criminal justice system through arrests and judicial proceedings. Nationally, "broken windows" policing techniques, in which police ticketed or arrested people who created civil disorder on the theory that disorder would propagate serious crimes, led to enforcement of more low-level offenses. Fines and fees for the offenses rose in tandem. Because of the procedures and processes collecting the penalties entailed, however, local governments often lost more money than they gained. The penalties disproportionately burdened and destabilized people living at the bottom of the economic ladder, and places with large African American and Latino populations relied most heavily on the money. Following the police killing of Michael Brown in Ferguson, Missouri, an investigation by the Department of Justice found that because of a "substantial sales tax shortfall," local officials asked the chief of police to increase ticketing for minor traffic violations. The resulting charges fell nearly exclusively on African Americans.

* * *

Miles waited for permission to enter a payment plan for the driving fees on the valid charge. He filled his days draped over his one chair at home, flipping through his folders of important papers and notes for clues about the gun warrant, paying people to drive him to construction sites, and taking the bus when he could not find anyone to drive him. Many people he knew relied on carpooling to get to construction jobs, even as the carpool drivers frequently also risked losing their licenses for driving without insurance. He hated his lack of control over his own schedule, and he could not pick up materials when his bosses asked or run out to buy them more gasoline. When he had to take the bus, poor connections made jobs across town unreachable.

He needed to keep moving, though, earning as much money as he could and then rotating which bills he paid each month. "You sit still, it'll catch up with you," he said. He had payment plans for his groceries, his utilities, his cell phone, his property taxes, and, he hoped, the auto-insurance penalties.

When a bill arrived for delinquent tuition for the online construction courses he watched, he wadded up the bill with delicate hands and threw it away, muttering, "How many times are you going to tell somebody you don't make the money you used to?"

Missing work, he waited again to ask the judge to remove the fines and fees she had already found improper. After she removed them he walked to another courthouse that handled criminal cases, which he had learned about on his phone, to ask about the old gun charges. In his understanding, the clerk he spoke with at the criminal court could not find the warrant because the charges had never been "bound" over to that court. In Detroit arraignments on both misdemeanors and felonies occurred in the district court, where Miles had just had his traffic hearing and where he had mailed his letter to the chief judge asking for help. If a district court judge found sufficient evidence at a preliminary hearing to believe a defendant committed a crime, the judge "bound" the case over to the criminal court and terminated the district court's jurisdiction over the case.

Miles's district court records predated the reorganization of that court, which occurred simultaneously with the city's bankruptcy to improve the collection of fines and fees and increase computerization. His records seemed to indicate that the criminal court remanded his case to the district court, which then sent the case back to the criminal court. In the criminal court, because the police officers did not show up to try the case, the judge dismissed it. He dismissed it "without prejudice," however, which meant that the prosecutors could bring the case again. No judge or jury had tried the charges on the merits, so no double jeopardy protections attached. The judge had neither acquitted nor convicted Miles. This meant that Miles could face another trial and potential conviction.

About a month after the dismissal, the district court opened a new warrant for his arrest on the same charges. The warrant did not enter the state-wide electronic system. In all the years since then, no further procedures took place: no preliminary hearing and no binding over of the case. The clerk Miles spoke with at the criminal court suggested that Miles go to the police station and ask an officer there if he could find any warrants against him.

At the station, the policeman who assisted Miles initially could not find any warrants, and then suddenly he did. Miles strained to overhear what happened next. As he understood it, the policeman phoned the prosecutor's office and described a warrant from 2003. The person on the other end of the line said the case had languished so long that no one would prosecute it.

Back home, Miles received a notice accepting him to a payment plan for the fines and fees attached to his genuine violation. To reinstate his driving privileges he bought new insurance, but he would have to let it lapse when the seven-day grace period ended. This time he could not afford legitimate coverage. Back behind the wheel of his truck, but now risking arrest for driving without insurance in addition to arrest on the open gun warrant, he rushed to install drywall at houses around town.

A few days later the warrant for his arrest on the 2003 gun charges entered the state-wide electronic system, and the prosecutors' office reissued the charges against him. Miles was still monitoring his record on his phone, skating his long fingers across the screen, and he saw what had happened. He did not know what else he could do. "The loss goes to me every time," he said. "That's my fault because they changed the court?" He returned to the criminal court, looking tired and thin. He spoke with a clerk who gave him a printout of the criminal court's original dismissal when the officers did not show up for the trial, and she penned on it in cursive, "This person was *never* charged in this case." She affixed a gold seal that made the documents look official and indicated that she would ask the state police to remove the case from the warrant system. The clerk's job description listed her responsibilities as assisting felons with court information, processing expungements, and managing transcripts and case files. She previously worked checking in patients at a doctors' office and in customer service at a cell phone store.

Miles viewed her paperwork as a second dismissal of his gun charges, though no judge had ruled on them. He placed the papers she gave him in a fresh folder in his truck, in case he got pulled over. If he faced any more setbacks, he realized with some irony, he did not know how long he would be able to survive without breaking the law.

* * *

A 15-minute drive north of the courthouse, Joe parked in front of his friend's bakery, near his house. He flicked off the radio, which he had been listening to with characteristic intensity. The station, AM 910, advertised as "the voice of Detroit," even though a white businessman from the suburbs owned it. It featured call-in shows hosted by local politicians and activists, including a former Detroit City Council president imprisoned for taking bribes. People called in yelling and shouting. A former Detroit police chief quit the station mid-broadcast. "However they package this thing, it's the crooks, the ex–police chiefs, the councilmen who got caught doing whatever," Joe said, smiling.

But increasingly he was growing exasperated with local politics. His wife, Naomi, who had finally joined him in Detroit, was having a difficult time adjusting to the crime and fear that seemed to penetrate her daily life there.

Joe and Naomi had met in Kenya, in the small village where she grew up. She lived in Germany for a long time, then returned to Kenya to teach English. She and Joe rendezvoused in cities around the world, but Detroit offered her only experience of America.

When she arrived in Detroit, Joe showed her the neighborhood: "A musician lives in this house, a nice old lady in this house, a crack addict lives in this house, and this house is abandoned." Since then she had found work at a nursery school in Fitzgerald near Joe's still un-renovated commercial space and the city's redevelopment project, another part-time job at the opera house downtown, and weekend work with an urban farming education center.

She considered America the land of milk and honey, a place of upward mobility, and so it surprised her to feel unsafe there. Though African, she did not feel an affinity with the neighborhood's African Americans. Near Joe's commercial space she saw drug deals take place, and she perceived a gun culture that seemed to pervade the city. On the street where she and Joe lived she witnessed a neighbor get shot in his driveway for reasons no one could explain. Around the corner another man shot the mother of his child, and then the mother's mother and his own cousin. When Joe and Naomi discussed the crime in their neighborhood, he observed that the city program that enabled businesses to install video cameras helped individual businesses by pushing crime further away but had no capacity to address the roots of the crime itself.

In spite of the violent environment, Joe and Naomi observed his daughter finding opportunity in Detroit. She bought a house for $500 in Fitzgerald and gardened there intensely, surrounded by land bank–owned lots slated for conversion to natural landscapes. Though the area struck Joe as too dangerous, she lived alone with her pit bull and jogged in the neighborhood carrying Mace. She seemed unfazed by a shooting that occurred two houses down from hers and the fact that the previous occupants of her house lived there with no electricity or plumbing. She had left the restaurant where she tended bar for a job at a new distillery downtown, then left the distillery to waitress at another new restaurant. At the new restaurant she earned even more money in tips, serving customers that included the highest city officials, the consultants involved in the Fitzgerald project, and wealthy suburbanites who ventured into the city.

Joe still believed in Detroit and mostly liked his life there, but for every resident like his daughter, he knew many others who did poorly. The wife of the African American family in the house to his left had promised her husband, a native Detroiter, she would try living in the city for five years. Then they would reassess. As soon as the five years elapsed they moved to the suburbs with their two little girls. The couple already worked in the suburbs, shopped in the suburbs, and ate in the suburbs. The family seemed like the kind that was supposed to help bring back the city.

* * *

The Preacher of Prairie Street preached about crime, guns, leaving, and staying in relation to his own life and also his neighborhood, Fitzgerald. Joe and the preacher sat on the preacher's front porch as some young men from the congregation mowed land bank–owned lots on either side of the house. In the mild autumn weather, with the scent of fresh-cut grass perfuming the air as the crack of a gunshot sounded in the distance, the preacher reminisced about the neighborhood.

Joe had met the preacher cleaning alleys and lots, and now he leaned forward with rapt attention, listening to the preacher talk. Joe's saws sat beside them. He no longer left anything in his truck, following a mid-afternoon break-in while the truck sat in front of an insurance office.

The preacher's block had only three houses left. The preacher got his house for free, a gift from an older neighbor who no longer wanted her closest neighbor nine lots away. Crack cocaine had swept through the neighborhood, carrying the preacher and his fortunes in its wake. Before he joined the clergy he sold drugs, and in the mid-1990s he could earn $500 in 15 minutes just standing on his corner dealing. When he got shot, he found God and became a preacher. As a preacher he could travel for the first time, and he saw people living in places that looked to him like paradise. Most people he knew never left the neighborhood. They could not drive because they lacked cars, or car insurance, or the wherewithal to pay child support, and they risked arrest if police pulled them over.

The preacher's house fell outside Fitzgerald's quarter-square-mile redevelopment area but looked in its direction. Joe now supported the project, but most aspects of it had fallen behind schedule, and the city's ambitions had grown more modest. Developers had begun renovating only three houses, had not started construction of the bike path, and would open the park a year late. They would no longer de-molish houses with a special technique billed as useful for creating neighborhood jobs and preserving materials for reuse. The developers would market half the number of renovated houses at affordable prices that they had originally planned. Affordable meant $55,000 or more, a relatively high price in a neighborhood with an average income of $14,000.

The obstacles the Fitzgerald project was encountering laid bare the complexity of seeding change in desolate urban neighborhoods, even relatively strong ones with major in-stitutions like Fitzgerald. Liens tied up title to many of the properties. Over a year into the project, the developers owned just nine of the 320 houses they needed to renovate. The developers also lacked experience dealing with so many houses at once. Just boarding up vacant properties took them two months longer than they expected. The college and university that bounded the redevelopment zone struggled under the same problems that plagued the neighborhood. At Marygrove College enrollment had declined, and a plan to increase revenues by renovating buildings into student dorms proved too expensive to carry out. Instead the administration terminated all undergraduate programs and cut the staff to 12 full-time graduate faculty, which meant lower population density and fewer people spending money in the neighborhood. University of Detroit Mercy, meanwhile, cut tuition to try to buoy enrollment, which comprised a few thousand students.

Fitzgerald had a 17 percent unemployment rate, but the developers had hired fewer than 10 local residents. Though 40 percent of Detroit's population did not have access to the Internet at home, the developers required candidates to apply for jobs through an online portal. The developers planned to install Wi-Fi infrastructure in the neighborhood. While volunteering there, Joe had introduced himself, sweaty from his work, to the redevelopment project's spokesperson. She described meeting her first Fitzgerald resident in a tone that suggested to him an anthropologist encountering her first indigenous Papuan in New Guinea. He told her loudly that she needed to establish a number that people in the neighborhood could phone to communicate with her. He asked her to help him get a nearby streetlight fixed.

Speaking increasingly quickly, Joe told the preacher about a subsequent meeting he attended about bringing jazz music into Fitzgerald. The music program might launch the following summer. An African American woman whom he met doing tree work yelled, "I'll be dead by then," from the audience. He understood how urgently people wanted anything that seemed new and different yet no longer expected fast changes.

* * *

As Joe finished his coffee at a meeting with a journalist, still wearing his customary black beanie, his cell phone rang. The ringtone played a tune on a harmonica. On the other end of the line came the voice of his neighborhood district manager, a position Mayor Duggan created as Detroit prepared to exit bankruptcy three years earlier. Seven district managers now oversaw community efforts within separate portions of the city. Joe had left his manager a message, complaining at length about "sabotage" of the playground he wanted to build. He had grown increasingly outspoken about neighborhood issues.

With the arrival of the first major snow, winter had descended on the city, and community politics had stalled Joe and Anthea's plans for a neighborhood playground. First the neighborhood community council dragged its feet filling out necessary forms. Then the council president, an older woman originally from Georgia, failed to schedule or attend required meetings with the land bank. The council blamed the land bank; the land bank blamed the council. Anthea had told the council president about her idea to convert the abandoned house next to the playground into a literacy center, expecting encouragement and help. Instead the president said, "Let me know how that goes," and offered no further assistance. Joe and Anthea had learned that the house would cost $40,000 to acquire and needed a complete renovation. A group of investors who owned hundreds of houses in the city had won the house in the tax foreclosure auction and done nothing with it.

With his commercial space in Fitzgerald still empty, Joe offered to host a community meeting there. The snow kept the council president from attending. A smattering of women in their 60s who came every time braved the weather, materializing almost magically on folding chairs in the raw space. In spite of the storm, Joe still wasn't wearing a coat.

One of the women announced that to ensure Joe's playground never got built, she would join the vacant lots committee he now chaired. He had done some tree work for her, and they otherwise got along. Nevertheless she refused to have her grandchildren play next to the abandoned house that Anthea wanted to repurpose. Joe couldn't keep from pointing out that the next three houses also stood empty and that to prepare the site for the playground he had removed garbage so voluminous that anyone could have hidden in it. Then he stopped himself and did not ask why she would allow her grandchildren to play by themselves at a playground or why for years the neighbors did nothing about the empty house. "This is Detroit," he said instead, biting his tongue for once. "If we operate on the worst-case scenario of what might happen, none of us should leave this room, so let's work where we can." A few days earlier a local teenager nonfatally shot four other teenagers in an argument at the annual Noel Night celebration, a Midtown festival near the art museum with carriage rides and music and theater performances.

Joe felt more and more discouraged by the apparent disconnect people had between thinking of ways to make things better and then acting. Recently he had seen a little girl playing in a collapsing, burnt-out house in the neighborhood because she had nowhere better to play, and he met a bright, funny five-year-old boy who told Joe his mother had a violent boyfriend. Joe found the child's understanding of adult aggression troubling. Meanwhile neighbors dominated the meeting with complaints about garbage cans left out too long and kids playing basketball in the street, rather than tougher issues.

Joe had taken to repeating the words of a local ex-gang member turned community activist whom he heard speak on a panel. "All anyone has to do is care," he said. Joe found hope in the idea that caring could alleviate seemingly insoluble problems. Following his new mantra, he advocated for the resignation of most Detroit politicians and others in leadership positions, university presidents, heads of community block clubs, and the young, educated professionals he knew who worked in high-profile community redevelopment jobs and lived in condominiums downtown. He thought few of them did anything to help the residents of the city. "If the job is too big for you, and you can't keep up, Boston Market's hiring," he told people.

In his neighborhood, one of Detroit's most stable, he watched a silent loop of old people desperate to leave, young people with nothing to do, crack addicts, and prostitutes. Everyone else sat complacent in a community he perceived as one large gas leak, where someone could light a match at any time.

15

The Way We Live Now

From her position beached on the sofa watching the snow, Tasha entreated Reggie just to let God work it out. He was running himself ragged, his eyes growing red and raw. He looked like he had lost weight. With every passing day, he and Tasha drew nearer to losing their home and also their livelihood. Someone from the company that owned the house had mailed them a copy of the deed, and at the end of the school year, when Reggie's daughter graduated from high school, the adoption payments the family received would end.

Reggie was hustling to earn money to create a buffer against the move and the expiration of the adoption payments. He drove the minibus for as many hours as the company would give him, and he tried to drum up further painting work for the weekends. He did not have a license to do the painting, but he asked people he knew to let him help them with their houses and refer him to their friends. On Thursday evenings he still practiced with the gospel band at his church, and every Sunday he performed at services.

Reggie had phoned the man who corresponded with him about the house to ask about buying it back from him. Reggie knew the $7,000 winning auction bid far exceeded the house's worth, but he told the man he would come up with that amount anyway. He got rebuffed and stopped himself from offering any more money. He resigned himself to walking away when the time came, while the new owner profited off his family's house.

Hoping he would see a place his family could move that he could afford, Reggie began driving up and down the surrounding blocks in the old minivan. That December it had already snowed more than average, and the forecast kept predicting more snow. As he navigated the unplowed streets, clutching the wheel to keep the van from slipping, he did not know what he was searching for or how he would pay for it. Though the number of mortgages in Detroit had risen through the year, the number had not yet reached 1,000, and less than a quarter of the home sales in the city used mortgages. The average Detroit sale price still fell below the $50,000 threshold at which banks typically began lending. Reggie knew he could not buy a house with a mortgage. Land contracts also seemed risky now that he knew about scams. He didn't think he could afford to rent a house, though, because he would need first and last months' rent and security. With the drawbacks of every option swirling in sync with the snow beyond his windshield, he tried to stay calm and banish any expectations of what kind of place he might find or how it might look.

At home he smoked more than usual and kept drumming his big hands against the glass coffee table. Then his cousin showed up from the suburbs with a proposition. The same cousin had introduced Reggie to Courtney Taylor, the woman who wrote the land contract on his house, and bore responsibility for Reggie's family's circumstances. Without any sign of remorse, he offered to flip Reggie a house he had won in the tax foreclosure auction.

The cousin had recently started bidding in the auction and generally rented out the houses he won. That autumn he had acquired eight houses, and he offered just one of them to Reggie. Reggie agreed to buy it for $5,000 on a land contract. Immediately the tension in his chubby-cheeked face eased. He smiled when he told people he had found a new house, and his dimples returned.

* * *

Reggie went to see the new house. Next door sat an overgrown vacant lot, and a shuttered school sat two houses down. The school had closed 12 years earlier, and the abandoned building and an empty flagpole remained accessible from the street. Behind an open chain link fence lurked three acres of neglected playing fields. The school's oldest alumni, mostly white, maintained a vibrant online community, circulating pictures of the building's construction in the 1950s and memories of teachers and school plays. Meanwhile, across the street from the school, several houses had vegetation growing out their windows, and graffiti blacked out the text of a drug-free-school-zone sign.

The house itself had two bedrooms and one bathroom, faded white siding the color of raw dough, and a tired roof roughly the same shade. Wiping his thick hand on his jeans, Reggie fished the key from his pocket and opened the door. Inside abandoned belongings were strewn across every surface. The walls and ceilings had holes where scrappers cut out plumbing lines. Ripped-up carpet exposed cement floors, and rubble marked the place where a wall once divided the kitchen from the living room. A family of raccoons scuttled through the wreckage.

Reggie beamed. Regardless of how the house looked now, once he paid off the land contract he would own it, and becoming a homeowner meant a great deal to him. The occupied houses on the block had well-maintained yards. Best of all his daughter could still get to her high school for her last semester. Moving schools so soon before graduation would have set her back, and though she did not have plans for when she finished, everyone in the family looked forward to seeing her move on with her life.

Reggie did not mind paying his cousin $5,000 for the house, even though he thought his cousin won it for $2,500. He did not expect anything free in life, and a small profit for his cousin seemed fair. He liked the fact that his cousin made him responsible for the property taxes. He did not want to depend on someone else to pay them on time, as he had at the house he lost. In a few months when the first tax bill fell due, the bill would cost more than the whole house, but he understood that to rebuild the city needed to increase revenues.

He vowed to make the house a blessing for his family. He steeled himself for the renovation. It would require repeating all the work he did on the old house and then doing more. He needed to erect new walls, paint and carpet everywhere, and buy a furnace and a hot water tank. The house also needed a new roof and new plumbing.

He would have to scramble to have everything ready for his family to move in before the new owner of the old house kicked them out. As Reggie installed a lock at the new house, he did not know that auction records indicated his cousin paid just $500 for it.

* * *

Looking tired, Cindy sat drinking a Diet Coke in the bar at the Moose Lodge fraternal organization dressed in slacks and a pullover cotton sweater. She had lost so much weight from mowing and hauling and gardening in the neighborhood that most of her clothes no longer fit. As outside Detroit grew steadily colder, inside the air around her grew thick with cigarette smoke, which hung atmospherically in the darkened room. She had an hour to kill, and the bar offered a good place to rest between her volunteer work and committee meetings.

The respite the Lodge provided from the neighborhood came as a relief. The clubhouse sat on the border between Brightmoor and the suburb of Redford. No one from Neighbors Building Brightmoor belonged to the Lodge, and its membership seemed almost exclusively white. Cindy's triumph in becoming the president of Neighbors Building Brightmoor had already faded.

She had seen a few foreign-looking families on her block, the women dressed in headscarves, and considered getting her gun from the closet to protect herself from them. Detroit had few immigrants, though the mayor and governor supported immigration to increase population. Cindy posted "We don't want them here" on her social media accounts and on Neighbors Building Brightmoor's. In response the district manager phoned to ask her to explain herself; the neighborhood organization's members formed an inclusion committee and visited the neighborhood mosque. The woman Cindy fought with while helping her install blinds, Breonna, wrote updates on the inclusion committee for the organization's newsletter.

"We already got enough crime and violence," Cindy had said, in her gravelly smoker's voice, to the district manager. "You want to add to that?" The neighborhood already had families living in abandoned houses, houses without lights or running water. She thought the city and the neighborhood needed to focus on supporting their own. After living through white flight, the drug epidemic, abandoned houses, and scrappers, and working to clean it all up, she refused to welcome new people who she felt didn't want her there. "You want to pull your head out of your ass?" she said about the inclusion committee.

It had been a difficult time in the neighborhood. The previous night she had awakened at three in the morning and called the police on a group of "nasty tall things" who "sagged their pants" and made noise on the street. Then today the same boys had hit their drug customer over the head with a pipe, stolen his wallet and cell phone, and taken off running, leaving the customer's prostitute still sitting in his truck. The husband of the young family who lived next door to Cindy phoned to tell her.

She repeatedly clashed with Breonna and frequently had to walk away to keep from slugging her. For the first time Cindy noticed that no one in the group but the former president ever called her or tried to be her friend. Her forehead wrinkled when she thought about it.

She was considering resigning the presidency and stepping down from the board of the organization she felt so proud to join. Neighbors Building Brightmoor members seemed to feel entitled to come in and do "whatever the hell" they wanted, and she didn't understand that attitude. She did, however, acknowledge, with a confused expression on her face, that many of the neighborhood residents who had lived in the area for longer did not try to do anything at all.

* * *

A few days later, in a landscape as different from Brightmoor as a summer day by the lake, Cindy was cleaning a mansion in Bloomfield, the most expensive community in Michigan. The house did not even seem dirty. Nevertheless she cleaned the bathrooms, mopped the floors, and scrubbed down a kitchen the size of her own house. She checked to convince herself that only one family lived there. As she returned her cleaning equipment to the trunk of her Escort, avoiding a stack of Neighbors Building Brightmoor newsletters, snowflakes landed on her long braid, covering it in tiny polka dots.

Cindy cleaned houses for $16 cash for as many hours as she could get, which wasn't many. None of the houses she cleaned was in Brightmoor or even Detroit. Hemmed in by the snow, she made her way carefully from Bloomfield to another suburb 30 minutes away. From there she would continue to another house in another suburb. The last house belonged to a neurosurgeon. Once she left a Neighbors Building Brightmoor newsletter on his kitchen counter and picked up a donation that way.

She was trying to work out how she felt about the organization she still led and what she and her neighbors had accomplished. As she returned home to Brightmoor at the end of the long day of cleaning, she turned onto Brightmoor's main commercial street and thought back to all the businesses that operated there when she was growing up. Wet flakes blurred the windshield, but she could still picture the old supermarket, the bowling alley, the Copa Lounge and the Bonton Lounge, the Fundamental Baptist church. Only Sonny's Hamburgers, where she hung out as a teenager playing the jukebox and waiting for her boyfriends, remained open amid all the snow-covered, boarded-up buildings. She smiled at the memory, and a pretty girl's face shone through all the hardship that had settled on top.

She turned off the main road into the part of the neighborhood where she grew up with her mother, down the street from her grandparents' house. After Cindy turned 18 her mother died in a drug-related crime. On the small lot where her house had stood new Habitat for Humanity houses now crowded together. The new houses looked worse than the older ones, which though decaying at least had architectural flourishes and character. Cindy stared at it all, unblinkingly. The park a few doors down still had its tennis court, now buried under snowdrifts, though the pavilion beside the court had long ago disappeared. She and a friend who lived near the court used to sell Kool-Aid from a wagon to the tennis players before the friend's family moved to the suburbs to avoid busing. A few blocks down, Cindy's grandparents' lot now lay empty and barren. Neighbors had blocked off the street to keep people from using it to evade police chasing them. The peony bush and the rhubarb that had grown along her grandparents' fence had disappeared. Before joining Neighbors Building Brightmoor Cindy had never gardened, but she remembered eating the canned fruits and vegetables her grandmother put up every summer. She could picture her grandfather and uncle turning the dirt to prepare for the new season. Gardening still triggered in her complicated emotions of death and rebirth and loss.

On the way back home Cindy passed a block with only one house, a vacant husk. Snow-speckled refuse piled up in the middle of the road. On another block another abandoned house had yellow foreclosure notices tacked to the door. Then a car on her tail interrupted her memories. "You want to be a dick, just go around me, this is a side street," she yelled out the window. "You ain't gonna pay my bills when I skid out." Spending the day in pretty neighborhoods with oversized houses and seeing the contrast had darkened her mood.

When she reached her driveway she teared up a little, then regained control of herself and pulled her car to the side. When her husband, Dick, got in from the night shift, he could park his car in front of hers, though by then the driveway might need to be shoveled again. She would leave early the next morning to clean more houses.

Inside the house she brewed a pot of coffee and found her reading glasses. Then she settled into the gray sofa with her laptop to answer Neighbors Building Brightmoor emails. Her cats and dog crowded around, as her long nails and rings clicked against the keyboard.

"Here's one of my little buddies," her sister Suzy said as she walked into the living room and stopped to pet a cat. Just then the dog started chasing another cat.

"Hey, hey, hey, I'll kick your ass, you knucklehead," Cindy yelled. "That's Wendy, and Wendy don't play." Slipping out the door, Suzy told her that Cindy's stepdaughter, Dick's daughter, had stopped by the house. She and her husband needed a place to stay and she wanted to talk.

* * *

As Cindy bristled at Suzy's news and the snow continued to fall, Charles's property taxes finally caught up with him in Morningside. He sat in a rocking chair on his front porch bundled into his fur hat, a workman's coat, and fuzzy gloves. The new owner of his house, a shivering Floridian about 30 years old who picked up four other houses in the auction that year, sat beside him. Charles had just given him a tour, pointing out various repairs the house needed. Though it was December, the porch felt warmer than the unheated living room, so they were finishing their conversation outside.

The tax foreclosure machine still bulldozed its way through Detroit's neighborhoods, though as more and more properties entered the land bank fewer houses remained in private ownership eligible for foreclosure. A philanthropic organization had offered the city money to cover the down payments on payment plans to enable homeowners with delinquent property taxes to keep their houses. The county treasurer declined the funding, saying the deadline for entering payment plans that year had already passed.

Giggling nervously, Charles asked the new owner if Charles could work for him and fix up the house. Top to bottom, Charles knew how to renovate houses. Though he didn't like getting on them, he could install roofs. And though he didn't consider himself a backyard guy, he could build swimming pools. The owner told him he already had a team in place to renovate all five of his houses.

The future for Charles's house, it seemed, would play out the same way as development downtown. A contractor from the suburbs would come in with a set crew, leaving Detroiters with the odd construction task for someone they knew. In spite of his objections to emergency management, Charles had hoped the bankruptcy would bring back jobs to the city for people like him. Completing the legal forms on his phone, he had incorporated a company for his renovation work and named it after his grandparents.

Now he viewed the bankruptcy simply as a way to show a balanced budget to the rest of the country, so that private investors would direct their money to downtown Detroit. Downtown looked spectacular to him, "I mean beautiful, like everything you want it to look." When it snowed, "not only do they clean up the snow, they actually haul it away." Downtown had police, and in the neighborhoods it looked as though a war had taken place. The city had cleared its own debt, but people like him still could not find the jobs they needed to pay their bills. A city of homeowners had become a city of renters, all struggling to afford cars and insurance to trudge to the suburbs for insufficient work.

How could his friends have agreed to pension cuts in the bankruptcy, he wondered, in exchange for investment in the areas of the city where they didn't live? He thought they should protest, then decided they'd only come away with sore feet. He clocked the bankruptcy as the time of death for "we the people" and "united we stand."

Walking back inside the unheated house, Charles sweetly told its new owner, with his small head bowed, that if someone had to have the house, he felt glad it would be him. Charles meant it. He hoped the new owner would have the best experience of a lifetime. Charles did not tell him that he doubted the owner could ever flip the house. Who would want to buy it with five other vacant, vandalized houses across the street, their gutters twisted and their yards full of debris?

16

I'm from the Government, and I'm Here to Help

JANUARY 2018

With the snow still falling, Reggie implored Tasha to visit the doctor. The stress of the upcoming move was making her asthma worse, leaving her prone on the sofa, but she wanted to stay out of the hospital to help pack.

"You trying to make me go, but I know what they going to do, they going to keep me," she said from the sofa. She raised the volume on a television show about chocolate to drown out Reggie. Briefly she looked away from the screen to yell, "You make me go, I say no!"

"But that means you need to be kept when you're breathing like that. You got to go. You can't just stay here and catch no air because you don't want to go."

"I find some air, I'll give it to you."

"I don't think it works like that."

The new house did not have functioning utilities, and Reggie would do anything to avoid subjecting her, vulnerable, to an unheated house. He drove his minibus for longer and longer hours, staying in the bus to protect himself when he made pickups in the dark. He had developed gray smudges underneath both eyes. But he still did not have enough money to pay the deposits that turning on the utilities required. Because earlier tenants of the new house left large bills unpaid, the utility companies demanded large payments before they would turn any services back on.

To save more money he stopped paying for auto insurance. Doing so jeopardized his job, but he had no other expenses to cut. Aside from the utilities, the new house was progressing. With characteristic bravado, his cousin William had chased out raccoons and cleared branches near the windows to prevent the raccoons from returning. William's son hauled out all the refuse, which had insulation and raccoon urine mixed in. Reggie bought new carpet and gradually installed new pipes. Unable to afford a new roof, he covered the old one with a blue tarp.

As Reggie placed his livelihood at risk to prepare the house, Tasha chose to entrust her fate to God. She visualized everything working out. God worked in mysterious ways, and she convinced herself that great things could happen at the new house.

"This is going to be a better year!" she yelled from her spot on the sofa. She turned down the volume on the television. "In God's hands, I say it is."

"And *I'm* going to make sure it is best I can," Reggie said more quietly.

With the new place still lacking heat, electricity, and running water, though, he did not know what he could do. He decided to try fighting in court for more time in the old house. He had never set foot in a courthouse before or drawn such attention to himself. On the day of his hearing he sat in a windowless mediation room, uncomfortably dressed, fighting the best his genial personality allowed. He felt too scared and frustrated to keep track of the name of his opponent who sat across from him at the conference table.

Reggie emerged shaken but with an agreement to pay $200 for two more weeks in the house. He needed more time than that, but his nameless adversary had made clear that at the end of two weeks, bailiffs would toss Reggie's family's belongings to the curb.

* * *

Two weeks later, Reggie and Tasha drove to the new house after church. Even though they had only finished moving the night before, Reggie played the drums at the service. Dizzy with relief at having the move behind them, they joked and giggled in the car, and Tasha spoke much more than usual.

The house now looked like a carbon copy of the old one but with less space. The living room had the same mauve walls and brown carpet; the glass coffee table, television, and black leather sofas occupied similar spots. Tasha confessed to Reggie that in church that morning she thought about the new house instead of contemplating the Scripture.

"It's like the old one, it's just everything is on one floor now."

"And we don't have no dining room," Reggie said.

"Yeah, where that wall at, that was stairs going up to our old bedroom."

They had moved in the snow. Tasha's son, Tasha's brother, Reggie's cousin William, and many more nieces and nephews all helped. Reggie rented a U-Haul and made one trip in it, loaded with as many belongings as it could fit. Then he returned it and drove back and forth between the houses in his clanking van several more times. William disconnected the hot water tank from the old house and brought the tank over to the new house, but he had to abandon the furnace. To function it needed a basement, which the new house did not have.

Reggie also left the lawn furniture he used when he hosted family get-togethers. Without a garage at the new house, he had nowhere to put the furniture where it wouldn't get stolen.

After they had moved what they could and their relatives left, Reggie and Tasha celebrated in the dark and cold. Without a working stove, they bought themselves sandwiches, corned beef in honor of St. Patrick's Day. As they ate sporadic drops of snow and rain pelted them through the roof.

Tasha gave Reggie a deadline. She wanted a lasagna for her birthday. He made her one every year, extra cheesy and meaty the way she liked it. To prepare it the house would need gas and running water. Plumbing in the bathroom would also be helpful. Until the house had those things she would suffer, much like the 1 in 10 city residents who had their water shut off that year.

"I promise it'll get more comfortable soon."

"Baby, with everything on one floor now, I don't got to sit here and listen to you. I can just go straight to my room!"

She would spend the rest of the day under the covers in the back bedroom. The move had worn her out.

* * *

Cindy's stepdaughter fainted in the bathtub after she and her family moved into the next-door squat. Cindy's sister Suzy rode with her to the hospital.

"Why was Suzy's ass involved?" Cindy wanted to know, her gray-flecked ponytail swishing. Since her stepdaughter and her family started squatting next door Suzy seemed to be backsliding. When she came home to Cindy's house from the squat, Suzy went directly to her room and closed the door. She emerged staggering, weaving an erratic course through the house. She helped herself to cigarettes from the plastic bag in Cindy's maroon purse. Her stepdaughter stopped waitressing when she got married, and her husband was often gone from home.

Cindy wanted Suzy gone. Dick had heart trouble, and he was refusing surgery. Cindy needed to look out for herself, not babysit a grown woman, she said with a hard set to her eyes.

Though Cindy would be the last to admit it, it seemed to pain her to watch Suzy lose all the progress she had made. Suzy quit the paid position she had earned at her outpatient program, phoning other patients to remind them of appointments. She told her supervisor that the calls made her throat hurt. Without the job, Suzy could no longer make money and chip away at the fines she owed for her various infractions. Even the prison had charged room and board plus a booking fee. That practice originated in Michigan and had spread throughout the country as a way to offset the costs of associated municipal services, but the income risked incentivizing improper arrests and enmeshed former inmates in a cycle of debt and incarceration. Suzy no longer did the gardening and mowing she had taken over from Cindy or attended typing and computer training classes.

For 15 years Cindy and Dick patronized a diner in Redford, the suburb adjacent to Brightmoor. The waitress serving them had worked there almost as long. As Cindy ordered a spinach and feta omelet in a booth by the window, the glass steamed against the cold. Outside, cars plowed their way through the snow on the five-lane road. "Some people aren't happy with their own life, so they got to make everybody else around them miserable," Cindy said, looking into her hash browns and trying to hide her fears about Dick's heart.

* * *

Signs saying "Boycott All Brightmoor Farmway Farms" began appearing throughout the neighborhood, referring to the collection of neighborhood farms. A family that lived behind a farm had grown tired of smelling compost from inside their house. The farm had expanded, amoeba-like, and spilled over onto adjacent lots. People in the neighborhood who kept goats and chickens began to receive citations from the city. Animal control showed up to confiscate livestock. Even the former president of Neighbors Building Brightmoor lost her farm animals and threatened to leave the neighborhood. Other neighbors kept their animals anyway, waiting to get caught. Their deliberate violation of the rules shocked Cindy. It evidenced a privilege that made her feel even more different from the group's other members.

Whispered complaints rumbled from block to block through the neighborhood. Cindy overheard people saying that Neighbors Building Brightmoor amounted to no more than "a bunch of white yuppies coming in here and taking over a black neighborhood." She realized she agreed. Why would anyone want to spend more for local produce at the neighborhood farmers' market when the grocery store offered coupons for two-for-one deals? She knew most of the farm products did not sell. The farmers needed the Brightmoor Artisans Collective's facilities to can their unsold vegetables. Otherwise the vegetables would rot.

"Honky" or not, she knew lots of people who lived in the neighborhood before Neighbors Building Brightmoor's members started arriving. She began asking them more questions and chatted with an African American man who lived across the street from where a young, white couple bought an intact house, an abandoned house, and a vacant lot.

"It looks like shit over there," he said, pointing to the couple's homemade ecological drainage system. To keep rainwater out of the sewers they had mounded dirt between the curb and the sidewalk and planted long-rooted perennials on top. "I have to look out my window and see that dirt every day," the man said.

"Well, there you go," Cindy said, shaking her head. People

like that just did what they wanted no matter what an original resident thought. Why didn't they ask first, she wondered?

Attendance at Neighbors Building Brightmoor meetings had fallen to about 15 people. Once-committed members defected to the Brightmoor Artisans Collective. When Cindy attended a neighborhood engagement training session downtown, she introduced herself as a representative of Neighbors Building Brightmoor. "Isn't that the hipster farmer group that doesn't exist anymore?" she heard the teacher say.

Then the news circulated that volunteers at Brightmoor's farmers' market had not allowed a couple Cindy knew to sell honey there. The honey came from a few blocks away in Redford, so it did not have Brightmoor origins. The couple had won a house in Redford in the tax foreclosure auction, beating out the next-door neighbor. Then the neighbor firebombed the house. After that the block had only two houses plus the couple's chimney. Making the best of their situation, the couple kept bees on their empty lot. Barring their honey from the farmers' market struck Cindy as of a piece with the pettiness and power plays that had already alienated her.

Dick's poor health also troubled her. Without Dick there would be nothing to keep Cindy in the neighborhood. Without him she wasn't even sure that she could stay. Her small salary alone would not cover the property taxes on her house. She and Dick had never requested a reassessment. They expected her community work to raise the house's value, so they thought it best to leave the assessment alone. Without Dick Cindy also worried her stepdaughter might force her out of the house. Cindy envisioned her breaking in when Cindy left for work and tossing everything Cindy owned but the rings on her fingers to the curb. Scrappers would immediately scavenge everything.

Cindy looked at a list of inexpensive, land bank–owned

houses in the neighborhood on file with Neighbors Building Brightmoor. To make any of the houses livable, she realized, she would have to wait for spring to come, save at least $20,000, and somehow acquire the skills to renovate a house herself.

Having stayed and tried for so many years, she decided to move on. When she explained her decision, her jaw tightened. She began shopping online for a camper trailer that she could take to off-season campsites or even out of state. She had a half sister in Mississippi who worked for a Spanish-owned company.[†] Cindy thought she might be able to park in her driveway and find houses to clean nearby. The following month's Neighbors Building Brightmoor newsletter would be the organization's last, and it would not list a president.

As Cindy spent time online, however, she realized that a camper trailer would cost more than her house. Even used ones started around $7,000, more than she could afford.

She had lived in Brightmoor for 55 years. She considered herself a "survivor."

* * *

Charles also did not go far. With most of his belongings still at the old house, he was staying with a friend who lived a few miles away. To get his hair cut from his usual barber, he was spending the morning in the old neighborhood. After his haircut he sat at a Formica-covered table at a diner on the road that separated the neighborhood from Grosse Pointe Park. He slurped a coffee through his cancer-scarred jaw and whispered to his white waitress that he would be out of her way soon.

Though he enjoyed catching up with his barber, the haircut

[†] The previous year the company had threatened to move its 22-year-old operations to another location, and local officials had scrambled to offer new tax breaks to entice the company to stay.

did not fully lift Charles's mood. He was still smarting from a fine he received from the county for failing to file a guardian's report on his mother. Why would he write the report? He did not have anyone to guard! His mother remained in Alaska with his half sister, unknowingly channeling social security checks and other assets into his half sister's household. Nothing about the situation made sense to him, and he missed his mother intensely.

In his whole life he had never spent as much time away from her, and he didn't plan to let the situation persist without a fight. He had learned that he could serve anyone with papers and then they would have 30 days to appear. Though earlier battles he fought to block some companies in Texas from sending his mother's money to his half sister ended only in insult and defeat, he thought since then he had developed into a stronger litigator. People in Texas did not like him, but he didn't have to sue in Texas again.

After he readied all the paperwork he planned to deploy a "curveball." The "curveball" entailed suing his half sister in federal court in Michigan, rather than in state court. A federal court might act with greater fairness, he believed. He gesticulated excitedly as he explained his reasoning. Once he served the complaint and the clock started for her to respond, he would line up social media to expose his half sister's behavior and contact federal agencies, including the director of the FBI. "I know how to redo houses, I know how to build in-ground swimming pools, and I know how to litigate," he said. Though at times he succumbed to an overwhelming sense that the system had failed him, he mustered the energy to continue to try. He was gearing up for a fight and steeling himself to make all kinds of enemies, but he felt that his religious belief would carry him through.

As he left the diner he thanked the waitress and the host

several times. The temperature had been dipping and climbing, and snow kept falling and melting. Bracing himself, he began walking to a friend's house, bopping along as usual but looking more stooped than before. He wore his fur hat and his black trench coat, and he smiled and said hello to the only person he passed on the sidewalk. When the owner of Charles's old house drove by in a black pickup truck, Charles waved to him too.

Charles's friend had agreed to drive him to a copy shop in the suburbs. Charles could pay to use a computer there to research more law. The shop offered things like paper clips and services like stapling for free, and he adored it there. He never got anything free in Detroit.

He expected to face forces in his lawsuit that, unlike him, had the judicial system on their side. Nevertheless he could not conceive of losing his mother for the rest of her life.

He had faith that he could go up against "any crook with a suit on" who crossed him. He could not lose all the time.

17

Nice Work if You Can Get It

FEBRUARY 2018

Joe's stubbled left cheek looked swollen, and the rest of his face looked wind burned. Sitting in a Chinese restaurant in New Jersey, he tried to chew his soup on only one side of his mouth. It was Saturday night, and he had just gotten his tooth pulled. The filling had fallen out in Detroit months earlier, and without a dentist there, he suffered through the pain until he couldn't any longer.

He had returned to New Jersey for a couple weeks. In the aftermath of a series of snowstorms he thought he might make some money doing tree work there. Detroit also had plenty of snow, but it was proving hard for him to earn a living in the city. Most people he knew there could not afford to take care of their trees. If a limb fell they simply stepped around it. Sometimes elderly ladies saved their social security checks for months to pay him. The money they gave him did not even buy a tank of gas. The last time he did a job there someone stole a saw he left out, and the customer paid him only half his fee.

Joe hoped his time in New Jersey could underwrite his family's life in Detroit. He was struggling under the burden of auto insurance that cost more than he earned in several months and more than he paid in New Jersey to insure a $200,000 crane. He could not afford his property taxes or his utilities. After maxing out all his credit cards he received shutoff notices for the first time in his life. To keep his electricity on his daughter put $600 in his bank account. But then his boiler cracked, and his family survived six weeks without heat. Like his neighbors he was learning the art of shuffling bills, paying a few bills at a time while avoiding service cuts. His complexion looked grayer, his eyes more tired.

He and his wife, Naomi, had a new baby, and he worried about the baby's future in Detroit. He had not realized that he had to reapply for Obamacare every year. When he did not re-enroll, his family lost its health insurance. To cover the baby he turned to something he understood to be Medicaid, but none of the doctors' offices he phoned accepted it. Looking ahead, he wondered about the baby's education and realized that he and Naomi would probably have to homeschool her. He had heard the interim superintendent of Detroit's public-school system say, more or less, that turning the system around would take six to eight years. He understood her to mean that kids not even born yet had no chance.

New Jersey felt like a different planet. Since arriving his accent had strengthened, and he had reverted to pronouncing dollars "dollahs." The people who bought his company had plenty for him to do. His phone rang consistently with work, and he found an array of potential professionals to assist him. His customers gave him tips. His stay in New Jersey made him realize he had "normalized" Detroit. Then he began to notice that New Jersey also had budget problems, and its public transit system struggled with debt. When people on the sidewalks did not say hello as people in Detroit did, he found it jarring. New Jersey seemed like a collection of strangers orbiting around each other.

His daughter called from Detroit with news. She had stopped by his house to water Naomi's orchids. In his mail she found a letter approving the nonprofit status he sought for his playground. A woman from Colorado he met online paid the filing fees for him and helped fill out the paperwork. With the new status he would be able to lease the lot for the playground himself, rather than relying on the neighborhood council to act on his behalf. His daughter also reported that the land bank had sold a renovated house near his for $80,000. The price fell short of the $109,000 the land bank had asked for the property, but the sale represented remarkable progress for the neighborhood. In some parts of the city property values and tax assessments were rising, and more people were paying property taxes.

As soon as Joe saved enough money in New Jersey he would return to Detroit and resume pushing forward on his plans there. He hoped he could settle his family and finish the playground before too much more time passed.

* * *

As winter dragged on prospects for Joe's commercial space began to improve. Back in Detroit, he attended a twice-weekly networking meeting in a building called the Green Garage. He nibbled on food that other entrepreneurs had grown in the alley outside.

After two years with his commercial building listed with Motor City Match, the city's small business program, Joe met a man called Kevin. Kevin owned McDonald's franchises in Detroit and the suburbs, and he gave motivational speeches. With a thin mustache and thick glasses, he looked about twice as wide as Joe and about half as tall. He had grown up in inner-city Chicago, worked his way through college as a bus boy and waiter, and eventually married a Detroiter. Then he had decided to sell the McDonald's franchises and open his own restaurant. He submitted a funding proposal to the city's program, pledging to earmark 15 jobs for former convicts whom he would train and mentor. The program helped people like Kevin fill financing gaps by providing matching funds and locate suitable real estate. He won a $50,000 matching grant and began calling landlords on the organization's list of local building owners. Joe called him back.

With Joe's entrepreneurial plans finally, potentially taking off, the Green Garage offered useful comradery and advice. The organization served social and environmentally minded businesses from an old Model T showroom. The building had been renovated with reclaimed materials and retrofitted with green building enhancements. Solar panels dotted the roof. Even before Detroit exited bankruptcy 55 nascent businesses, most drawn from industries like art and design and social work, joined the organization. Additionally, the city had also attracted other organizations that nurtured startups with connections to the auto industry.

Despite all the excitement, however, Kevin did not have enough money of his own to renovate Joe's buildings, and the $50,000 grant covered few of the costs. The space still needed new roofing and a new facade, plumbing, and basic electrical work. Joe still could not pay off his own credit cards.

Together he and Kevin tried for another meeting with staff from one of the community development financial institutions. The CDFI was working to apply the same approach it used to facilitate development in Midtown in Joe's neighborhood and the area around the Fitzgerald project. The CDFI had money to spend on streetscapes, commercial corridors, parks, and residential stabilization efforts. It invested in similar improvements in the two other "tipping-point" neighborhoods the city targeted for revitalization efforts, and it was raising funding for future efforts in seven further neighborhoods. Simultaneously the staff members were trying to finance extensions to federal low-income housing tax credits set to expire at thousands of affordable units in Detroit. The expirations threatened imminent rent increases in a city where the median income still hovered around $28,000. In 1986, when the federal government launched the tax-credit program, legislators expected the country's housing crisis to resolve within a generation. It did not.

Joe and Kevin got a meeting with the CDFI's staff and pitched their plans. With Joe standing nearly a head taller than Kevin, they presented an unlikely pair. The meeting went well, though, and the CDFI offered them a loan to cover the "soft costs" of renovation work, costs such as environmental study fees and an architect's wages. The loan had an interest rate of a little more than 6 percent. Staff at the CDFI would help them apply for grants and connect them with city officials. Before long Joe and Kevin also met with staff from the city planning department, who introduced them to private developers for mentorship and advice.

Bringing other people into the project, however, added costs. Joe and Kevin now had to hire a property manager and conduct surveys, requirements Joe complained about. It struck him that the system seemed set up to create expenses that the businesses that could underpin a successful community could not afford. Those businesses were run by local people who lived where they worked and catered to neighbors who had little disposable income. Though a friend of Joe's started a coffee shop in Joe's neighborhood with the same matching grant Kevin received, few other businesses had opened there, and no other businesses had opened near the Fitzgerald project.

Joe took on a new mission to advance an alternative system of affordable commercial real estate akin to affordable housing. Though he expected the restaurant would eventually open, he worried that he might wind up bankrupt before it did.

* * *

Friday evening arrived with a reprieve from work but heavy rain. Watching a video with Delilah, Lola kept dozing off. She tucked her daughter into bed, then fell asleep dreaming of new meals to cook. For Sunday dinner she would make smothered pork chops, homemade mashed potatoes, and corn. If she ever found a new job or moved out of her house, she would celebrate by preparing a soul food feast with banana pudding cheesecake and homemade sweet rolls.

A loud crack woke her from her dreams, followed by a crunching sound of shattering glass. Scrambling clumsily toward the living room in the dark, Lola saw a car accelerate in a tight circle around her front yard. The living room window lay in pieces on the stained beige carpet. Further investigations revealed a burst light bulb in the bathroom and a bullet gently vibrating in the bathtub.

She phoned one of her many childhood friends and told him that her house had gotten shot. It would take him a while to drive over from the suburbs, where he moved when his corporate career took off. As she waited she considered the gang that operated in her neighborhood, the Seven Mile Bloods. The gang dubbed the area 4820-Die, a play on the zip code 48205. Generally the neighborhood seemed quieter and more peaceful to her than the nickname implied, but now she wanted to turn tail and move back to the suburbs. She knew, though, that she could not afford to move, and she needed her family nearby to drive her to work and help take care of Delilah. Still waiting for her friend, Lola tried to console herself by staring at pictures of her daughter on her sparkle-covered cell phone with a broken screen, which had the password "Mommy LovesDelilah."

"People don't want you to have nothing," Lola told her friend when he arrived. She wished she could put the people who wanted to shoot and fight into an open field. They could battle each other there, away from everyone else, and let the children and the "mommas" live. She confided to her friend her worries for her daughter, who could have been sleeping in the path of the bullet. Her friend sat by the broken window the rest of the night.

In the morning, Lola brought Delilah to her sister's house late. Lola looked unusually tousled in black jeans, a black hoodie, and white sneakers. When her sister asked why, Delilah piped up and told her, "We had a situation." Lola found that "crazy for a seven-year-old," but that night Delilah put a miniature Elsa from the Disney film *Frozen* on Lola's keychain to encourage her to "let it go."

Lola tried to convince herself things could still go better for them. She lectured herself, saying that she would find a new job that paid enough to move to a different neighborhood. She would prove her toughness and act humble and prayerful. But until then she needed to keep her daughter safe, and now the house lacked protection. Until the company that owned the property came to fix the window or she found the money to fix it herself, someone could tap the window and walk right into the living room.

* * *

To keep Delilah occupied inside a couple weeks later, Lola asked her to clean her room. Lola tried to sound strict, but she seemed more adoring. Once Lola cleaned the kitchen and the living room, she said, then they could watch movies together. Though spring would arrive soon, it had snowed, then rained, then froze, and Lola did not know "what Detroit got goin' on."

Delilah felt to Lola like the only thing she had done right. So much else had gone so badly. She wished she could buy a car and provide a safer, more comfortable place for her daughter to live. Since the bullet pierced the window, Lola had seen a drug deal take place on the sidewalk by her front yard. She ran straight outside, hands on hips, and ordered everyone away from her house, yelling that she had a child inside. The house sat on the corner by a stop sign, and now Lola's pulse quickened whenever people stopped in front of it.

She hated her new landlords and simultaneously worried about how long they would allow her and her daughter to stay at the house. They had not yet come to board up the window, and when she called to remind them, no one answered the phone and no one returned her messages. The property manager, a young southerner called Shane, refused to shovel snow and never bothered to collect her security deposit. He told her to pay her rent through an online payment system that did not work, told her to wait, then suddenly threatened eviction if she did not immediately hand over cash. She knew better than to pay in cash and phoned her grandfather so that she could drive a money order right over, but soon afterward Shane texted her, "Game over, squatter. You're evicted." The president of the property company assured her Shane did not mean it; Shane had texted her drunk.

Lola started drinking copious amounts of water. She was trying to suppress her appetite so that she would not have to buy as many groceries. A coworker noticed and offered her half a slider. Delilah seemed to notice too, though Lola made an effort never to cry or show fear in front of her. Delilah tried to cook noodles for her and offered her the birthday money she had tucked away.

When Lola finished cleaning she phoned a childhood friend who worked at a hotel to ask about getting a job as a manager. Out the window of her grandfather's car, Lola had noticed new hotels under construction downtown and in Midtown. Developers were repurposing old buildings into boutique places to stay, and analysts predicted that as Detroit gained notice from more tourists, the city would need 1,200 new hotel rooms within the next three years. Lola told her friend she considered herself a "people person" who had "x factor" and had succeeded at everything in the past; she had no trouble organizing other people. The hotel did not have any openings.

Dressed in a black fleece jacket and black stretch pants, with her hair still not done, Lola immediately tried to identify alternatives. The hotels she found had numerous online complaints and she could tell that they needed to renovate. It would be difficult for her to "get in there" and think she could "move them" into doing things differently.

With an eye toward eventually retiring comfortably, she tried to come up with a new plan. A sign she had noticed beside the lottery said that any outstanding medical bills, student loans, and tickets and fees to government agencies would be deducted from winners' earnings. Lola, laughing and sounding more like her young age, said she would feel glad just to pay all that and go home, though she also wanted to take Delilah to Disney World.

* * *

Several Sundays later, following church, Reggie's nephews came over to help him clean up his new yard. Inside, Tasha was cooking chicken on a newly working stove. The smell of butter and garlic wafted out the kitchen window, mingling with the scent of freshly clipped grass. Before long bags of branches and weeds neatly lined the curb, and the boys began clearing the vacant lot next door. A car drove by with its radio bumping; they stopped their work and stared. "Now that's something different I hadn't had to deal with before moving here," Reggie finally muttered. Then he recovered himself and reworded his outburst: "That's something I will have to get used to."

Neither Reggie's careful attitude nor the Rockwellian domestic scene masked the unease that had descended on the family. Tasha wanted her grandbabies to visit, but the smaller house did not offer much room for them to play, and the yard seemed unsafe. Neither Reggie nor Tasha had met any of the neighbors. Everyone on the block seemed to keep to themselves, and Reggie missed the sense of community he felt in his old neighborhood. A few nights earlier, though, he had received troubling news about his old house.

When Reggie's family moved out their elderly neighbor bought a new dog, a Doberman pinscher, to feel safer with fewer people around. With the dog not yet fully trained, he took the dog outside in the middle of the night and noticed smoke spewing from the back of Reggie's empty house. He phoned the fire department. When the firemen arrived, they found that someone had unlocked the front door of the house, set a fire in the back bedroom, and then re-locked the door.

The fire destroyed the house, and Reggie thought it looked suspicious even though there was insufficient evidence to prove it. Normally when people committed random acts of arson they kicked open doors and left the doors open, rather than unlocking them and locking them again. Representatives of the company that won the house could see the problems with the roof from outside; they could not see the problems with the foundation, however, until Reggie and his family left and the representatives could enter the house. In refusing to allow Reggie to pay for more time there they had seemed in a hurry to begin renovating. After his family left, though, work had never begun. It would seem easier to offload the property than fix the cracked foundation. Or, perhaps, to abandon it altogether and collect insurance from a damaging fire.

Why didn't the new owner sell the house back to Reggie, Reggie wanted to be able to understand. Instead the owner displaced a family and ruined a neighborhood. The effects of the blighted property would spread throughout the block. Powerless to do anything else, Reggie vowed to reclaim the lawn furniture he had left in the old garage, which had not burned down. The elderly neighbor offered to watch over the furniture until Reggie could pick it up.

In reality, though, what Reggie really needed was a furnace for the new house. He still did not have enough money to buy one, even from back-alley places that sold scrapped ones. Faced with the prospect of spending the winter without heat, he and Tasha considered leaving Detroit. Both of them had lived in the city all their lives.

Tasha had a son in Arizona who worked in "heating and cooling," and through her pink phone he tried to persuade them to join him there. Tasha found the idea of year-round sunshine and winter sandals in Arizona intriguing. She wanted to experience a misting pool and taste new kinds of food. Reggie's daughter would graduate soon, and though Reggie lit up when he talked about her, his brother had already set up a bed for her at his own house in Detroit. She spent time there with her cousins. Reggie knew Detroit lacked opportunities, but he also understood that selling the new house would be difficult. He and Tasha needed money from the new house to pay for a move. The phone rang, interrupting their conversation. William's son's car had stopped on the freeway. He needed Reggie to drive the old van over and get him, and Reggie lumbered outside, his keys in his hand.

18

New Beginnings

APRIL 2018

The police took Miles to jail. He had just checked his mailbox at home on Rosemary Street and was feeling relieved not to see any new bills or notices. His truck was leaking antifreeze, but a contractor had called to ask him to pick up some windows and doors. Miles turned out of his driveway and onto his empty street. Six blocks later a police car drove up behind him. The lights on the police car flashed.

So far that year about 120 police officers had quit the Detroit police department, joining the more than 800 who resigned during the previous five years. Unlike the surrounding suburbs Detroit provided a small salary to students in the police academy. Upon graduation, however, the city paid its starting officers 25 percent less than suburban departments did, and the suburbs also offered easier work. Between 2015 and 2018 Detroit taxpayers spent over $2.5 million training officers who left city service within two years. The city did not have enough officers, and half the officers it had were rookies with less than five years' experience.

Nevertheless, police officers took the time to run Miles's plates and found an active warrant for his old gun case. From jail, Miles used his phone call to ask his mother to bring over the papers with the seal, the papers that the clerk at the criminal court had given him six months earlier. They showed the criminal court's dismissal of his charges and not the district court's subsequent reinstatement of the charges. Thinking the papers would hold up better at home, he had recently taken them inside after driving around with them for months and added them to the stacks of records on his glass coffee table. Now he assumed that once the police saw the papers, they would let him go, but his mother told him that no one at the jail would accept them from her. Miles remained in his cell, unable to afford his $7,500 bail.

About 10 men crowded into the cell with him. Sometimes he got a mattress; other times he lay on the concrete floor or on a steel bench, his long legs dangling off the side. The men shared one toilet and one shower, and when they used them they pulled a sheet around themselves for privacy. The sink attached to the top of the toilet. From a leak on the floor above, sewage ran down the walls, and the whole cell stank. The jail should have closed in 2014. In 2013, however, with the replacement jail already three times over budget, work at the new site stopped until a new construction company could take over. In the interim Dan Gilbert of Quicken Loans, along with the owner of Detroit's basketball team, argued that a new jail so close to downtown would suppress the city's revitalization. Eventually a complicated plan would gel for Gilbert to build the jail in a different location and the city to pay most of the costs. Gilbert would turn the former site of the new jail into a mixed-used development. Until all that happened the original jail remained in operation.

As the days stretched on Miles's goatee grew wild, and his mother worried about him getting lost in the system. His case had been scheduled for trial again, 14 and a half years after the original judge dismissed it. Miles's mother called her sister in Maryland and asked to borrow money for bail. Miles's aunt had retired from the local police force, but she had returned to work, unable to support herself on her own savings. Together she and Miles's mother scraped together enough money to pay a bail bondsman and hire an attorney. Miles's daughter moved into Miles's house to protect it against arson and theft.

Just as the bail payment should have enabled Miles to return home until the trial, a fugitive arrest warrant against him in Ohio surfaced. Four days elapsed before he could go home, wearing a tracking device around his shrunken ankle. First he had to wait for permission to leave the jail with the warrant outstanding. Then he had to wait for a device to be removed from someone else to free one up for him. His trial would take place one day after his release. Freedom from jail, if only for a day, confirmed for him his faith in God.

The day of the trial, the judge again dismissed Miles's case "without prejudice" on grounds that it could not proceed without officers there to testify. Miles had spent two weeks and three days in jail.

* * *

Out of prison and with the trial behind him, Miles raged. His voice dropped into a lower register and his phrases grew more lilting. He wanted to sue for a violation of his rights. If his mother and aunt had not helped him, he thought, he would probably still be languishing in jail. One missed bill on his payment plan, and he would have lost his house. Twice now his family spent all the money they had on lawyers and bail, and twice the case could not even proceed. He did not claim that he had never gotten involved in anything wrong; he claimed a mistake from 14 and a half years earlier should not keep following him around. He wanted to pay his bills and go to work. He had tried to deal with the warrant for the old charges on his own. "You can't just keep locking me up whenever you feel like it and hold me two weeks or whatever you want to do," he said. "You can't just grab anyone off the street and put them in jail until they straighten out they paperwork." He did not seem to realize that because both dismissals, in 2003 and 2018, came "without prejudice," the police could arrest him on the same charges again at any time. No judge or jury had tried him on the charges yet.

As Miles struggled to get his life back on track, in April 2018 the city's financial oversight commission voted to release the city from the commission's supervision. For six years the commission had scrutinized the city's budget and some of its contracts. For three years in a row the city had balanced its budget, and now it had even banked a small surplus. "I'm pleased to say this financial emergency is resolved and I look forward to the city's continued success," the state treasurer said. Oversight, however, could resume at any time on a majority vote, and the commission's supervision of the city's school district continued.

"Man," Miles kept saying meanwhile, as he pored over the bills arrayed on his coffee table, marking his place with a long fingernail. He needed to pay back the money his family spent on bail and the attorney, but he had lost the money he would have earned if he had not gone to jail. A project to renovate an apartment building he expected to work on had started during his incarceration. Now he would have to wait to get back into the project manager's rotation. Without anything to do, Miles passed out his business cards at the home improvement store, and he asked all the workmen he saw who they worked for and whether that person needed further help.

In interviews on Detroit's balanced budget Mayor Duggan credited his discipline in forgoing action on residents' requests to avoid overspending. He described how he told people, "'Look, this city ended up in financial crisis because its elected officials didn't have the courage to say to you that with the revenue we have, we can't afford to do that.'" Bankruptcy, however, traumatized local residents, he said, and he did not recommend it. He announced a new job training program and within just 24 hours, 1,500 residents signed up for it. Even if Miles found more work, though, it seemed impossible for him to pursue it: He had two weeks to turn himself in at a court in Ohio. Otherwise he could be arrested again on the warrant that appeared during his bail process.

Fourteen years earlier, after the judge dismissed Miles's original gun charges in Detroit, Miles moved to Dayton, Ohio. He planned to gain a new start for himself by studying to become an appraiser at a local community college. In combination with the building and residential rehabilitation skills he already had, he thought an appraiser's license could help put him on a more successful path, and the license seemed easier to obtain in Ohio than in Michigan. Dayton also had more opportunities and more construction work than Detroit. A few months into his first semester, police pulled him over as he drove his 11-year-old Honda. During the stop they allegedly discovered crack cocaine inside a bag of marijuana. Miles freely admitted to using marijuana but claimed not to know about the crack or ever to have used any. Because he had no prior offenses in Ohio, the police seemed to suggest outpatient rehabilitation as a potential sentence. They also told him, however, that a drug conviction would disqualify him from further financial aid to attend college. Without that money he would not be able to afford anywhere to live in Dayton, and he assumed the drug charges would prevent him from finding a job there. Rather than wait to learn his sentence, he moved back home to Detroit.

Miles did not know how long he would have to spend in Dayton dealing with the warrant or what the consequences for him would be. He did not have anyone to stay with, and he could not afford a hotel. He hoped he could make the trip in a day. He was trying to pay the bills outstanding when he went to jail in Detroit and prepare to pay the new month's bills. Lost wages threatened his payment plans for his house, drivers' fees, and home utilities. Now he needed to spend money to travel to Dayton. Nervous energy made him compress his lips and worry the papers in front of him.

Because the Ohio warrant never caught up with him in Michigan, even during all his contact with the police over the auto insurance penalties, he assumed the case was not serious. Once he got his name cleared in Ohio, he thought he would explore staying there. The idea seemed to calm him. Dayton would still probably offer better work at higher wages than Detroit. Once he established his new life there, perhaps his daughter would join him. For a second time, though, everything would turn out worse than he imagined.

* * *

As Miles arranged his trip to Dayton, Lola drove to the district courthouse in downtown Detroit. Driving again after so long made her feel "extra popping." She had saved enough money, combined with her tax refund, to pay $3,000 cash for a scratched-up white Chrysler with 60,000 miles on it. As she parked she considered painting the car with sparkles and glitter and making some eyelashes to put over the headlights. Then she got arrested.

Lola just wanted to resume driving, but she rode to jail in the back of a police car. She had visited the courthouse neatly dressed and made up and asked politely why she could not register her new car in her name. A clerk looked her up in his computer, and police from a nearby suburb drove over and got her. She had never gone to jail before and her situation stunned her. She knew that if she got a ticket she had to pay it, and she had.

Over a year earlier, in the middle of the night, Lola picked up a friend she knew from work without bringing her license with her. Her car conked out on the road, and she got a ticket. She paid it and moved on. Then as she drove to the hospital for her first surgery she got pulled over again. The policeman told her that her license had been suspended and instructed her to bring the license and her registration to court. Dealing with the surgery, she forgot. A judge opened a warrant.

Lola's jail cell did not have a clock, and she did not know how much time passed while she waited inside. She used her phone call to contact her mother, who immediately corralled Lola's sister, Lola's ex-boyfriend Michael, and Michael's mother to help rescue Lola. By pooling their available cash, they had enough to bail her out.

"I couldn't picture you in a jail cell," Lola's ex-boyfriend Michael said at the jail when she got released. "You too bougie." Lola talked excitedly about what happened to her, but her shapely figure bent a little closer to the floor, and her mouth turned down a little at the corners. Michael drove her home, poked around in her kitchen, and walked back outside to his car. He returned with a carload of groceries. Recently, grieving his grandmother's death, his "best friend," he had stopped going to work and lost his job as a line cook at a chain restaurant. Now he had a temporary job making sandwiches for a food distribution company.

Lola and Michael had dated for seven years. They met on the sidewalk when he stopped her from punching someone. "Baby girl, you seem like a classy lady," he had said, and they had exchanged phone numbers. She had still been wearing the pantsuit she dressed in for work that day. His mother told Lola not to get herself stuck with him. She had too much going for her. Her grandfather disapproved and thought she was settling. After Michael had a baby with someone else Lola decided to break up with him.

Now Michael invited her out for barbecue the following week. In the meantime she returned to court for a hearing on the warrant. She pled guilty, and the judge imposed fees. Altogether the episode cost her $1,250. In March Governor Snyder had signed legislation that eliminated responsibility fees and also cut personal income taxes, but the fees remained in effect through the following October. In Detroit outstanding debt from the fees totaled $120 million, and 18 percent of the city's adult workforce owed the money.

To pay everyone back Lola prepared to do a lot of braiding. She lined up a friend's twin daughters and another customer. When her paycheck arrived she paid her rent, then transferred the rest of the funds to her mother. Her license proved valid so the court returned some money, which she gave to her sister. It would take time before she could repay Michael and his mother, and the fees would eat away at her paychecks for months. Until she paid off the fees she could not drive, but she drove herself to work anyway. She wondered what might transpire with Michael.

* * *

In the weeks since Lola met her ex-boyfriend Michael for barbecue her house had transformed into one big commotion.
On Saturday morning Michael served his son, his daughter,
and Delilah copious amounts of pancakes and bacon. Then he
turned around and started cooking sausages and eggs. "I can't
afford to feed you all," Lola yelled, loudly enough to be heard
above the din from the kids and the clangs from the pans and
mixing bowl. With all the ruckus at the house she nearly forgot about her hair, then bent curlers around it a few times and
decided that would have to do. Temperatures in Detroit were
climbing, and her summer clothes showed off her tattoos. She
wore a tee shirt that spelled out Bad-Ass Babe in glitter letters.
In spite of her feigned outrage, a smile kept creeping across
her face. Even her tattoos seemed to sparkle.

At the barbecue restaurant Michael and Lola had talked
for hours. Just before the dinner, he brought over new clothes
for her and sent her to a salon. In full makeup with her hair up
she looked like a different person that night: curvy, glamorous,
and relaxed.

Michael lived with his sister, but since the dinner he spent
alternate weekends at Lola's house, cooking meals for everyone and laughing when the kids climbed into bed with him
and Lola. He made popcorn and the whole mixed family
watched movies together. Lola professed to anyone who asked
that she had no expectations of the relationship, but in a tone
that implied she was trying to convince herself. The baby that
broke them up had just turned three months old, and Michael
still went back and forth to the baby's mother's house.

Whatever the new situation would become, Lola could not
host it. With the additional people her house felt tiny, and the
problems with the property company continued. In spite of
endless promises over several months, no one had ever come
to board up the window with the bullet hole through it. She

worried about Delilah stepping in the glass shards that daily appeared in the carpet, no matter how much time Lola spent picking them out, and in low moments she dreaded Child Protective Services seizing her daughter because of a cut foot. Summer was descending on Detroit, and the property company had never fixed her air conditioner. When she cleaned out her deep fryer she found rat droppings behind it. Then she arrived home from work and smelled something rotting. She found backed-up sewage flooding the basement and photographed it.

The president of the property company tweeted messages like "Bringing back the love to Detroit" and "We would like to thank the mayor for the opportunity to help Detroit rebuild," but his staff's behavior undercut his spin. It emerged that the property manager who'd drunkenly threatened to evict Lola had embezzled money, collecting payments for work he never performed and pocketing rent tenants paid in cash. A new manager replaced him and made Lola pay to fill out a new rental application. She did not know Lola's rent, and then she raised it. She mailed documents to Lola without stamps, so the documents never arrived, rarely returned phone calls, and threatened eviction. To make matters worse, someone knocked on Lola's door and told her to pay him her rent. He told her the company she thought owned the house did not own it. The same man repeated the scam on her friend who lived nearby.

When Delilah came home from her free evangelical day camp and announced that the nonprofit that sponsored the camp was renovating houses and renting them out at affordable rates, Lola dropped everything to claim a house. She drove directly to the bank to get a money order, though she wasn't supposed to be driving. From the bank she sped to the organization's offices and submitted an application on the spot, breathless but chatty with excitement. If she could, she would have packed and moved that day.

The organization denied her application. The staff reviewed her credit and found that a debt collector had brought a successful action against her. With her eyes drooping, demoralized, she nevertheless noticed an actual for-sale sign on her sister's street. She phoned the number on the sign, then met the agent. A woman from the suburbs who did side work in voice-overs, the agent specialized in selling bank-foreclosed homes. She told Lola that instead of paying rent, Lola could pay off her own house for only a little more money each month than she currently payed in rent. The agent described a nontraditional form of mortgage financing that depended only on proof of on-time utility and cell phone payments. When Lola told people about it she spoke in a higher and higher pitch. To focus on qualifying for a mortgage she decided to stick it out in her broken, too-small house. Because the agent did not ask for money, Lola found her honest.

* * *

All day Saturday Lola braided hair for extra cash with her own hair straightened and flipped under near her chin. With tired fingers, but still immaculate fingernails, she arrived at a restaurant downtown for a party. At nearly 10 o'clock on a Saturday night, large families and groups of 10 people and more packed the restaurant, which had few white patrons. Lola worried that her hoodie smelled like the fried chicken Michael had cooked at her house. She scanned the menu for a strawberry martini, then raved about the spinach artichoke dip. She waved to a waitress who used to work for her as an agent at her first call center.

The restaurant, a brewery, sat within a seven-building complex downtown. Nearly 50 years earlier Henry Ford's grandson spearheaded construction of the towers beside the Detroit River. Calling the towers the Renaissance Center, he intended them to anchor the revival of the city. "Detroit has reached the bottom and is on its way back up," he said in a speech marking the opening of the complex. Over the following decades the bridges that would connect the towers to other downtown businesses never got built, and the project never stimulated an urban resurgence. A perimeter barrier, added to protect against rioting, isolated the towers from the rest of the city. In the mid-1990s General Motors bought the complex for substantially less than the construction costs and moved the company's headquarters there.

Chatting brightly from inside the storied space, Lola spoke mostly of Delilah. Lola had planned to send her to Flint to spend the summer with her biological father. Worried about the water quality there, Lola instead decided to keep her home.

Lola hoped that by the end of the summer her daughter would feel excited to return to the suburban charter school. An education advocacy group had found that fewer than 10 percent of Detroit's third graders read at grade level. In an attempt to lure back to the city some of the roughly 32,000 local children who attended suburban schools, Detroit officials were implementing a new pilot program, in which a school bus in northwest Detroit would collect lower- and middle-school students from the schools closest to their homes and drop them off at any of six district schools and four charter schools. On the way home the bus could drop the students at a community center that operated an after-school program. The arrangements for the new bus service would cost $1,000 per student, paid for by their schools. The bus's path did not include Lola's neighborhood.

Detroit's new schools' superintendent had undertaken a review of all the property the school district owned. The results indicated half a billion dollars in needed renovations, which the bailout money would not support. A judge described the conditions at some of Detroit's schools as "nothing short of devastating" but nevertheless denied district schoolchildren's claim to a constitutional right to literacy. Later in the summer the superintendent would have to shut off the water at the schools because of elevated lead levels in school water fountains.

Lola still wanted a suburban yard with a barbecue grill, a finished basement with a television, a driveway with a big basketball hoop, and freedom from worrying about her daughter's safety and her own. She committed herself to making the best of her current living situation and saving to move in a few years. She realized the future would probably not hold a shared life with her ex-boyfriend Michael. He had too much to figure out for himself first.

Lola also still wanted a new job. As the country enjoyed strong employment, and in downtown Detroit thousands of new workers pursued new projects, the unemployment rate in the city remained above 7 percent, and more than half the city's working-age residents no longer bothered to look for jobs. Two-thirds of city residents continued to commute to low-skilled positions in the suburbs while 200,000 suburbanites enjoyed high-skilled positions in the city. A friend who worked for Chrysler, however, had referred Lola for a production job at the local plant, and Lola was advancing through the hiring process. Her grandfather balked at the idea of his granddaughter on a factory floor, but the job would pay more than the call center and the commute would be easier. Besides, she drove a Chrysler now.

In another year, when she turned 30, she hoped for better. She set herself a one-year deadline for finding her direction, making better use of her degree, and achieving her goals. She did not want to turn 30 still wanting a home and a career. Once she had both in place she would plan her retirement.

The Renaissance Center party ended, and Michael arrived to drive her home. She had various leftovers with her, which she had cheerfully asked the waiter to pack separately so different dishes did not touch. Michael opened the passenger door for her and introduced himself to her friends.

19

Bait and Switch

MAY 2018

For the scheduling conference on his 14-year-old drug charge Miles rode a bus four and half hours from Detroit to Dayton. His truck could not have survived such a long journey, and he still could not afford valid auto insurance. He also feared getting pulled over by Ohio police on the warrant and taken to jail. If he rented a car or borrowed one and the police locked him up, he would have to worry about the car from his cell. Besides, he knew no one in Ohio to bail him out.

"Man," Miles repeated, in a low, deep voice. His family had spent all the money they had dealing with the Detroit gun charges. In Dayton he would have to rely on a court-appointed lawyer. The lawyer assigned to him specialized in bankruptcy and personal injury law. He shared an office with a family dentist across the street from a gas station. Miles met him for the first time in the courthouse hallway. From his backpack Miles withdrew a crisp folder. He handed the lawyer papers Miles had annotated in tall cursive, which evidenced his pristine legal record since leaving Ohio, apart from his inability to afford auto insurance. He told the lawyer about his repeated contacts with Detroit police and explained that he went to the police station on his own to ask about the warrant for the gun charges. No one at the station had said anything about extraditing him to Ohio. Neither Miles nor the lawyer seemed to take the Ohio charges very seriously, and they casually entered the courtroom together.

Inside, the prosecutors pressured Miles to plead guilty to felony charges. He asked his lawyer for time to think. Miles did not know the details of the allegations against him or the evidence behind the allegations. The lawyer insisted that Miles had to know if he had crack cocaine with him. He stared at the lawyer and reminded him the events took place 14 years earlier. Miles said he only remembered getting pulled over by the police. He told the lawyer he wanted the case to proceed to a trial.

Afterward Miles walked to a local bus stop near the courthouse, caught a bus to Dayton's regional bus station, and boarded another bus back to Detroit. In all he would spend more than nine hours on buses that day and three hours waiting for them. In Detroit he switched to another local bus and walked from the bus stop to his house at 2:30 in the morning.

Back home, with bloodshot eyes and dressed in a faded hoodie, he tried to distract himself by searching for work, but he still did not know anything about the charges against him. He did not feel that his lawyer was answering any of his questions. Miles considered filing a freedom-of-information request for his case file, and meanwhile he spent time praying and handing out business cards. He needed a job, and with the Ohio drug charges on his record he needed one from someone who would not conduct a background check. Local news reports of construction worker shortages in southeast Michigan puzzled him; he was not finding anything to do. Though his record would not keep him from working as a private security guard, a position also considered a bright spot in the local economy, the companies paid minimum wage and no benefits.

Finally the lawyer phoned with the original police report and read portions of it aloud to him. In 2003, according to the first part of the report, the police found Miles in possession of 1.91 grams of crack cocaine. In the next section of the report the weight of the drugs jumped to 3.48 grams without explanation. In the final section of the report the police summed the two amounts and charged him with possession of more than five grams of crack cocaine, a serious felony. On the phone the lawyer hesitated to predict a probable sentence.

Miles swore he would never have five grams of crack with him. He had never even used the drug! And if he did have that amount of crack he would not have stopped for the police, or at least he would have tried to hide it. "This is why we believe in God," he said and refused, again, to take a plea for felony charges.

* * *

At home Miles studied the police report, which the lawyer had finally emailed him. As he read through it, he penned copious notes on a legal pad in capital letters. Just before the arrest, the report said, he took a sharp left turn to the west while driving south and nearly collided with the police car. For failing to yield to oncoming traffic the police pulled him over. They smelled alcohol on his breath and asked him to get out of his car. When he did he immediately put his hand in his pocket. The officers searched his pocket and found a wallet and a brown paper bag. The wallet contained an identification card but no driver's license. The bag contained 3.48 grams of a white rocky substance the officers believed to be crack cocaine. They field-tested the substance, handcuffed him, and took him to jail. A subsequent report from a lab confirmed the substance as a 0.92-gram piece of crack and another 0.99-gram piece of crack. The lab billed Miles for the cost of the tests.

Sitting bent on the front corner of his only chair with documents splayed in front of him, Miles was calling up maps on his cell phone and drawing diagrams on his legal pad of the sharp turn the report described. Any near collision with the police car seemed impossible to him, given that the police car was driving behind him when he turned. He wanted to know if the intersection had traffic lights or stop signs and whether the police said he ignored them. Otherwise he thought the police car would have had to yield behind him to allow him room to turn. Furthermore if he was driving south and turned left, he would have been turning east, not west. He also noted that despite smelling alcohol on his breath, the police did not perform a sobriety test.

Above all, why did the officers charge him with possession of more than five grams of crack cocaine? The officers first noted 3.48 grams of crack cocaine; the lab test indicated only 1.91 grams. Miles knew five grams of crack was a lot of cocaine. It was more than a person would buy for himself. Someone with five grams of crack intended to sell it.

Using his phone Miles photographed the questions he had listed on his legal pad. Toward the bottom of the page he had written: "IN NO WAY AM I TRYING TO TELL YOU YOUR JOB I JUST BELIEVE WE HAVE A DIFFERENT AMOUNT OF TIME AND INTEREST INVOLVED. THIS IS MY LIFE/FREEDOM, THIS MAY BE A HOBBY TO U." He tried to email the picture to his lawyer, but he did not know how to attach the picture to the message.

He texted the picture instead. When the lawyer finally responded, Miles thought he downplayed most of Miles's concerns. He dismissed the east-west discrepancy as a simple mistake. He explained that in the intervening 14 years since Miles's arrest, the state's sentencing guidelines had changed. According to the United States Sentencing Commission a 100:1 sentencing disparity between crack and powder cocaine led to a "racial imbalance in . . . prisons." Nationally African Americans accounted for nearly 80 percent of crack offenders and fewer than 30 percent of powder cocaine offenders. To rebalance sentences, Ohio, like many other states and the federal government, in 2011 relaxed sentences for small amounts of crack. In Ohio in 2003, however, even one gram of crack cocaine triggered serious felony charges. Though the federal sentencing guidelines applied retroactively to federal drug charges, Ohio's guidelines did not apply retroactively to state charges. Miles's felony charges therefore may not have depended on the five-gram drug weight. The inconsistencies in the weight of the drugs, the lawyer conceded, raised concerns. He said he would file a motion to suppress the evidence. He had learned that in the years since Miles's arrest the officer who wrote the report retired.

Miles curled his long torso around his cell phone and began researching officers' protocol on drunk driving. A text from the lawyer interrupted him. The police no longer had the drugs in evidence. The lawyer predicted the prosecutors would reduce their plea offer from a felony to a misdemeanor. If that happened, Miles texted back, he would agree to plea to the misdemeanor. Then he could resume his life without a felony on his record.

* * *

Meanwhile in Detroit's Southwest neighborhood, Robin parked his pickup truck in front of a three-story brick house that his company owned. He had rented out rooms there since 2009, when he bought the house out of mortgage foreclosure. Now he had a contractor and a fleet of suburban workers making changes so that the company could squeeze more money out of it. The men were redoing the kitchen, carving an additional bedroom from the attic, and blocking off the basement to create a separate garden apartment. After saying hello, Robin waited in his truck for a roofer. He wore his usual uniform of black jeans, a black quilted coat, and work boots, which blended in with his dark hair and beard. While he waited he puffed on his e-cigarette and fielded phone calls from other contractors.

In the 1940s the neighborhood attracted Mexican families who came to work in the auto industry. Over the following decades successive waves of Latin American immigrants joined their descendants. While Detroit lost population and abandoned houses accumulated in most neighborhoods, families stayed in Southwest and fought to maintain it. When Mayor Bing shuttered city parks to save the city money and try to thwart emergency management, in Southwest, neighbors banded together to assume responsibility for the local park and keep it open. Despite its pervasive poverty, blue-collar mien, and industrial pollution, the area rated as one of the city's more vibrant, with small groceries, taquerias and bakeries, and colorful murals. The city planning staff chose the neighborhood as one of the three strong neighborhoods, like Joe's, in which the city would undertake concentrated redevelopment efforts.

Robin found Southwest still somewhat "funky," but its walkability, rare in Detroit, attracted his attention. Most of the properties in the neighborhood looked to him like they needed $100,000 renovations. Still on the phone with a contractor discussing the direction a door should swing open, he admired a brick building with the name Hortencia etched into its facade.

"Hey, man, what's up?" a middle-aged Mexican American man driving by in a pickup truck yelled out the window to Robin. A tenant of his, the man pulled over to chat. Five years earlier, at the same time Robin bought the house he was renovating, he had also bought several bank-foreclosed row houses behind it. The tenant and his wife had been living in one of them for nearly 30 years. He and Robin now chatted briefly from their respective trucks, mostly about the brickwork on the apartment across the street, which needed repointing.

Leaning somewhat precariously out his car window, Robin gave his regards to the man's wife. He tried to disguise the awkwardness he felt. He planned rent increases for the row houses, and he knew that the couple could not afford the highest price. He had considered giving them a year's notice, but he could not forego the extra rental income. He had a business to run, and for the previous five years he had never raised the rent. He had probably been charging them too little.

Robin believed the neighborhood could attract young professionals or young students, and they would pay more for the properties his company owned. He could spin a pitch for the house under renovation that focused on its new kitchen: "You can sit at the bar in the kitchen having drinks. Somebody's cooking. Doesn't that sound nice?" He planned to raise the rent there from $1,000 a month for four bedrooms to $2,500 for five.

The roofer had failed to show so Robin headed out. He had inherited his truck from his father-in-law. Robin liked driving the beat-up vehicle and the image it communicated. He had rebuilt the engine himself, but transmission problems were overtaking it. This time the truck started, and he slowly rolled toward another property he needed to check on. On the way he detoured past the old school he had planned to buy and convert into apartments until scrappers got hold of it. Another developer had bought it for half the price Robin offered for the intact building, but it still sat empty, only now it no longer had windows. The graffiti on it had grown thicker. Robin felt he had reached the end of the line with residential property. He had ridden its wave since the mortgage-foreclosure crisis. Faced with tenants' acute needs for affordable, stable housing and buildings with unending restoration and carrying costs like the abandoned school, he had decided to seek his fortune in commercial development instead. In commercial real estate he could write leases for long-term tenants and pass through to them costs associated with running the buildings, like property taxes and insurance.

* * *

"Hey, Andre, hey, brother, mind if I smoke?" Robin greeted his broker, a young African American man who emerged from a Cadillac dressed in a natty suit. As Robin switched from an e-cigarette to a traditional cigarette another broker pulled up, a white man from the suburbs called Norman. Together the three men stood talking by their cars in the belly of a 45,000-square-foot warehouse that Robin had recently acquired.

Above them soared a concrete ramp the width of a long-haul truck that led to the second floor. Beside them lay a mess of shipping containers. Local high school students would weld the containers into a gathering space that Robin's friend planned to open nearby with food and drinks, a local artists' bazaar, and a DJ booth. Down the street sat the Michigan Urban Farming Initiative, where corporate volunteers from around the region grew food they gave away for free. Unlike other local farms that sought to empower neighborhood residents and increase access to affordable, nutritious food, the white founder of the initiative envisioned the farm contributing to higher real estate values in the area.

Robin acquired the warehouse and an acre of land next door as a first step in transitioning from residential housing into commercial real estate. He bought the building from a "motivated seller" who won it in a lawsuit just before scrappers stole all the cast iron downspouts. The building flooded, and Robin took it off the seller's hands for a discounted price. Robin structured the deal to optimize his taxes and immediately had a crew draining all the water from the building, clearing out garbage, and installing heat and electrical wiring. The workers replaced the missing downspouts with plastic ones.

Narrating the history of the building to the brokers like the filmmaker he once had been, Robin pointed out the building's hidden features. Originally the building had belonged to an outdoor advertising company. The company's trucks could drive inside, and trenches in the floor would catch melting snow from their tires. The trucks then used the ramp to ascend to the second floor and reload. Two small rooms sat off to the side on the ground floor. Already Robin had rented them out, and he told the brokers about his tenants. One, an electrical engineer from Ohio, was trying to build the world's fastest electric motorcycle in his room there. He also lived in the space, and Robin had built him a shower. The other tenant, an edgy New York artist, used the second room to fulfill orders to her risqué side business.

Robin wanted tenants, he told the brokers as he fingered his beard, who ran startup businesses with interesting stories to tell, businesses that would contribute to Detroit's revitalization. He mentioned companies involved in fine furniture design and glassblowing as examples of "artisanal stuff" that could trigger new kinds of development in the neighborhood.

Norman, the broker from the suburbs, reminded Robin that he represented a charter school that was seeking a larger space, and the three men traipsed toward the basement. As they picked their way down steep stairs by cell phone light, a gas-like smell grew stronger. Steel fuel tanks, still full of fuel, lay beneath the basement floor. The same contractor renovating the house in Southwest was trying to determine a safe way to extract the tanks.

Leaving the smell behind them, the three men trooped back upstairs and up the truck ramp to the building's second floor. Raising his arms and circling the room, his work boots thudding heavily, Robin described it as a marquee space. He envisioned the second floor for events, he said, but first he would have to install an elevator, which would be difficult. As he began to describe his plans for skylights and sight lines a series of phone calls from contractors interrupted him.

"What would a similar space in Los Angeles cost you?" Norman asked Robin after he got off the phone.

"A shitty house on the outskirts of L.A. would cost more. A building like this wouldn't even exist." He had paid about $290,000.

"That's the amazing thing about this city. Its history is all coming to light now and bringing guys like you from California who never even thought of Detroit," Norman said.

"Yeah, destination stuff can work here. People want to have a nice, refined dinner in a shit part of town. That's why I think this can be an event space. It feels like authentic Detroit, but it's not as dangerous as some areas."

* * *

If Robin followed his heart, he would develop the warehouse not into an event space or a charter school, but into a techno club. Earlier he and his son had flown to Berlin and met with the owner of a famous techno club there. In the 1980s near Robin's building three African American teenagers invented techno music. Its rhythms nodded to the hum of the city's auto plants, but the music found more success in Germany than it did in America. The Berlin club's owner, Dimitri Hegemann, had therefore taken an early interest in Detroit. Since the 1990s he had visited the city numerous times.

Hegemann believed that investing in nightlife as Berlin had done could attract more tourists to Detroit. In 2012 he launched the Detroit-Berlin Connection, a series of conversations in Detroit about repurposing industrial spaces into arts venues. He flew a group of Detroit officials to Berlin to see Berlin's nightlife and hear the Detroit techno artists performing at his club.

Already Hegemann had sought out local sites for a new club at the old Fisher Body Plant 21 and Packard Automotive plant, not far from Robin's warehouse. General Motors once manufactured auto bodies at the Fisher Body plant, but now the city owned the property. The Packard plant, once a modern facility for building luxury cars, stretched across 40 derelict acres. No one had bid for the property in the 2013 tax foreclosure auction, but later a Peruvian investor acquired the property for a few hundred thousand dollars. Since 2014 he had spent $4 million clearing and securing the building, but it still lacked windows and doors. Though Hegemann had opened his Berlin club on top of the remains of a former power plant, stabilizing either Detroit building—asbestos-laden, scrapped, and with contaminated soil—seemed difficult and costly.

In filmmaker mode, Robin pitched Hegemann on his new warehouse space instead, spinning a colorful narrative even though he knew that converting the space would cost about a million dollars. A techno club that held about 400 people twice a month would not generate profits to justify the renovation costs. Without a clear path to revenues Robin's original investor would not offer the money to build out the space. Robin petitioned for a liquor license anyway and fought to change the building's zoning. His mellifluous filmmaker voice grew brighter when he talked about it.

But if Norman's charter school client offered market rent, Robin's head would prevail and he would not say no. Half of him privately salivated and wanted the income. The other half wept and wished the school would simply go away. He knew that techno clubs and schools did not mix. If the school rented the downstairs, he couldn't build the club. Gently he explained his techno vision to Norman and told him about the drug culture that the venues typically attracted, rocking his weight forward onto his toes.

"I understand the school's not part of your vision," Norman said.

"I'm not saying it isn't. I don't have the luxury of not caring if no one rents it."

"Then I'm gonna present this building to my guys at the school. I'm also gonna present it to an investor of theirs who may want to buy it and put them in here."

"You know the field next door where I plan to put a parking lot? That was a public elementary school that got torn down about 15 years ago. There are a lot of possibilities here. I haven't figured it out yet."

"You don't have to. You can just let the market do it for you."

20

Detroit Versus Everybody

JUNE 2018

On an overcast humid morning in June another celebration was underway at the old train station. On the outdoor stage a cellist was bowing a rendition of "Don't Stop Believin'." Bill Ford, Henry Ford's great-grandson, received a standing ovation from a crowd of about 5,000 people. The Ford Motor Company had purchased the station. The company planned to develop it and some surrounding buildings into a hub for researching and testing driverless and electric cars.

An emblem of Detroit's struggles no longer, the station now seemed poised to play a role in the next chapter of the city's history, a history that first accelerated when the automobile supplanted train travel. Eventually the station would mark the eastern terminus of a mobility corridor that stretched west through Ford's suburban headquarters, past the airport, and out to mobility research sites at the University of Michigan. Ford might hire about 5,000 people to work in Detroit.

Those employees would pay income taxes to the city and spend money there, and journalists giddily reported that the company's investment might effect a fundamental transformation of the city. Perhaps Detroit would once more rise on the coattails of the automobile, though an automobile of a new and different kind.

"Detroit is open for business for good," Bill Ford told the crowd gathered for the celebration while at Charles's former house Charles packed up his family's belongings. A crew was fixing the house's roof, and the compressor made it difficult to hear. The men had already dismantled the broken garage door, leaving the driveway strewn with nails. Once the workers finished using the dumpster in the front lawn Charles would sweep up the nails and throw away his family's possessions that he did not want to save. He was having trouble deciding what to do with the furniture he referred to as "bedroom soots." He looked older and more tired than before, and the whites of his eyes seemed almost yellow.

Amid whirring, refrigerator-like sounds he sorted through some old cargo crates he found in the attic. The crates were designed to travel on trains. Inside the crates he found his father's newspapers from the 1960s and his mother's old magazines. One of the newspapers covered the assassination of John F. Kennedy. As Charles sorted and stacked the new owner came and went, moving among all his houses. Though Charles had explained that he liked to keep the lawn even with the grass of his only neighbor who still mowed, the new owner had cancelled the lawn-mowing service that Charles had used for decades. He made it clear that he needed Charles out of the way.

The owner's message echoed for Charles from the old train station throughout Detroit. He had grown up in the Motor City; now the city seemed to be becoming "Tech Town." Soon self-driving electric shuttles would ferry Quicken Loans' employees between their office towers downtown and parking garages. Charles knew he could not access new jobs in the city like the ones the Ford Motor Company promised to bring to the old train station. Company spokespeople liberally predicted that the new headquarters would attract young professionals from Silicon Valley, luring them away from there and other bastions of high tech.

To afford rent and electricity, car insurance, gas, and food, Charles assumed people like him still needed factory jobs for a Big Three auto company. Those jobs had grown increasingly scarce, and the economic future of Detroit and the country seemed to lie in other types of work that required other types of education and skills. Even if the city flourished again Charles felt he would no longer find a place there.

He concluded sadly that "they" wanted people like him to go, to leave Detroit. Otherwise "they'd" give people like him opportunities that would make it possible to stay. If real estate values rose within the city, anyone who had fallen behind financially would be flushed out. If the city looked better, it would look better for the newcomers who had the opportunities. "How much do you want?" he wished he could ask people. "When is enough, enough?" Already a company in New Jersey was trying to sell a vacant lot adjacent to the train station for $2 million.

The judge had not helped Charles get his mother back. Everyone seemed for sale. The country had become entirely focused on profit, a place where the wealthy accumulated more wealth.

Charles felt ready to go. He hoped he could find a new home somewhere that offered more peace and happiness. He took a shovel from the garage to dig up the rosebush his father had planted in the backyard 28 years earlier.

* * *

Back at Robin's commercial building, Robin and the two brokers were standing on the roof gazing down on the surrounding
North End neighborhood. The Detroit broker Andre pointed
out buildings people bought on land contracts to develop into
artisan spaces. In 2016 an abandoned manufacturing building
reopened as offices for creative firms as well as community and
event spaces. Another building became a social club. Between
phone calls Robin explained with excitement that the building
with the social club still had its original mezzanine. Then he
used his cigarette to point out the old Jam Handy soundstage.
During World War II Jam Handy produced instructional films
primarily for General Motors and training videos for the U.S.
Army. In the 2010 tax foreclosure auction a friend of Robin's
had bought the soundstage for $13,000 and reopened it for
events and performances. Robin's friend had screened original
Jam Handy films there, including a black-and-white depiction
of the creation of a car set to Wagner music and a tribute
to mid-century modern design and the 1959 Chevy Impala.
He had also hosted a winter solstice celebration with guided
meditations set to a live DJ.

"This area's really happening now, really starting to pop,"
Norman, the suburban broker, said in a tone of some disbelief. The North End stood in a gap between more gentri-
fied areas to the north and the development pushing outward
along Woodward Avenue from downtown through Midtown.
The last stop of the QLine streetcar fell just two blocks south
of the North End. Between 2011 and 2016 roughly a billion
dollars in real estate deals had taken place in the neighborhood.
Another friend of Robin's had recently bought four properties
for $20,000. The properties needed $50,000 of renovations,
but a bank had loaned money for the work, which surprised

Robin. He did not realize that the neighborhood could attract traditional lending. Many people viewed the neighborhood as the next Midtown, though people said the same thing about the part of town where Joe lived.

Historically the North End offered an aspirational neighborhood for corporate leaders and politicians, as well as Jewish professionals and African Americans who found success in Detroit. Motown musicians like Diana Ross and Aretha Franklin also moved in, and in the 1930s the neighborhood provided a home for a thriving music scene of rhythm and blues and soul. Eventually highway construction divided the neighborhood, causing many businesses to relocate, and the music venues disappeared. Highway construction through urban neighborhoods throughout the country offered a way to address blight in the urban core. Instead of improving urban neighborhoods or ameliorating the social conditions that manifested in blight, publicly funded highways paved over the neighborhoods and displaced their residents. In the North End collapsing industrial buildings, graffiti, razor wire, and weeds took over. Though strong housing stock still remained, ready for rehabilitation, vacant land predominated. The population, mostly low-income African Americans, supported only one grocery store, and the store was cooperatively owned. Even prior to the city's bankruptcy, though, an arts community was beginning to develop, drawn to the old industrial buildings concentrated around the railroad tracks.

"This city has everything already here but capital and a vision," Robin said. He pointed out the historic Art Stove Building, an ornate brick structure built in 1907 as a showroom for cast iron stoves back when Detroit had a reputation as the stove capital of the world. The building now had new owners who intended to convert it into small work areas for entrepreneurs and yet another event space.

"It takes guys like you to really pioneer out here," Norman said to Robin. "These neighborhoods don't recover overnight, but this is a fun city."

"Most of my friends want to move away," Andre said. "I feel like I'm obligated to stay."

"That's one of the cool things about Detroit, the pride that people have," Norman said.

Returning to the conversation, Robin agreed. "It's the people, man, they're the greatest thing about this city. Their spirit. It gives me chills."

Norman explained that 24 years earlier he moved from Chicago to the Detroit suburbs. At first he felt like a visitor, but now he knew he had become a Detroiter. He hoped his kids would move to the city after they finished college. "There's so much opportunity here," he said.

"That's exactly who wants to be here," Robin said. Then he turned to Andre. "Why would you leave the place that made you? It's in your fabric. It's your town."

* * *

Later the same afternoon Robin pulled his truck in front of his and his wife's new house, a mile from downtown. He adjusted his duct-taped side mirror and for a few minutes he sat and watched his contractor riding a bulldozer through the forbidding, untamed yard. A water main had burst in front of the house, and the deep water gave the impression of a moat. Nine empty lots on both sides of the house contributed to a grandeur at odds with the vacancy and dereliction of the area.

The water main had broken days earlier, and Robin called his wife to let her know that the water continued to run. "That's bullshit," she said. "It's not getting into the house, is it?" They had bought the property for $1,500 from a friend of a friend, who bought it from someone who won it in the tax foreclosure auction. Robin and his wife had decided they wanted more of a sense of living out in the country than the West Village provided. Even though the new property sat closer to downtown, the area felt like prairie land, and Robin had taken to referring to the house as a farmhouse. For the previous 20 years or so the house had stood vacant, and no other houses remained on three surrounding blocks. Those properties had reverted to fields and foxes and pheasants, and he found the atmosphere magical.

Robin thought the house needed nine more months of work and $150,000 in further investment before he and his wife could move in. A crew had removed about 52,000 pounds of plaster from inside, taking the house down to the studs, and it still didn't have a roof or windows, electrical wiring or plumbing, or any walls. The back porch had collapsed over the entrance to the basement, but Robin nevertheless talked excitedly about the house's underlying construction. The thickness of the lumber in the frame exceeded current building standards, and the floors only needed refinishing. A pair of workers were scavenging rocks and garbage from the yard in preparation for Robin's wife's garden, and Robin had stashed a 100-year-old claw-foot bathtub and a 1950s stainless steel Detroit Jewel stove for the house at his commercial space. He also planned to install a bay window, laundry room, garage, and new porch.

Patiently, he was working to acquire the surrounding empty lots. The two adjacent to the house had not yet shown up in the land bank's database. One lot further down had, but the land bank's side lot program required him to buy the lots next to the house first. Then he could purchase the two lots adjacent to those, and on down the line. Eventually if he acquired all nine, he would own more than an acre of land just south of Poletown. In that neighborhood, 40 years earlier amid sit-ins and demonstrations, construction of a General

Motors plant had displaced 140 businesses, 6 churches, a hospital, and 4,200 residents, many of whom had lived in the neighborhood for generations.

Robin took a sip of water from a glass water bottle and continued driving. After several blocks he passed an old bank building from the 1920s that provided storage space for an absent owner. Though the building had boarded-up arched windows and graffiti, it featured intricate brickwork and moldings. Robin coveted it for an office, and he had been trying to identify the owner.

Further east Robin stopped at the coffee shop near the yellow house where he and his wife still lived. A branch of a suburban chain, the shop opened during the bankruptcy on the same block as the restaurant that opened around the same time. The shop's owner spent $100,000 renovating the desolate storefront. Now a mural of a tropical bird adorned the ceiling of an airy, bright space, and Robin seemed to know nearly every customer inside. All white, they sat drinking lavender lattes and turmeric milks, cloistered under the light thrown by filament bulbs and the screens of their chrome laptops. From one of the tables someone waved to Robin. It was the man who owned the restaurant. "Oh my god, so much love," Robin said, bounding toward him.

Robin found Detroit to be still one of the great cities. He sensed there the traces of the grand ambitions of the past: the attitude that anything could be possible. In Detroit iron had been smelted into steel and welded into cars powered by gas extracted from boulders. Though that era had ended he could feel a new buzz accelerating through the city and becoming part of the zeitgeist of America and its future. When people talked about Detroit's regeneration, they were talking about an area no bigger than a splat on a windshield where development was taking place. He wondered what remained achievable. He knew he had his work cut out for him.

* * *

After another four and a half hours on the bus, Miles arrived in Dayton for his trial. He carried a backpack containing the food and water he had bought from a gas station as he left his house a little before four in the morning. The shop at the bus station cost more and had not even opened by the time his bus pulled out of the station.

He had returned to Dayton because the prosecutors never offered him a misdemeanor plea as his lawyer predicted. Instead they maintained that Miles's failure to appear in court in 2003 to contest the drug charges justified the disposal of the drugs. The old police reports would provide the only evidence for the trial. Given the conflicting weights in the reports, however, Miles had decided to take his chances.

When he arrived at the courthouse he passed through a metal detector, gracefully climbed a flight of stairs, and took up a position in the hallway by his courtroom. The room would not open for another three hours, but the next bus from Detroit would have arrived too late. As he waited in the hallway he read the newspaper on his phone and picked at his fingernails, a nervous tic. A crowd gathered to watch the sentencing in a robbery-murder case in a nearby courtroom. He continued to wait.

He thought about the time he was losing, time in which he could earn the money to pay for his punishment, the money that he depended on to keep his house. He leaned his head on his hands and thought about the career he might eventually lose, the career that made anything possible. Before he left Detroit for the trial, a man he used to work for had referred him to a friend in California. Ten to 15 years earlier, before the real estate market crashed, Miles's former boss bought numerous properties in Detroit. He believed the city's property market generated better returns than the bank. Now that man's friend was buying houses in Detroit, and Miles hoped he would hire him. Miles also worried about his daughter. She seemed relieved when he returned from jail, but since then she had gotten into a fistfight. Her job at the suburban taco chain was not going well. Her future also seemed uncertain.

A sudden buzz interrupted his thoughts. The potential jurors in his case were arriving in the hallway. If he listened carefully he could pick out individual complaints about missing work and individual speculation that the case seemed serious. He noticed only two African Americans. Panicking, he realized that most of the jurors would doubt anything he said in court. They would not be able to relate to events that would never happen to them.

Then Miles's lawyer materialized and called him to the side of the hallway for a brief chat. The courtroom was opening for the trial. The lawyer told him that if Miles lost, the judge would send him straight to jail without letting him return home to organize his affairs. Again the lawyer advised him to take the felony plea. Without the drugs in evidence the lawyer had nothing to dispute in court.

In the hallway, as they discussed the plea, Miles noticed the potential jurors watching him. They seemed to realize that he might be the defendant in their trial. "Man," Miles said under his breath. He already felt a stigma coming from Detroit. They would assume he moved to Dayton to start trouble, not to attend school. "I wasn't just a guy from Detroit, but if you say Detroit you automatically get blackballed," he explained. He had been tagged guilty, he felt, before he even had his say in court, and he decided that he best surrender. He could not risk losing his house as he would if he went straight to prison. With his normally proud gaze cast downward, he told his lawyer he would plead guilty to the felony charges and go home.

By the time he got back, he had changed his mind. He realized that he had stopped fighting at the moment it mattered most. He texted his lawyer and asked him to tell the judge that the plea was a reflection only of indigence, not guilt. "This is not a measure of who Miles is," he instructed his lawyer to say. "It might be a question of who Miles was, but it's not an actual marker of who Miles is today." Miles begged for a chance to explain to the judge how he needed to stay out of jail in order to work and pay the delinquent property taxes on his house; he had no choice but to plead out. The lawyer refused, warning that the judge still had to decide the sentence.

* * *

A few weeks later, with the court process behind him, Miles was installing ceramic tile and drywall at an apartment building. When he finished he would hang cabinets and lay laminate flooring. The work came through a management company he had worked for before so he did not have to undergo a new background check. A Canadian investor owned the eight-unit building.

At sentencing Miles had received one year of probation, $600 in fines, and a community service requirement. He could not leave Michigan, and he had to pay for monthly drug treatment sessions with a counselor and for random drug tests, and report to a probation officer. The procedures struck him as ridiculous: Since the drug charge in 2003 he had stopped drinking on his own, and he had never gotten in trouble again for drugs. He swore he had never used a drug more serious than marijuana. He wished the meetings and tests could at least wait until the winter when construction work slowed down. With the weather warm, he needed all his productive time to work and save money to cover himself during the off-season.

No matter what he did, he felt he would never get ahead. He did not know how he would pay the $600 fine when he still had to return the money his aunt paid for his bail in Detroit and for his lawyer there. His aunt did not have savings and needed her money back to pay her bills, but he also had another property tax payment coming due. The interest on the taxes outstanding before he owned his house threatened to sink him.

By autumn he would finish work on the apartment building and need to find a new employer. A new employer might investigate and uncover the felony on his record. Every time he drove to work, he carefully obeyed every traffic rule and checked and rechecked his rearview mirror, sitting tall and upright, worried about getting caught without auto insurance and finding himself back in court. He did not realize that he could be arrested again on the gun charges at any time.

Yet as the annual Ford Fireworks began lighting the sky for the Fourth of July, he understood that the earth would keep spinning no matter what happened to him. It would be up to him to keep the pace. He hoped he could at least hold his position.

Epilogue

We Hope for Better Things[†]

We consider America a place of opportunity, but increasingly, where we live within the country determines the level of those opportunities. A map of the country shows a spiky and uneven terrain. Innovation hubs with educated populations have gained spectacular wealth. Other places have not weathered deindustrialization, automation, or the recent financial crisis. Cities with large populations of historically disadvantaged racial and ethnic groups, low educational attainment, and heavy reliance on nearly obsolete industries have not adapted to changes in the global economy.

Among such cities lies Detroit. Its unstable, unsafe neighborhoods; limited lending; shortage of businesses and jobs; and inadequate schools, police resources, services, and transportation have prevented many of its residents from making full use of their talents. Reggie has lost savings and time trying

---

[†] Detroit's motto, emblazoned on the city seal and city flag, is "Speramus Meliora; Resurget Cineribus" (We hope for better things; It will rise from the ashes).

to make a series of houses habitable for his family. Cindy has devoted most of her energy to policing drug use, prostitution, and dumping on her block. Consider what Lola could have accomplished with further training for higher-skilled work or without a two-hour commute.

A short drive outside Detroit, the landscape abruptly changes. In the suburb of Bloomfield Hills, 30 minutes to the north, the median income climbs above $160,000. Forty-five minutes to the west, Ann Arbor boasts a major university and a growing tech sector, with automotive innovation, medical device companies, and software interface development. When resources cluster in isolated enclaves, economic segregation reinforces economic inequality. School districts with insufficient resources keep local children from future opportunities. The children's parents find it more difficult to get to work, especially without adequate public transportation.

The Congressional Budget Office has estimated that every $1 million in federal spending to states adds several full-time jobs that stabilize communities. Every dollar raises GDP between $0.40 and $1.10. Investment in education and health care generates even more value over the long term.

Rather than investing in cities like Detroit and the people who live in them, however, the federal and state governments have withdrawn supports. Local governments like Detroit's have found themselves abandoned to their own insufficient budgets, searching for solutions to the problems that afflict their residents and, by consequence, themselves.

* * *

Against a backdrop of decades-long campaigns to lower taxes, reduce urban spending, and limit the role of government, the federal government ultimately responded to the most recent financial crisis with austerity. By 2015 federal spending amounted to more than $1 trillion less than it did in the years following the recessions of the early 1980s.

Because of state balanced budget laws, reduced payments from the federal government to the states cascaded toward cities. Cities already faced budget shortfalls from depressed taxable property values, employment income, and investment returns in the municipal bond market. Cities began selling parks, raising fees, and laying off workers, and they delayed spending on infrastructure and pension contributions. Many turned to complex financial deals to plug gaps in their revenues, and often the deals, like Mayor Kilpatrick's off-balance-sheet pension scheme in Detroit, appeared destined to fail. When they did, the federal and state governments increasingly left cities to solve their troubles on their own in bankruptcy.

Once rare, municipal bankruptcy became more common. It represented a culmination of a range of austere policies toward cities. Without a federal bailout forthcoming for Puerto Rico, the Obama administration and U.S. senators in the Democratic Party supported bankruptcy for the territory, so that it could at least write down some debt. In 2011 Jeb Bush and Newt Gingrich advocated for bankruptcy in part to discourage tough union bargaining. In his bid for the GOP presidential nomination the same year, the former governor of Minnesota Tim Pawlenty talked about bankruptcy as a way to sidestep pension liabilities.

Cuts at the federal level, passed on to the states, and from the states to cities, through bankruptcy landed at the feet of individual workers and retirees.

* * *

In Detroit, efforts to avoid bankruptcy made the city's situation worse. To show state auditors a more balanced budget, city officials pushed cuts that exacerbated problems. The officials withdrew investment in revitalization in parallel with federal and state aid reductions.

As Mayor Duggan recognized, Detroit depends on increased population density in order to generate sufficient property and income tax revenues to pay the city's debt and provide services across a large geographic area. Population density, in turn, depends in part on jobs and quality of life. The city had already lost jobs prior to and during the financial crisis. To pre-empt emergency management, city officials reduced the municipal workforce. One out of every three city employees lost his job; the layoffs affected more than 4,000 people. Fewer residents paid the city income taxes or spent money in the city; with less manpower city services worsened, and fewer active workers paid into health care and pension funds to support benefits for existing retirees. Over decades the city had lost population and associated tax revenues; then tax increases to recoup revenues encouraged more people to leave, further depressing the revenues. Cutbacks in public transportation also prevented residents from getting to work and to school. The city could not, on its own, make up the ground lost from cuts to state aid, rock-bottom real estate prices, job loss, and risky financial deals.

Resources, people, and money, by contrast, supported earlier progress the city made. In 2001 local business leaders raised money for a park downtown, which eventually attracted companies into nearby office towers that the companies renovated. Employees, new restaurants, and further building renovations for white-collar housing followed and rents rose, all of which contributed to the city's budget.

In 2005 the scion of a suburban real estate family used family money to open the barbecue restaurant in the Corktown neighborhood where Lola ate with Michael. The restaurant attracted customers from the city and the suburbs and did $1.8 million of business in the first year. Unlike typical private investors, the family moved into the neighborhood and also financed several small neighborhood businesses. Within a few years the area had grown more vibrant and generated higher property and income taxes for the city.

In Midtown, a nonprofit development group and local education and health institutions developed a scheme that provided discounts to the institutions' employees to buy or rent neighborhood properties and loans to renovate the properties. The density of the neighborhood increased and its housing stock improved. In 2009, with the support of philanthropic contributions, Wayne State University extended campus security patrols to the surrounding neighborhood and upgraded security technology. The changes made the neighborhood safer and helped it attract further development and small businesses, a boon for the municipal budget.

* * *

Bankruptcy, by contrast, does not address the circumstances that overwhelm a city's budget. In the wake of bankruptcy cities have sought to maintain their newly balanced budgets by welcoming speculative property investment and enforcing fines and fees for civil infractions, avenues for raising revenues that have inflicted further harm on cities like Detroit and residents like Reggie, Lola, and Miles. Reduced spending has further limited public services and further reduced the capacity of those communities to contribute to their cities' reinventions.

Following the recent financial crisis Vallejo, California, turned to bankruptcy after a naval shipyard closed and the housing market that buoyed the economy crashed. The city emerged from bankruptcy with a plan to balance the budget through comprehensive spending cuts. The city slashed the police department by 50 percent, closed firehouses, and terminated funding for libraries, youth groups, arts organizations, and senior centers. The city's sole remaining police station opened to the public a meager two days a week, and crime and prostitution surged. Unemployment also rose, triggering more housing foreclosures, and the real estate market fell further. Credit rating agencies warned of a possible second bankruptcy. More recently Vallejo's proximity to San Francisco's inflating property market has improved Vallejo's circumstances, independent of the cuts.

The ingredients needed to produce successful cities are more complex than those needed to produce successful businesses. Even among companies, however, restructuring debt has helped only companies that already enjoyed the building blocks for profitability—companies with problems that could be characterized as purely financial and not structural. Airlines, for example, have returned to profitability following bankruptcy because the public has continued to depend on air travel to reach faraway places. By contrast the Eastman Kodak Company, a photographic film manufacturer until digital photography decimated its business, has struggled in the wake of bankruptcy to reinvent itself as an imaging technology company. The company has reduced its staff to just 3 percent of the size of its workforce in 1982.

Many companies have repeatedly entered bankruptcy before permanently going out of business. Between 1979 and 2017 about 40 percent of the companies that attempted to reorganize in bankruptcy did not survive the bankruptcy process, and nearly 30 percent of those that did later entered into bankruptcy again. Recently large numbers of retail companies have reentered bankruptcy several times. Those companies have suffered from global economic changes like declining foot traffic, the rise of big-box stores, and the growth of e-commerce competitors. Companies that have turned to bankruptcy because of relatively easy problems to fix, like supply chain inefficiencies and e-commerce glitches, however, have tended not to return to bankruptcy.

For analogous reasons, bankruptcy has seemed most useful to cities for addressing onetime debt imbalances, not the broader-scale decline that cities like Detroit have suffered. In 2011 Boise County, Idaho, filed for bankruptcy because it could not pay a $4 million judgment. Similarly Jefferson County, Alabama, tried to use bankruptcy to resolve losses from complex derivatives it used to hedge interest rate risk on sewer revenue bonds.

Even under those circumstances, bankruptcy has risked further costs. Beyond the direct expenses of lawyers and other court fees, bankruptcy can damage cities' reputations and create uncertainty that depresses real estate values and dissuades investment. Bankruptcy has triggered reductions in cities' credit ratings that have made future borrowing more expensive, and when the markets' concerns have spread across the state, the cities' surrounding economies have also suffered. Moreover, as those protesting the bankruptcy process in Detroit recognized, transferring power from elected officials to a bankruptcy judge infringes on democratic ideals and has the potential to carry further racial undertones in majority-minority cities.

* * *

Within bankruptcy's parameters, Detroit's succeeded and even surpassed expectations. The bankruptcy ranked as the largest municipal bankruptcy in history, and the emergency manager used it as an opportunity to analyze municipal choices. Participants, particularly the bankruptcy judge, acted with sensitivity to local politics, and settlements attracted new money to support higher returns to pensioners than the city's own finances would have allowed. Related media coverage of the city's struggles elicited support from the public and the philanthropic sector, which contributed funding that ameliorated some of the austerity that would have followed.

Mediation by sitting judges sped the bankruptcy process to completion in just 14 months, which reduced costs to under $180 million. Several times, the bankruptcy judge refused to confirm settlements with two financial creditors involved in the off-balance-sheet pension deals, which saved the city money. The Grand Bargain contributed nearly $820 million to prevent liquidation of the Detroit Institute of Arts' collection and mitigate potential pension cuts, bolstering future tourism and local education and preventing thousands of pensioners from falling below the poverty line. By joining the Affordable Care Act's Medicaid expansion, Michigan officials enabled a federal backstop to cuts the bankruptcy made to municipal retirees' health care benefits. The bankruptcy plan included a detailed framework of ideas to restructure the city's operations. The plan reduced the city's required debt service payments to free up money for other uses.

Detroit is both similar to and different from other struggling cities across the country, and its differences have contributed to better outcomes during and after bankruptcy. Detroit has played an outsized role in the American imagination, falling from luxury-Cadillac highs to abandoned–auto plant lows, and the city's bankruptcy captivated national attention. Reports of reduced services stimulated an outpouring of national support. Cindy has devoted countless hours to organizing volunteers from across the country. The bankruptcy has increased local tourism, including from abroad.

The presence of well-resourced philanthropic organizations with funds to contribute to the city made the bankruptcy unusual and more humane, though in some cases the organizations assumed decision-making power from local elected officials. Few cities would have had similar local connections to national philanthropies such as the Knight, Ford, Kresge, and Kellogg Foundations. In the wake of the Grand Bargain, philanthropic initiatives have supported concentrated revitalization projects in several neighborhoods, including the Fitzgerald neighborhood, and provided funding that fostered community input from residents. Private donations have paid for new police cars and ambulances. Since the bankruptcy Detroit's development and grants office has expanded to capture further money to invest in the city.

As of this writing one could fly to Detroit and check into a hip downtown hotel, hop a streetcar to the Museum Mile, and finish the day in a renovated art deco building drinking a farm-driven cocktail and eating a $149 porterhouse steak. City officials' priorities of strengthening core areas, building on assets, preserving viable neighborhoods, and identifying green uses for excess land have increased the appeal of some parts of the city. The officials have recruited staff from across the country with talent and technical skills. They have launched new programs and attracted new private investment. One could move through the more central areas of the city without witnessing the problems that persist in the remaining 95 percent, in which 95 percent of residents live.

Commentators have continued to tout Detroit as either wholly a comeback story or wholly an urban failure. Neither narrative seems correct.

* * *

On the one hand, the name Detroit has increasingly become synonymous with grit and cool. On the other hand, the rising fortunes of greater downtown have seemed to do little to help the majority of the city and its remaining residents, and sometimes even to have harmed them. The deeper causes of the city's decline persist, and many fall outside the city's authority. In other words, bankruptcy could not possibly have corrected them.

Many positive developments entail branding and perception, and this can drive future private investment, tourism, and both corporate and individual moves into the city. The luxury watch company Shinola found that "made in Detroit" marketing tested well in focus groups. The philanthropic sector has gained attention for Detroit as a place for progressive urban planning experiments. Images of seeds planted in reclaimed buildings, abandoned houses repurposed as art projects, and artisan distilleries have contributed to an idea of the city as a new Brooklyn, New York.

This new image, however, does not seem to be improving individual outcomes for long-term residents or reversing the structural drivers behind their struggles, including the causes of blight and collapsed private lending. The poverty rate in Detroit now exceeds twice the national average. The city's median household income reaches less than half the national figure.

Gaps in safety, high-quality schools, and employment have continued to thwart economic mobility and deter population growth. Detroit still has the highest violent crime rate of any major city in the country, and in 2016 the crime rate increased more than 15 percent. Local teachers estimate that half the children in Detroit's schools have had an incarcerated parent or caregiver. Ninety percent of local eighth-grade students still score non-proficient in mathematics and reading. Meanwhile, the city's workforce participation rate remains the lowest in the country. The city still has too few jobs, and many new employers among the handful that have established themselves there have reported a deficiency in skilled local residents. Only

13 percent of Detroiters currently have bachelor's degrees, and suburban residents continue to fill the majority of jobs in the city.

Many in Detroit, like Charles, Reggie, Joe, Cindy, and Miles, have not felt their lives improving, and in some cases they have felt them getting worse. The actions of some outside investors who have participated in the tax foreclosure auction, for example, have perpetuated blight and abandonment, unraveling cohesion in neighborhoods like Reggie's. The investors' actions have further diminished the safety and well-being of lifelong residents, with little corollary benefit to the tax base.

As the downtown revival slowly spreads to adjacent areas, many neighborhoods stand derelict, public transportation remains inadequate, and the population continues to decline. Studies have shown that the resurgent popularity of cities across the country has not helped the parts of those cities afflicted with concentrated poverty.

* * *

"The path forward for Detroit seems to be Techtown, not the Motor City," Charles said. Sadly, he and others do not have the skills to participate in an economy evolving in new ways. Insufficient outlets for small-scale construction skills, for example, have provided a recurrent theme among Detroiters' stories. Such people in Detroit and elsewhere have needed more help transitioning to the new economy that is leaving them behind. That challenge echoes beyond urban areas: The 2016 election signified a growing proportion of Americans who felt forgotten.

Meaningful economic mobility for individual residents would stabilize cities' budgets. If Miles could find sufficient construction work, he could afford to renovate his house, contributing to property values in his neighborhood; pay for proper auto insurance, rather than wasting productive time and local resources on civil court processes; and better support his daughter in a successful transition to adult life. With access to finance, Joe could open a community-oriented business, reversing blight and instability in his neighborhood and producing more tax revenues for the city. Charles could use his warmth and wit for civic good. Their personal progress could translate into their city's progress.

"You paying Peter to pay Paul and then you're just staying afloat," Miles said, describing his precarious personal finances. "And if you get a flat or a ticket or something else, your life change. It puts you in a hurdle." This sounds much like the cycle of borrowing to finance existing debt that Detroit engaged in, which the city's emergency manager, Kevyn Orr, found unsustainable.

With the federal and state governments fracturing under partisan pressures, commentators have increasingly cheered cities as enablers of bottom-up changes and as innovators creating their own policy solutions. Cities have accomplished many great things, but the idea of cities reinventing themselves all on their own seems a form of magical thinking, divorced from the reality inherent in the structure of the federal system. Cities have not had the authority to accomplish everything that would help their residents. State-level decisions govern areas such as local taxation, property regulation, allocations to local public universities, and land use. No amount of innovation, for example, would enable Detroit to vary the state auto insurance scheme under which city residents currently suffer. Miles's inability to afford auto insurance triggered fines and fees that threatened his livelihood and his housing, outcomes that in turn impacted the city's income and property tax revenues.

"You try to be a person ready to move on in life," Miles said. "You lost so much, and you still got to try to go forward, but you got all this dragging you backwards." Miles offers a metaphor for Detroit, and his struggles mirror the difficulty of a city achieving a fresh start. His future, and that of the other individuals chronicled in *Broke*, matters for the future of Detroit. The causes behind their difficulties, and thus the city's, are complex, and city officials cannot solve them on their own.

* * *

If we believe that the success of individuals like Charles and Miles will improve the success of cities and towns, and the success of the country, and if we take seriously a commitment to equal opportunity, we must commit to solutions for struggling places beyond abandoning cities to bankruptcy. Alternatives exist within the reach of local, federal, and state governments.

First, Detroit needs roughly 100,000 new jobs. Even at low wages, the jobs would significantly contribute to the local economy and tax base. Increased purchasing power would boost demand for local retail and commercial services, strengthen the housing market, and generate more income and property taxes. The new salaries could even contribute to reducing crime. Augmenting employment, however, depends in part on making public education better, improving transportation to existing job opportunities, providing more training, and facilitating increased access to capital for entrepreneurship.

Those prerequisites for increased employment cost a lot, but reducing or eliminating tax subsidies would free public money to support improvements. The city has diverted tax revenues to private businesses even as studies have shown that 90 percent of subsidized projects would have occurred without the incentives. The incentives have reduced the city's budget, diminishing the funding available for education and for services like transportation and training. Nationally, tax incentives have resulted in cuts in primary and secondary education spending of more than 10 percent, with future consequences for individuals' wages and tax contributions, and therefore for government spending. Amid evidence that most company executives have based corporate location decisions on workforce and infrastructure quality, not on subsidies, cities might do better investing their revenues in their own workforce development and infrastructure. Lola provides an example of someone who could find better, higher-paying work, benefiting herself, her daughter, and her city.

Second, city officials could accomplish more with allies at higher levels of government who could aid in addressing structural problems that fall outside local control. Regulatory decisions at the federal level affected the mortgage lending market in Detroit, for example. Michigan's policies have deprived the city of tens of millions of dollars per year in income taxes, including from suburban workers; contributed to harmful speculative property investment and the destabilization of neighborhoods; and incentivized people to leave the city for the suburbs for reasons including cheaper auto insurance. Yet federal and state actions could instead support the city's progress.

Detroit has benefited in areas that federal and state programs already support. More than $260 million from the federal Hardest Hit Fund have brought down close to 12,000 blighted houses in the city. Brightmoor residents celebrated when, after years of meetings and letter-writing campaigns, the derelict neighborhood school got demolished. Federal Community Development Block Grants have contributed to the redevelopment of the Fitzgerald neighborhood near Joe's house. The federal Affordable Care Act has extended medical insurance to the city's incarcerated population, a change credited with saving the city money and reducing recidivism. Bonds backed by state transportation revenues have funded recent infrastructure improvements in commercial corridors, including new bike lanes and wider sidewalks and repairs to streets and sidewalks. City officials have predicted the state investment will help return to the city billions of dollars in retail spending that currently occurs in the suburbs.

Despite recent cuts, the federal government still devotes a considerable portion of its budget to cities through direct payments and grants. After President Trump threatened to withdraw federal contributions from cities that did not follow immigration law, Seattle, for example, calculated that it would lose about $280 million in federal support. Federal spending that appears less obviously urban oriented also reaches cities through programs related to terrorism, crime, and acute environmental restoration projects, among other areas.

Even without increasing urban spending, the federal government could coordinate existing programs to enable cities to leverage federal funds in a more integrated way, more closely tailored to revitalization goals. Scattershot funding categories could be united into a framework for addressing urban problems. The federal government often makes decisions without assessing their local fiscal impacts. No process currently exists to facilitate an analysis. Nevertheless recent discussions of raising the age of Medicare eligibility, for example, would increase costs to local governments, which fund medical benefits for retirees and their families until the retirees become eligible for Medicare. An executive order could create a mechanism for evaluating and reporting local consequences of federal choices.

The rules that govern how the states spend federal money could better incentivize urban renewal strategies. Federal tax credits that subsidize the construction of affordable housing require states to administer the credits with priority to projects that "[contribute] to a concerted community revitalization plan." The federal government has never clarified the meaning of the requirement's language, and most states have therefore ignored it. Allocating tax credits, for example, to people who buy and renovate houses to live in, in neighborhoods with high incidences of foreclosure and vacancy, could contribute to neighborhood regeneration. We have seen examples of the problems caused by non-owner-occupied houses in Charles's and Cindy's neighborhoods.

Finally, state representatives from areas surrounding distressed cities hold power either to advance solutions or to thwart them. Many people cross geographic borders for work and read regional media, but regional coordination to improve transportation and planning and address racial and economic segregation has proved rare when it has involved the redistribution of resources. In Michigan the state legislature has consistently voted against Detroit's interests.

To encourage regional cooperation that benefits cities, the state and federal governments could strengthen incentives for state officials to act to further regional interests. Governors, congressmen, and the president have the political authority and economic resources to foster closer collaboration. In fact, the regional transportation plan that failed in southeast Michigan grew out of federal efforts to condition federal transportation grants on the establishment of regional "metropolitan planning organizations" that could develop shared initiatives for regional transportation. More federal programs could include funding criteria to catalyze regional efforts toward urban recovery.

* * *

Current political trends do not play in favor of federal or state action to help cities. As urban America enjoys diminishing electoral strength, the geographic distribution of globalization's winners and losers has cleaved urban and rural values to reinforce the electoral imbalance. Reduced attention to urban priorities has led to changes such as elements of the 2017 federal Tax Cuts and Jobs Act. Earlier, taxpayers who itemized their deductions could subtract from their federal taxes the state and local taxes that they already paid. In effect, the federal government relinquished revenues to the state and local governments. The new legislation, however, limits state and local tax deductions. The revenue losses that result will threaten further cuts to local welfare services and further reliance on fines and fees to raise money, rather than on income taxes grounded in considered tax policy.

The position of the country's struggling cities and the rise of bankruptcy have reflected the current political moment. Perceived inequalities have engendered an American mind-set of scarcity that identifies resources as limited and interprets wins in one place as losses in another. This mentality of all against all has pitted rural poor against the so-called urban elite and deprived cities of national and state support, when in fact few cities rank as elite. Since the late 1910s more Americans have lived in cities than outside them. It is in cities that most Americans receive their educations, find jobs, buy homes, connect to other people, and grow old. Cities have acted as drivers of national economic growth, yet we have allowed many cities to fall behind.

Quiet rumblings across the country, however, are gaining volume as more citizens begin to fight in other contexts the same austerity approach that bankruptcy represents. Four hundred miles southeast of Detroit, in West Virginia, teachers went on strike to fight for more funding for schools. The teachers marched to shrink the distance between local conditions and areas of greater opportunity, following years of disinvestment. Since then educators in Arizona, California, Colorado, Kentucky, North Carolina, and Oklahoma have joined West Virginia in defending their communities. As Cindy's experiences in Brightmoor have illustrated, however, citizens cannot act alone.

Detroit has a gripping story that permeates its remaining streetscapes—a story about American industrial might, war victories, grit, and resilience. Its future seems to reflect the future of the country. Perhaps that narrative, combined with strong local leadership and philanthropic attention, will prove sufficient to overcome long-term economic shifts and federal and state impediments beyond local control. Other cities in more forgotten corners, however, may lack even those supports. Less than a year after Detroit exited bankruptcy, Hillview, Kentucky, petitioned to enter it. Ultimately an agreement to raise local taxes, issue new bonds, and divert more than 8 percent of revenues to one creditor for 20 years forestalled the bankruptcy. Had Hillview entered bankruptcy, it would not have enjoyed Detroit's ability to trade against an art collection for new assets for pensioners or attract ongoing philanthropic commitments.

We cannot allow the country to fragment into areas of varying opportunity. We cannot continue to withhold resources from desperate people and the desperate places where they live. Equalizing opportunities and narrowing divides should be fundamental to who we are as Americans.

Author's Note

My maternal grandfather often said, "The bottom line is what is best for the society we are serving." A child of the Depression, he taught me that government could be a force for good. As the secretary of welfare for Pennsylvania he created a program that the federal government later replicated and called Head Start. He spearheaded functional education programs for those on welfare, introduced music and art to public programs, and advanced services for the mentally disabled. He intervened so that a young woman could attend college without causing her family to lose their welfare benefits. She later attended medical school and continued to keep in touch with him.

Taking his lessons to heart, I became a lawyer. Bankruptcy law captured my interest because at heart it aspires to fair outcomes. The law differentiates among types of creditors and takes account of what the creditors likely knew about risks. I saw how bankruptcy also offers a corollary to the existence of credit in our society. Credit enables economic growth but in excess can contribute to economic disruptions. I became concerned with the varying access to credit that various entities enjoy, which exacerbates income disparities. Eventually I went on to teach bankruptcy law as a law professor.

In 2013 Detroit and its impending bankruptcy, along with the fiscal challenges many other cities faced, started to dominate news headlines. Newspaper articles adopted a dramatic tone about rising municipal debt, but they rarely discussed the people who lived in the cities. Before long books began to appear about Detroit's bankruptcy process, and the books also made no mention of the people caught up in it. After the city exited bankruptcy, the reporters and pundits returned home. Bankruptcy dropped out of the news before its effects could be fully evaluated.

The accounts of the Detroit bankruptcy went one of two ways. Most described the legal process in optimistic, corporate terms: After being rightsized, a new Detroit would rise from the ashes of the old, mismanaged city. Others expressed greater outrage: After the suspension of power of Democratic elected officials in a majority African American city, in favor of control by the appointee of a Republican governor of a majority white state, public spending would fall and outsiders would scavenge Detroit's remaining assets.

Both characterizations of the bankruptcy missed the fundamental point that for changing the future of a city, bankruptcy offers a limited tool. Bankruptcy offers a legal process for restructuring debt. It does not address the deeply rooted problems that reduce municipal revenues. Cities cannot be viewed in isolation; they inhabit the lowest rung in a hierarchy incorporating federal and state powers and remain subject to federal and state policies. The federal government has targeted spending cuts to states as a means for reducing discretionary spending, and states have passed down the cuts to cities by reducing revenue sharing and aid to education. The economies of cities are small and open; the real economy has become regional and potentially global. Cities can tax only within their city limits, but the economy in which they operate crosses international borders. Federal law influences the range of options available to city officials, and state law can discourage urban investment.

Why did nobody probe why Detroit ran out of funds to pay for essential services, what options the city had to generate more money, and whether the bankruptcy process could help the people of Detroit in the long term? I decided to write a book exploring those questions.

* * *

In 2016 when I began working on *Broke,* the presidential election was reaching its climax, and both candidates were exploiting cities like Detroit in their messaging. Hillary Clinton challenged the narrative of America in decline at a speech in Detroit; Donald Trump attended a service at a Detroit church and told residents of distressed cities everywhere they had "nothing to lose" by voting for him. Trump played up gaps emerging between elites in a handful of thriving cities and the rural poor, neglecting gaps among cities' residents.

As I spent time in Detroit I could see how cities could lack resources of their own to solve structural problems that had proliferated, and bankruptcy did little to provide further resources to end the downward spiral. In fact, bankruptcy exacerbated negative trends that would not otherwise have been inevitable.

The cases and legal theory I had taught in law school bankruptcy classes failed to capture the stakes. A case might refer to a group known only as "employees," or theorists might struggle with the consequences of the law for "unsecured creditors," but neither the case nor the theory communicated what losses personally meant to those parties, especially those inexperienced in lending and without enough savings to absorb losses they did not expect.

How could we approach bankruptcy and isolate such people from our concern? How could policy makers hype bankruptcy as the solution to struggling cities without understanding the efficacy or basic consequences of its use? Numerous articles were touting the benefits of bankruptcy for cities, and scholars and politicians espoused bankruptcy even for states. We had overlooked urban residents and considered the issues in the wrong way.

To find answers I began spending more and more time in Detroit. The Detroit airport sits far outside the city limits, halfway to Ann Arbor and the buzzing quads and opulent buildings of the University of Michigan. A direct bus runs between the airport and Detroit just once an hour, and only during peak periods. Out the bus window nearly empty landscapes stretch for miles. As houses come into view, instead of typical American suburbia empty lots and the remains of houses appear one after another.

I had not set out to focus on real estate, but it quickly became clear to me that real estate encapsulated many of the causes of Detroit's bankruptcy and the challenges the city has confronted in bankruptcy's wake. In Detroit, where 80 percent of residents were African American and 40 percent lived below the poverty line, the population that subprime lenders targeted in the lead-up to the financial crisis predominated. Less well known is how high rates of predatory lending eventually left the city with a large pool of abandoned properties that outside speculators bought in bulk. Rather than investing in the city, many speculators wrung resources from it and then abandoned it. Often they tried to offload derelict properties onto naïve Detroit residents through contracts that did not carry the protections of mortgage lending or landlord-tenant law.

Detroit also had to enforce strict tax foreclosure procedures enacted by the state legislature. The 2016 election, two years following the city's exit from bankruptcy, occurred just as roughly 36,000 Detroit properties entered foreclosure, not for delinquent mortgage payments but for delinquent property taxes. A local data company called Loveland Technologies surveyed the occupants of the foreclosed properties. Its representatives visited more than 8,000 occupied houses slated for auction. No federal assistance materialized to keep those people in their homes, and the unpaid property tax revenues that the foreclosures represented impeded the city's ability to maintain a balanced budget.

Ask a Detroit resident about his housing and chances are good that he will tell you a sad story. In only a few decades a city of homeowners has transformed into a city of majority renters. The loss of homes has propagated vacancy and blight that has depressed local property markets and destabilized neighborhoods. Even following bankruptcy the city has had no authority to stop the cycle of abandonment on its own.

I started to explore the interplay of these various currents with a small group of Detroit residents and over time moved on to exploring further issues with the people I had gotten to know. The executive director of the United Community Housing Coalition, a local housing nonprofit, agreed to let me join the agency's efforts to canvass houses in foreclosure and observe counseling sessions at its downtown offices.

I drove from house to house, neighborhood to neighborhood, with a young housing counselor, bouncing along in her rickety Volkswagen Golf. She had maps indicating foreclosed houses to visit but no way to reach them all before the county began auctioning them off, and we raced to knock on as many doors as we could before time ran out. We visited houses with windows and houses without them, houses with tidy lawns and houses with weeds and waist-high grass, and houses with toys on the porch and houses strewn with garbage. We talked to residents with running water and those without it, and we talked to people trying to keep hold of houses for relatives in prison and people who had given up in the face of excessive property tax assessments. We met a woman with six children who had moved six times the previous year and whose most recent landlord sold her house without telling her to an investment company that did not pay property taxes.

We talked to a man who bid in a previous tax foreclosure auction on the house next door to his grandparents'. He entered the bid while bleeding from a gunshot wound in the emergency room and lost to a bidder representing an investment company that immediately had the pipes removed from the house and then disappeared. For the past three years the man had been mowing the lawn at the house and parking a car out front to deter potential squatters and protect his grandparents, but now he prepared to lose the house in the tax foreclosure auction again.

While canvassing I met Reggie, as he and his family were pulling into their driveway in a rusted 2001 minivan. Reggie became the first person I decided to follow for the book. He had bought his house outside the traditional mortgage market, which no longer functioned normally in Detroit. I met more people at the Housing Coalition's offices.

The Coalition occupies a small space in a faded, block-long art deco building divided from downtown by Interstate 75. Families who arrived at the Coalition would find crowds spilling from mismatched plastic chairs on scuffed linoleum floors, clutching money orders and thick folders of personal documents under the glare of fluorescent lights. After telling clients there about my plans for a book, I followed up by phone and arranged home visits. I met Lola when I sat in on her counseling session, and we got together for breakfast a few days later on her birthday. She had taken the day off from work.

Around this time, the better-organized local neighborhood associations, together with the American Civil Liberties Union of Michigan and the National Association for the Advancement of Colored People Legal and Education Fund, filed a lawsuit challenging the tax foreclosure process as racially discriminatory because of its disproportionate effect on African American homeowners. I spoke with leaders of several of the neighborhood associations and lawyers from the ACLU. In this way I met Cindy, who by then was running the neighborhood association in Detroit's Brightmoor neighborhood, and Joe, who actively participated in the Bagley Community Council, a northwest Detroit community association. The ACLU considered listing Charles as a plaintiff in the lawsuit. Charles introduced me to his childhood friend Miles.

* * *

In time my relationships with Reggie, Lola, Cindy, Joe, and Miles deepened, and my conversations broadened to urban issues beyond housing that urban revitalization seemed to depend on, including education, work, transportation, and safety. In those areas, too, numerous forces appeared to have acted on Detroit and other cities that both contributed to their decline and limited the effectiveness of bankruptcy. Detroit has lost revenues in parallel with every student who has left the Detroit school system for state-authorized charter schools, every resident who has more easily found employment in the suburbs, and every person who has migrated to the suburbs to reduce the burden of commuting to suburban jobs,

avoid the cost of auto insurance in the city, or protect themselves from neighborhood crime. Deficiencies in the public education system, the availability of local jobs, and the high cost
and difficulty of living in Detroit have stymied recent efforts to
encourage migration into the city to reinvigorate the tax base.

I noticed that being white and well-educated did not
shield Joe from the hardships faced by lifelong Detroiters.
Nevertheless he enjoyed closer access to politicians and neighborhood leaders and better relationships with his employers.
He introduced me to a property developer called Robin, along
with several other property investors he'd met while doing tree
work for them.

My relationship with Robin developed gradually. I became
interested in the fact that he was trying to do good, but doing
good profitably often proved difficult. His heart wanted to
build attention-grabbing projects that would improve life in
Detroit, but his head knew that he had a responsibility to his
funders to earn profits.

I bridged different worlds: People with money and power
had little insight into the lives of the poor, and vice versa.
An investment banker involved at a high level in the bankruptcy told me that Detroit just needed its residents to pay
their property taxes. An activist minister who protested the
bankruptcy spent an hour with me railing against it and then,
as I was leaving his church, took me aside and sincerely asked,
"Who profits from a bankruptcy?" Many Detroiters did not
understand the complexities of a bankruptcy process. When
I asked for their thoughts about it, I heard answers along the
lines of, "Oh, Detroit's always been bankrupt."

The fieldwork that supports this book encompasses more
than 200 interviews. I continue to talk with the people I got

to know in Detroit. During my recent brief bout with an illness people from the city checked up on me, and Charles kept texting new advice.

I interviewed numerous people not featured in this book, including further property developers, city officials, educators, architects, and activists. In this way I triangulated what the individuals in the book told me. Property records, court records, and news reports have also provided corroboration.

Detroit ranks as a notorious example of bankruptcy, but it is hardly alone. Bankruptcy should not be a foregone conclusion for cities, and my hope is that by understanding Detroit's experience we may push for better outcomes for other cities. Rather than penalizing distressed cities through forced austerity, actions at all levels of government could instead support them. Economic shifts and the aftermath of the financial crisis demand the opposite of current patterns, in which cities fight for themselves, competing to attract and retain businesses with limited returns while acquiring debt to fund basic services and infrastructure essential to the future, like good public schools. The lives that *Broke* chronicles show us what bankruptcy cannot accomplish. They show us the hard work of combatting individual poverty must take precedence over facile, short-term urban fixes.

Acknowledgments

My unending thanks to Miles, Charles, Robin, Reggie, Cindy, Joe, and Lola. It has been a privilege getting to know you. I hope that you will continue to keep in touch with me and to share your lives with me. Thank you for sticking by me while the work wended its way to a book, and thank you for lending your voices and your experiences to it, so that we can learn from you.

A couple hundred further interviews also inform *Broke*. A grateful thank-you to all the people who took the time to speak with me. I appreciate your insights and your generosity. The arguments in the book reflect your expertise.

Elisabeth Dyssegaard, my editor at St. Martin's, believed in *Broke* from the start, then helped me to make it better. Thank you for your gentle touch and broad vision. I am also indebted to St. Martin's managing editor Alan Bradshaw, whose labor has made the manuscript as technically perfect as it could be. Thank you for bearing with my dialogues around possible line edits and for readily supplying new words when a phrase simply did not feel right to me. Katherine Haigler improved the flow of the text, and it has been my tremendous luck to work with Danielle Preilip and John Karle, who have greatly supported me in attracting notice of the book. Carin Siegfried, thank you for your advocacy and enthusiasm in selling it, and for your friendship.

I particularly value the wisdom and advice that Samuel Freedman, Kevin Peraino, and George Black shared with me. It helped lead me to my agent, Anna Stein, who has been a steadying and responsive presence throughout the publication process. Thank you, Anna, for working with me to develop the proposal and for championing nonfiction authors endeavoring to write difficult stories. Thank you also for connecting me to Nicole Dewey at Shreve Williams. Working with and learning from you, Nicole, has been an honor and a pleasure.

The Marron Institute at New York University has provided an ideal home from which to research and write *Broke*. I am indebted to the people of the institute, who have helped me in various ways. I want to especially thank Paul Romer and Brandon Fuller for welcoming me to the institute, Clay Gillette for sustained support, and Allison Weinger, Kari Kohn, Alex Wesnousky, and Nicole Eason for carefully and thoughtfully taking care of countless details. I appreciate the exceptional group of faculty, postdoctoral researchers, and staff at the institute, who have enriched the book through their feedback and encouragement.

Several relatives and friends hosted me at various points while I was writing *Broke* and offered kindnesses. Thank you to Michel Marks, George and Jamie Schuler, Judy Adams, Ali Krantzler, and Nancy and Jack Dickson for your hospitality. Paula Croxson provided a priceless early read.

The support of the Kresge Foundation made *Broke* possible. In particular, I want to mention and thank Benjy Kennedy for his receptiveness to the idea of a book and Rip Rapson and Ariel Simon for also backing it. It was my good fortune to partner with a foundation that eschewed influence to the degree that I did not interview anyone from it. I owe a debt of gratitude not only for the foundation's support but also for the freedom it afforded me.

I began conceiving of *Broke* while on a sabbatical from Cambridge University to Columbia Law School in New York, an invaluable opportunity that enabled me to begin traveling to Detroit and to pursue the idea of writing a book about the bankruptcy. It also enabled me to meet Michele Oberholtzer at the Detroit United Community Housing Coalition and Kim Buddin-Crawford at the ACLU of Michigan, who aided and abetted me in such a crucial way. Since then, I have continued to teach a bankruptcy seminar at Columbia, and the insights and reactions of numerous students have developed and deepened my arguments.

Thank you to the friends and family who soften the twists and turns of life, and who have been an incomparable source of support during recent critical moments. Thank you, above all, to Carol and Howard Kirshner, without whom nothing would be attainable.

Notes

═

Prologue: Springtime in Detroit

xvii *In the county tax foreclosure:* All references to county tax foreclosure auction winning bids reference data from the Detroit Open Data Portal and data maintained by the national parcel data company Loveland Technologies.

xviii *He did not know that:* All references to real estate (ownership, purchases, foreclosure) have been corroborated using the Wayne County Register of Deeds and the Detroit Open Data Portal.

xviii *Detroit entered bankruptcy:* Nathan Bomey, *Detroit Resurrected* (New York: Norton, 2016), offers a detailed account of the progression of the bankruptcy and related negotiations.

xviii *Bankruptcy offered a process:* Municipal bankruptcy is codified in chapter 9 of the U.S. Bankruptcy Code, 11 U.S.C., § 901–946 (2006). Good sources on chapter 9 include Randal Picker and Michael W. McConnell, "When Cities Go Broke: A Conceptual Introduction to Municipal Bankruptcy," *University of Chicago Law Review* 60 (1993): 425–495; Clayton P. Gillette and David A. Skeel, Jr., "Governance Reform and the Judicial Role in Municipal Bankruptcy," *Yale Law Journal* 125 (2016): 1150–1547; Michael De Angelis and Xiaowei Tian, "United States: Chapter 9 Municipal Bankruptcy: Utilization, Avoidance, and Impact," World Bank, 2013; Kenneth E. Noble and Kevin M. Baum, "Municipal Bankruptcies: An Overview and Recent History of Chapter 9 of the Bankruptcy Code," *Pratt's Journal of Bankruptcy Law* 513 (2013); John Gramlich, "Municipal Bankruptcy Explained," Pew

Charitable Trusts, November 22, 2011; Henry C. Kevane, "Chapter 9 Municipal Bankruptcy: The New 'New Thing'?" American Bar Association, *Business Law Today*, 2011.

xviii *Outside bankruptcy even one:* A good description of this process can be found in John A. E. Pottow, "What Bankruptcy Law Can and Cannot Do for Puerto Rico," *Revista Juridica UPR* 85 (2016): 689–704.

xviii *Seventeen months and nearly:* Eighth Amended Plan for the Adjustment of Debts of the City of Detroit, *In re City of Detroit, Mich.*, no. 13-53846 (Bankr. E.D. Mich., October 22, 2014), https://www.michigan .gov/documents/treasury/Detroit__Eighth_Amended_Plan_of _Adjustment_476086_7.pdf; Expert Report of Martha E. M. Kopacz Regarding the Feasibility of the City of Detroit Plan of Adjustment, *In re City of Detroit, Mich.*, no. 13-53846 (Bankr. E.D. Mich., October 22, 2014), http://www.detroitmi.gov/Portals/0/docs/EM /Bankruptcy%20Information/M.%20Kopacz%20Expert%20 Report%20to%20Judge%20Rhodes%20071814.pdf.

xix *No one knew in part:* Omer Kimhi, "Chapter 9 of the Bankruptcy Code: A Solution in Search of a Problem," *Yale Law Journal* 27 (2010): 352–395, provides a good source on the early history of municipal bankruptcy.

xx *In 1975 New York State advanced:* Gretchen Morgenson, "Lessons from the Bailout of New York," *The New York Times*, May 11, 2008.

xx *In 1978 after Cleveland:* "The State Role in Local Government Financial Distress," Report of the Pew Charitable Trusts, July 2013.

xx *But as voters moved:* On the rise and fall of federal support for cities, good sources include Charles Tabb, "The Wider Context of Urban Austerity," *City* 18 (2014): 87–100; and Jamie Peck, "Austerity Urbanism," *Rosa Luxembourg Stiftung City Series* 1 (2015): 1–25.

xx *Between 1980 and 1988:* William Tabb, "National Urban Policy and the Fate of Detroit," in *Reinventing Detroit*, ed. Michael Peter Smith and L. Owen Kirkpatrick (New Brunswick, N.J., and London: Transaction Publishers, 2015), Chapter 4.

xx *Mandatory balanced budget rules:* On cuts cascading from the federal government to the states to the cities, Phil Oliff, Chris Mai, and Vincent Palacios, "States Continue to Feel Recession's Impact," Report of the Center on Budget and Policy Priorities, June 27, 2012.

xx *Lacking support from federal:* Josh Pacewicz, *Partisans and Partners: The Politics of the Post-Keynesian Society* (Chicago: The University of Chicago Press,

2016). On municipal debt, "Report on the Municipal Securities Market," U.S. Securities and Exchange Commission, July 31, 2012; Emilia Istrate, "Municipal Bonds Build America," National Association of Counties, Policy Research Paper Series, Issue 1, 2013; Lisa Lambert, "U.S. Municipal Bond Market Shrinks to Smallest in Five Years," Reuters, December 11, 2014.

xx *During the crisis governmental support:* "The Local Squeeze: Falling Revenues and Growing Demand for Services Challenge Cities, Counties, and School Districts," Report of the Pew Charitable Trusts, June 2012; "Sector Comment: Outlook for U.S. Local Governments Remains Negative in 2013," Moody's, 2013.

xxi *In order to maintain solvency:* Kirk Victor, "Struggling Cities Strike Deals to Solve Fiscal Problems," *Governing*, March 2012.

xxi *In 2012, Stockton, California:* Bobby White, "Stockton Files for Bankruptcy Protection," *Wall Street Journal*, June 29, 2012.

xxi *By the end of 2012 three:* "What Happens When a City Declares Bankruptcy?" Talk of the Nation, July 11, 2012.

xxi *In 2013 Detroit broke Stockton's:* "Detroit Bankruptcy Is the Nation's Largest," *The New York Times*, July 18, 2013.

xxi *The problems Detroit confronted:* On mortgage foreclosure, "Spotlight on the Housing Market in the Detroit-Warren-Livonia, Michigan MS," U.S. Department of Housing and Urban Development, U.S. Department of the Treasury, January 2013. On property tax revenue, "Detroit City Government Revenues," Citizens Research Council of Michigan Report 382, April 2013. On income tax, "Detroit City Government Revenues," Citizens Research Council of Michigan Report 382, April 2013. On state aid, "Detroit City Government Revenues," Citizens Research Council of Michigan Report 382, April 2013. On job loss, "Detroit City Government Revenues," Citizens Research Council of Michigan Report 382, April 2013.

xxi *Without outside help:* For an updated list of municipalities that have entered bankruptcy, see "Bankrupt Cities, Municipalities List and Map," *Governing*.

xxii *Detroit's bankruptcy offered:* Gene Armromin and Ben Chabot, "Detroit's Bankruptcy: The Uncharted Waters of Chapter 9," Chicago Fed Letter Number 316, November 2013; Lydia DePillis, "Here's How Detroit's Bankruptcy Will Actually Work," *The Washington Post*, July 19, 2013;

Monica Davey, Bill Vlasic, and Mary William Walsh, "Detroit Ruling on Bankruptcy Lifts Pension Protections," *The New York Times*, December 3, 2013; John W. Schoen, "It's Feds vs. State as Detroit Heads to Bankruptcy Hearing," CNBC, July 23, 2013; George Lafferty, "Bankruptcy and Beyond: Detroit's Neoliberal Constraints and Democratic Possibilities," *International Sociology* 33 (2018): 171–181.

xxii   *A majority of Americans live:* "U.S. Cities Home to 62.7% of Population," U.S. Census, 2015, https://www.census.gov/newsroom/press-releases /2015/cb15-33.html; Kim Parker, Juliana Menasce Horowitz, Anna Brown, Richard Fry, D'Vera Cohn, and Ruth Igielnik, "Demographic and Economic Trends in Urban, Suburban, and Rural Communities," Pew Research Center, May 22, 2018; Jonathan Rees, "Industrialization and Urbanization in the United States: 1880–1929," *Oxford Research Encyclopedias*, July 2016. About half the children in Detroit fall below the poverty line.

xxiii *The people in Detroit:* Christine MacDonald and Jennifer Chambers, "Detroiters' Income Rises for Second Year but Poverty Rate Doesn't Improve," *The Detroit News*, September 13, 2018.

I. Emergency Management

4   *Tensions between the city:* Useful articles on the relevant tensions include Neena Rouhani, "Border of Detroit and Grosse Pointe Park Reflects Gap, Tensions Between City and Suburbs," *Newsroom of the Michigan State University School of Journalism*, July 31, 2017; Alana Semuels, "At Detroit's Border, a Barrier Separates the Haves from Have-Nots," *Los Angeles Times*, October 18, 2014; Bill Laitner, "Grosse Pointe Park, Detroit Find Common Ground, Dedicate Sculpture at Border," *Detroit Free Press*, August 3, 2017; Rose Hackman, "'Detroiters Stay Out': Racial Blockades Divide a City and Its Suburbs," *The Guardian*, February 3, 2015.

4   *But his half sister had:* Records pertaining to the property are on file with the author.

5   *In the late 1930s Charles's:* August Meier, Elliott Rudwick, and Joseph William Trotter, *Black Detroit and the Rise of the UAW* (Ann Arbor: University of Michigan Press, 2007).

5   *Detroit had grown fat:* For visual representations, the Detroit Industry Murals, pictured and described by the Detroit Institute of Arts, which exhibits them in "Rivera Court," available at https://www.dia.org/art

/rivera-court. For a summary of how industrialization led to urbanization, see John R. Meyer, "The Role of Industrial and Post-Industrial Cities in Economic Development," Harvard University Joint Center for Housing Studies W00-1, April 2000. For a concise description of the city attracting nascent auto companies, see Thomas J. Sugrue, "The Motor City: The Story of Detroit," The Gilder Lehrman Institute of American History, September 16, 2014. On manufacturing tanks, Thomas J. Sugrue, *The Origins of the Urban Crisis: Race and Inequality in Postwar Detroit* (Princeton: Princeton University Press, 2014).

6 *Charles's father found work:* "The Budd Company Records: 1912–1951," University of Michigan, Bentley Historical Library; Paul Clemens, *Punching Out: One Year in a Closing Auto Plant* (New York: Doubleday, 2012); "Budd Co. Files for Bankruptcy Protection to Modify Retiree Benefits," *Automotive News,* April 1, 2014.

6 *African Americans could not access:* On redlining then and now, J. Brian Charles, "Federal Housing Discrimination Still Hurts Home Values in Black Neighborhoods," *Governing,* April 30, 2018; Emily Bader, "Self-Fulfilling Prophecies: How Redlining's Racist Effects Lasted for Decades," *The New York Times,* August 24, 2017. "Expert Report of Thomas J. Sugrue in Support of Class Certification," *Adkins et al. v. Morgan Stanley,* Case No. 1:12-cv-7667-VEC, S.D.N.Y. (2014) provides a good summary of redlining and following elements of discriminatory practices in Detroit's real estate market at the time.

6 *Urban redevelopment projects under:* On urban renewal, Jon C. Teaford, "Urban Renewal and Its Aftermath," *Housing Policy Debate* 11 (2000): 443–465.

6 *The Supreme Court had found: Shelley v. Kraemer,* 334 U.S. 1 (1948).

6 *As the racial frontier:* For a general analysis of the aftermath of *Shelley v. Kraemer,* B. T. McGaw and George B. Nesbitt, "Aftermath of Shelley Versus Kraemer on Residential Restriction by Race," *Land Economics* 29 (1953): 280–287; Joe T. Darden, "Black Residential Segregation Since the 1948 Shelley v. Kraemer Decision," *Journal of Black Studies* 25 (1995): 680–691.

6 *Block-busting real estate agents:* On block busting, and connecting above racial politics to Detroit, Joe Darden, Richard Child Hill, June Thomas, and Richard Thomas, *Detroit: Race and Uneven Development* (Philadelphia: Temple University Press, 1987).

7 *Years later, to clear a site:* Paul A. Eisenstein, "1,700 Chrysler Workers Put in Final Day at Detroit Plant," *Chicago Tribune,* February 3, 1990;

Doron P. Levin, "Chrysler Opens Plant, Makes a Point," *The New York Times*, April 1, 1992.

7   *In the face of global shifts:* Sugrue, *The Origins of the Urban Crisis.*

8   *The German conglomerate restructured:* Terry Kosdrosky, "Budd Co. Changes Name, Reorganizes to Win Business," *Crain's Detroit Business*, November 25, 2002; Brent Snavely, "ThyssenKrupp Budd Closing Detroit Plant; About 350 Workers Affected," *Crain's Detroit Business*, May 15, 2006; Brent Snavely, "ThyssenKrupp Budd on Block," *Crain's Detroit Business*, August 28, 2006.

11 *Eyeing Detroit and the still powerful:* John Gallagher, *Reinventing Detroit* (Detroit: Wayne State University Press, 2010); William K. Tabb, "If Detroit Is Dead, Some Things Need to Be Said at the Funeral," *Journal of Urban Affairs* (2015): 1–12; "Michigan Gov. Rick Snyder Defends Right-to-Work, EM Laws on Fox News," MLive, March 21, 2013; "Union Contracts Could Be in Crosshairs as Gov. Snyder Intervenes in Detroit," Fox News, December 20, 2015.

11 *Local activists began gathering:* On this time period, see "Time: Detroit's Road Through Bankruptcy," *The Detroit News*, November 7, 2014. The events provoked significant criticism in the news media: Chris Savage, "The Scandal of Michigan's Emergency Managers," *The Nation*, February 15, 2012; Chris Lewis, "Does Michigan's Emergency-Manage Law Disenfranchise Black Citizens?" *The Atlantic*, May 9, 2013.

14 *As the threat of emergency management:* Sydney L. Hawthorne, "Do Desperate Times Call for Desperate Measures in the Context of Democracy?" *NYU Review of Law and Social Change* 41 (2017): 181–233, detailing Michigan's 2011 Public Act 4, ensuing protests, and Michigan's passage of 2012 Public Act 436.

14 *Nearly half the streetlights:* J.C. Reindl, "Why Detroit's Lights Went Out," *USA Today*, November 17, 2013.

15 *"dumb, lazy, happy, and rich":* "Kevyn Orr Apologizes for Calling Detroit 'Dumb, Lazy, Happy, and Rich,'" Michigan Radio, August 15, 2013.

2. Home

19 *Between 2005 and 2015, mortgage:* Good sources on subprime lending and the foreclosure crisis in Detroit include Christine MacDonald and Joel Kurth, "Foreclosures Fuel Detroit Blight, Cost City $500 Million," *The Detroit News*, June 3, 2015. Nationally, see Jacob S. Rugh

and Douglas S. Massey, "Racial Segregation and the American Foreclosure Crisis," *American Sociology Review* 75 (2010): 629–651; Katalina M. Bianco, "The Subprime Lending Crisis: Causes and Effects of the Mortgage Meltdown," *CCH Mortgage Compliance Guide and Bank Digest*, 2008; Rick Cohen, "A Structural Racism Lens on Subprime Foreclosures and Vacant Properties," Kirwan Institute for the Study of Race and Ethnicity at Ohio State University, National Convening on Subprime Lending, Foreclosure and Race, 2008.

22   *No law prevented such "zombie foreclosures":* Amanda McQuade, "The Antidote to Zombie Foreclosures: How Bankruptcy Courts Should Address the Zombie Foreclosure Crisis," *Emory Bankruptcy Developments Journal* (2016): 507–535; Judith L. Fox, "How to Kill a Zombie: Strategies for Dealing with the Aftermath of the Foreclosure Crisis," Notre Dame Legal Studies Paper 1519, June 24, 2015; David P. Weber, "Taxing Zombies: Killing Zombie Mortgages with Differential Property Taxes," *University of Illinois Law Review* (2017): 1135–1167.

22   *As the foreclosure crisis diminished:* Researchers conducted a study in four cities about the extent of investor interest in foreclosed properties and how they treated the properties and surrounding communities: Christopher E. Herbert, Irene Lew, and Rocio Sanchez-Moyano, "The Role of Investors in Acquiring Foreclosed Properties in Low- and Moderate-Income Neighborhoods: A Review of Findings from Four Case Studies," Harvard University Joint Center for Housing Studies, October 2013. Journalists further documented the scale of investment in mortgage-foreclosed properties: Morgan Breenan, "Investors Flock to Housing, Looking to Buy Thousands of Homes in Bulk," *Forbes*, April 3, 2012; Matthew Goldstein and Jennifer Ablan, "The Wall Street Gold Rush in Foreclosed Homes," Reuters, March 20, 2012.

23   *In the wake of the financial:* Lewis Wallace, "Why There's Almost No Mortgage Lending in Detroit," *Marketplace*, October 5, 2016; Joel Kurth and Mike Wilkinson, "Home Mortgages Remain a Detroit Rarity," *Bridge Magazine*, March 30, 2017.

24   *Land contracts enabled a rent-to-own:* Elizabeth Weintraub, "How a Land Contract Works for Buying Homes," *The Balance*, February 17, 2018. On the tainted history of the contracts, see Sarah Mancini and Margot Saunders, "Land Installment Contracts: The Newest Wave of

Predatory Home Lending Threatening Communities of Color," Federal Reserve Bank of Boston, April 13, 2017.

24 *Land contracts began filling:* On the rise of land contracts among low-income buyers in Detroit, Joe Kurth, "Loose Regulations Make Land Contracts a Tool to Exploit Low-Income Homeowners," *Bridge Magazine,* May 20, 2017; Lewis Wallace, "In Detroit a Risky Alternative to Mortgages," *Marketplace,* October 6, 2016; Kaye Lafond and Sarah Hullet, "Why Detroit Is 'Ground Zero' for Surge in Land Contracts," *All Things Considered,* June 14, 2017.

26 *Across the country speculators:* Jeremiah Battle, Jr., et al., "Toxic Transactions: How Land Installment Contracts Once Again Threaten Communities of Color," National Consumer Law Center, July 2016. On involvement of Fannie Mae, see Mancini and Saunders, "Land Installment Contracts."

27 *By February 2016 at least:* Matthew Goldstein and Alexandra Stevenson, "Cincinnati Sues Seller of Foreclosed Homes, Claiming Predatory Behavior," *The New York Times,* April 20, 2017; Matthew Goldstein and Alexandra Stevenson, "Market for Fixer-Uppers Traps Low-Income Buyers," *The New York Times,* February 20, 2016; Matthew Goldstein and Alexandra Stevenson, "How a Home Bargain Became a 'Pain in the Butt,' and Worse," *The New York Times,* July 7, 2017; Matthew Goldstein and Alexandra Stevenson, "Law Center Calls Seller-Financed Home Sales 'Toxic Transactions,'" *The New York Times,* July 14, 2016.

3. Census

28 *Summer 2013 brought warmer:* For example, Melanie Hicken, "Detroit's Workers and Retirees Face Big Cuts," *CNN Money,* July 18, 2013.

29 *Brightmoor nestled into the far:* On Brightmoor's history, John Gallagher, *Revolution Detroit: Strategies for Urban Reinvention* (Detroit: Wayne State University Press, 2013).

29 *Growing up a few blocks:* For a comprehensive background, Hubert G. Lock, *The Detroit Riot of 1967* (Detroit: Wayne State University Press, 1969); Sidney Fine, *Violence in the Model City: The Cavanagh Administration, Race Relations and the Detroit Riot of 1967* (Lansing: Michigan State University Press, 2007).

29   By the "Long Hot Summer of 1967": Also comprehensive, M. McLaugh-
      lin, The Long, Hot Summer of 1967: Urban Rebellion in America (New York:
      Palgrave Macmillan, 2014).

30   To assess the causes: Report of the National Advisory Commission on Civil
      Disorders, U.S. Kerner Commission, 1968. For context, Fred R. Harris
      and Roger W. Wilkins, eds., Quiet Riots: Race and Poverty in the United States:
      The Kerner Report Twenty Years Later (Westminster, MD: Pantheon, 1988);
      Paul A. Jargowsky, Poverty and Place (New York: Russell Sage, 1997).

30   Instead of increased integration: For an overview of white flight, Heather Ann
      Thompson, "Rethinking the Politics of White Flight in the Postwar
      City: Detroit, 1945–1980," Journal of Urban History 25 (1999): 163–198.

31   Detroit no longer had: For background, Joseph Radelet, "Stillness at De-
      troit's Racial Divide," The Urban Review 23 (1991): 173–190.

31   The Supreme Court agreed to review: Joyce A. Baugh, The Detroit School Bus-
      ing Case: Milliken v. Bradley and the Controversy over Desegregation (Lawrence:
      University Press of Kansas, 2011).

32   In the decades after busing: "A Land Use Plan for Brightmoor," Urban
      and Regional Planning Program, Taubman College of Architecture
      and Urban Planning, University of Michigan, April 2008, provides
      a good summary of neighborhood changes prior to the plan's publi-
      cation, including the crack epidemic, business closings, and property
      abandonment described in the text.

33   Soon afterward Governor Snyder: "Despite Budget Surplus, No State Bail-
      out in Works for Detroit, Says Top Lawmaker," Reuters, January 15,
      2014; "Michigan Gov. Snyder Vetoes Bailout for Detroit," UPI, July
      27, 2013; Jackie Calmes, "$300 Million in Detroit Aid, but No Bail-
      out," September 26, 2013.

34   New rumors began to spread: The art had already been appraised. Karen
      Pierog, "Detroit Art Sale Could Bring Less Than Half Collection's
      Value: Expert," Reuters, July 15, 2014; Rod Dreher, "Must Pension-
      ers Suffer for Art?" The American Conservative, July 27, 2013. On negoti-
      ations with creditors more generally, Nathan Bomey, Detroit Resurrected
      (New York: Norton, 2016).

35   He won awards for the resulting: An explanation of the deals from a po-
      litically left point of view can be found in Wallace Turbeville, "The
      Detroit Bankruptcy," Demos, November 2013.

35 *It's possible they should have:* Nathan Bomey and Matt Helms, "Judge Approves $85 Million Detroit Debt Swaps Deal," *USA Today*, April 11, 2014; Turbeville, "The Detroit Bankruptcy"; William K. Tabb, "If Detroit Is Dead, Some Things Need to Be Said at the Funeral," *Journal of Urban Affairs* (2015): 1–12.

36 *Meanwhile cuts to state aid continued:* An overview: Mitch Beam, "Starving Michigan Cities and the Coming Storm," *Bridge Magazine*, June 1, 2016, and deeper analysis: Joshua Spotichne et al., "Beyond State Takeovers: Reconsidering the Role of State Government in Local Financial Distress with Important Lessons for Michigan and Its Embattled Cities," MSU Extension White Paper, August 31, 2015.

36 *Orr filed for bankruptcy:* The filing, Chapter 9 Voluntary Petition, *In re City of Detroit, Mich.*, No. 13-53846 (Bankr. E.D. Mich. July 18, 2013), ECF No. 1, can be accessed at "Detroit Bankruptcy Docket," Justia, https://cases.justia.com/federal/detroit-documents/1.pdf.

36 *A state court found the bankruptcy:* Bill Vlasic, "Michigan Judge Rules Against Bankruptcy Push," *The New York Times*, July 19, 2013.

39 *That year Mayor Bing initiated:* For various viewpoints on Detroit Future City, see Daniel Clement and Miguel Kanai, "The Detroit Future City," *American Behavioral Scientist* 59 (2014): 369–385; Seth Schindler, "Detroit After Bankruptcy," *Urban Studies* 53 (2014): 818–836; L. Owen Kirkpatrick, "Urban Triage, City Systems, and the Remnants of Community," *Journal of Urban History* 41 (2015): 261–278. The final strategic framework can be downloaded from https://detroitfuturecity.com/strategic-framework/.

4. Detroit Hustles Harder

43 *To enter bankruptcy cities:* Eligibility requirements for municipal bankruptcy are codified in section 109(c), 11 U.S.C. § 109(c).

43 *Immediately before the start:* "Detroit Bankruptcy Foes Beg for Judge's Help," Associated Press, September 19, 2013.

44 *In response someone else posted:* Sources on the organization and its founding include: "Neighbors Building Brightmoor," Detroit Future City, 2017; Julia Billings et al., "Blight on the Block: A Resident's Guide to Reducing Blight," Master of Urban Planning Program, Taubman College of Architecture and Urban Planning, University of Michigan, April 2012; Neighbors Building Brightmoor, "History and News-

letter" (August 2014), available at www.neighborsbuildingbrightmoor
.org; Theodore Price, "Resident Led Urban Agriculture and the Hegemony of Neoliberal Community Development," Wayne State University Dissertation, January 1, 2016; Sara Hoppe, "The Revitalization
of Brightmoor," Purdue University, available through the Motown
Mission organization.

46 *Meanwhile, in November Mike Duggan:* For example, Steven Yaccino, "For
Detroit's New Mayor, Power with Conditions," *The New York Times,*
November 6, 2013.

46 *A month after the election: In re City of Detroit,* 2013 WL 6331931.
The written opinion followed a 90-minute ruling read into the record. Oral argument, *In re City of Detroit,* No. 13-53846, 2013 WL
6331931 (Bankr. E.D. Mich. December 3, 2013), available at http://
www.mieb.uscourts.gov/sites/default/files/detroit/docket1917.pdf.

47 *Orr proposed operationalizing a plan:* Nathan Bomey, *Detroit Resurrected* (New
York: Norton, 2016), explains the details of these negotiations.

47 *The city, they argued, should: Detroit Strategic Framework Plan,* Detroit Works
Project, 2012, sets out plans for various neighborhoods, and also Livernois.

50 *The newspapers scattered around:* Court transcript of the first swaps trial
hearing in the U.S. Bankruptcy Court, Eastern District of Michigan, December 18, 2013; court transcript of the second swaps trial
hearing in the U.S. Bankruptcy Court, Eastern District of Michigan,
January 3, 2014; court transcript of Rhodes's oral ruling in the U.S.
Bankruptcy Court, Eastern District of Michigan, January 16, 2014.

53 *The city had just secured:* Karen Pierog, "Bankruptcy Judge OK's $120
Million Loan for Detroit," Reuters, April 2, 2014.

53 *By rejecting the first two swaps:* On reaching settlements with swap creditors
and thereby freeing up casino tax revenues, see Bernie Woodall and
Joseph Lichterman, "Detroit Can Keep Casino Tax Revenues, Judge
Rules," Reuters, August 28, 2013. The casino tax revenues eventually
returned as a topic for negotiation in relation to another creditor, and
the initial part of Debtor's Response to Motion of Syncora Guarantee
Inc. and Syncora Capital Assurance Inc. for Leave to Conduct "Lim-
ited" Discovery Regarding Motion of Debtor for Authorization and
Approval of Forbearance and Optional Termination Agreement, *In re
City of Detroit,* 2013 WL 6331931, before it delves into the situation

vis-à-vis the other creditor, explains the background and controversy over the casino revenues well. The document is available at http://www.mieb.uscourts.gov/sites/default/files/detroit/docket244.pdf.

5. Bottom Line

60 *When the emergency manager, Kevyn:* Kevyn Orr, "City of Detroit Proposal for Creditors," June 14, 2013; Christine MacDonald, "Rhodes Needs to OK Payouts; Tax Tribunal Halts Detroiters' Appeals," *The Detroit News,* July 26, 2013.

60 *Rather than complying with the state:* On assessment see Gary Sands and Mark Skidmore, "Detroit and the Property Tax," Lincoln Institute of Land Policy Focus Report, 2015; Christine MacDonald and Mike Wilkinson, "Half of Detroit Property Owners Don't Pay Taxes," *The Detroit News,* February 21, 2013; Christine MacDonald, "Detroit's Property Tax System Plagued by Mistakes, Waste," *The Detroit News,* February 22, 2013.

60 *As a consequence, the city taxed:* On Detroit's property taxes see Timothy R. Hodge, Daniel P. McMillen, Gary Sands, and Mark Skidmore, "Assessment Inequity in a Declining Housing Market: The Case of Detroit," *Real Estate Economics* 45 (2006); James Alm, Timothy R. Hodge, Gary Sands, and Mark Skidmore, "Detroit Property Tax Delinquency: Social Contract in Crisis," Lincoln Institute of Land Policy Working Paper, 2014. Bernadette Atuahene, professor of law at the Chicago-Kent College of Law, has written extensively on this issue. See, for example, "Don't Let Detroit's Revival Rest on an Injustice," *The New York Times,* July 22, 2017.

62 *Life expectancy in the city:* Christine MacDonald and Charles E. Ramirez, "Life Span for Detroit's Poor Among Shortest in Nation," *The Detroit News,* June 2, 2016.

62 *In 2014, as the bankruptcy progressed:* A good source on property taxes in Detroit is Sands and Skidmore, "Detroit and the Property Tax."

63 *Between 2000 and 2012 the number:* For a good explanation of these trends, see Wallace Turbeville, "The Detroit Bankruptcy," Demos, November 2013.

64 *About three months before the emergency:* The hockey stadium financing has been widely reported. Good sources include Ryan Felton, "How Mike Ilitch Scored a New Red Wings Arena," *Detroit Metro Times,* May 6, 2014.

66 *Detroit's school system also suffered:* A separate book could be written on the school system. Recommended sources include later chapters of Jeffrey Mirel, *The Rise and Fall of an Urban School System: Detroit, 1907–81* (Ann Arbor: University of Michigan Press, 1999); Kate Zernike, "A Sea of Charter Schools in Detroit Leaves Students Adrift," *The New York Times,* June 28, 2016; Robin Lake, Ashley Jochim, and Michael DeArmond, "Fixing Detroit's Broken School System," *Education Next* 15 (2015); Shaun Michael Black, "An Examination of Urban School Governance Reform in Detroit Public Schools, 1999–2014," *Wayne State University Dissertations Paper 1429,* 2016; Leanne Kang, "The Dismantling of an Urban School System: Detroit, 1980–2014," University of Michigan Dissertation, 2015; John Grover and Yvette van der Velde, "A School District in Crisis," Loveland Technologies Report, 2015; Monte Piliawsky, "Educational Reform or Corporate Agenda? State Takeover of Detroit's Public Schools," *The Future of Educational Studies* 218 (2003): 265–283; and Allie Gross, "Out of Options," *Vice News,* December 19, 2016.

6. Exit from Bankruptcy

73 *In 1999 Michigan enacted:* Selected sources on tax foreclosure in Detroit: Margaret Dewar, Eric Seymour, and Oana Druja, "Disinvesting in the City: The Role of Tax Foreclosure in Detroit," *Urban Affairs Review* 51 (2014): 587–615; Erika C. Poethig, Joseph Schilling, Laurie Goodman, Bing Bai, et al., "The Detroit Housing Market," Urban Institute Research Report, March 2017; Carl Hedman and Rolf Pendall, "Rebuilding and Sustaining Homeownership for African Americans," Urban Institute, Southeast Michigan Housing Futures Brief 3, June 2018; Dianne Feeley, "A Hurricane Without Water: Detroit's Foreclosure Disaster," *Against the Current* 3 (2015): 10–11; Joel Kurth and Christine MacDonald, "Detroit Braces for a Flood of Tax Foreclosures," *The Detroit News,* September 8, 2015; "Real Property Tax Foreclosure Timeline," State of Michigan, revised August 21, 2013, https://www.michigan.gov/documents/taxes/ForfeitureForeclosure TimelinesChart_317028_7.pdf; Quinn Klinefelter, "Mass Tax Foreclosure Threatens Detroit Homeowners," *All Things Considered,* March 31, 2015; Mark Betancourt, "Detroit's Housing Crisis Is the Work of Its Own Government," *Vice News,* December 29, 2017; Laura Gottesdiener,

"Detroit Just Had the Single Largest Tax Foreclosure in American History," *Mother Jones*, April 21, 2015; Jessica McKenzie, "Detroit's Foreclosure Crisis and the Need for 'Information Justice,'" *CityLab*, March 8, 2017; Rose Jackman, "One-Fifth of Detroit's Population Could Lose Their Homes," *The Atlantic*, October 26, 2014.

73 *In September Mayor Duggan:* "Detroit Officials Regain Most City Control; Orr to Stay on Through Bankruptcy," Associated Press, September 25, 2014.

74 *A few days later city officials:* Stewart Bishop, "Barclays Ups Detroit's Exit Loan to $325M," *Law360*, September 30, 2014.

74 *Miles followed the instructions:* On show-cause hearings in the tax foreclosure process and the overall process more generally, good sources include James Alm, Timothy R. Hodge, Gary Sands, and Mark Skidmore, "Detroit Property Tax Delinquency: Social Contract in Crisis," Lincoln Institute of Land Policy Working Paper, 2014; Mark Skidmore, "Will a Greenbelt Help to Shrink Detroit's Wasteland?" *Land Lines*, October 2014; Monica Davey, "A Hearing on Housing in Detroit Draws a Reluctant Crowd," *The New York Times*, January 29, 2015.

76 *In 2017 the owner of a bulk acquirer:* John Gallagher, "Belgium Investors Learn It's Buyer Beware in Detroit," *Detroit Free Press*, April 12, 2017.

77 *Through the auction, the largest:* Mark Paul, "Detroit: Eddie Hobbs-Founded Fund Forfeits Scores of Houses," *The Irish Times*, January 13, 2017; Tom Perkins, "Are Real Estate Investors from Oakland County to Hong Kong Driving Detroit's Blight?" *Detroit Metro Times*, May 4, 2016; Joe Guillen, "Detroit's Other Blight Crisis: Commercial Decay," *Detroit Free Press*, November 19, 2015.

78 *The family strategically bought properties:* Joann Muller, "Why One Rich Man Shouldn't Own an International Bridge," *Forbes*, January 12, 2012; Frank Witsil, "Moroun Family's Lawsuit Aims to Block Building New Bridge to Canada," *Detroit Free Press*, January 6, 2017; Mitch Potter, "This Secretive Billionaire Family Owns the Ambassador Bridge," *The Star*, February 16, 2010.

79 *The bankruptcy treated the water system:* On trend lines, bankruptcy restructuring, and shutoffs: Cria Kay, Kely Markley, Malavika Sahai, Chris Askew-Merwin, et al., "Water Insecurity in Southeast Michigan," Master of Science of Natural Resources and Environment, University

of Michigan School for Environment and Sustainability, April 2018; Claire Sabourin, "Responding to the Detroit Water Crisis: The Great Lakes Water Authority and the City of Detroit," *Washington University Journal of Law and Policy* 51 (2016): 305; Dana Kornberg, "The Structural Origins of Territorial Stigma," *International Journal of Urban and Regional Research* (2016): 263–283; Sarah Phinney, "Detroit's Municipal Bankruptcy," *New Political Economy* 23 (2017): 609–626; Ann Rall, "Community Organizing and the Detroit Water Struggle," Report from the Front Lines, *Journal of Progressive Human Services* 29 (2018): 103–129; Suparna Bhaskaran, "Public Health and Wealth in Post-Bankruptcy Detroit," Haas Institute for a Fair and Inclusive Society at UC Berkeley Research Brief, November 2017; Lindsey Wahowiak, "Access to Water Surfaces as Human Rights Issue as Poor in Detroit Lose Services," *The Nation's Health* 44 (2014): 1–20.

81   *Eventually most creditors would agree:* Nathan Bomey, *Detroit Resurrected* (New York: Norton, 2016), details these.

82   *In 2016 the American Civil Liberties Union:* ACLU, "ACLU, NAACP LDF Sue Wayne County to End Racially Discriminatory Tax Foreclosures in Detroit," July 13, 2016, http://www.aclumich.org/article/aclu-sues-wayne-county-end-racially-discriminatory-tax-foreclosures-detroit; "ACLU, NAACP File Class Action Lawsuit over Tax Foreclosures," *WDET*, July 13, 2016; Greg Wickliffe, "Lawsuit Claims Detroit Tax Foreclosures Based on Inaccurate Bills," *MLive*, July 13, 2016.

82   *The Michigan legislature agreed to expand:* Monica Davey, "Medicaid Expansion Battle in Michigan Ends in Passage," *The New York Times*, August 27, 2013.

83   *It appeared that the collection:* On the Grand Bargain, see Maureen Collins, "Pensions or Paintings?" *University of Miami Business Law Review* 24 (2015): 1; Margaret A. Leary and Betsy Jackson, "Detroit: Part 2—the Grandest Bargain," *Journal of Urban Regeneration & Renewal* 10 (2016): 22–41; Rebecca Gosch, "An 'Immeasurable Sign of Great Hope,'" *Washington University Journal of Law & Policy* 51 (2016): 233; James L. Tatum, III, "Monetizing Masterpieces in Detroit's Bankruptcy," *The Urban Lawyer* 49 (2017): 267–282; Stefan Toepler, "Public Philanthropic Partnerships," *International Journal of Public Administration* 41 (2018).

84 *For about $180 million in costs:* Eighth Amended Plan for the Adjust-
ment of Debts of the City of Detroit, *In re City of Detroit, Mich.,* No.
13-53846 (Bankr. E.D. Mich. October 22, 2014), https://www
.michigan.gov/documents/treasury/Detroit__Eighth_Amended
_Plan_of_Adjustment_476086_7.pdf; Expert Report of Martha E.
M. Kopacz Regarding the Feasibility of the City of Detroit Plan of
Adjustment, *In re City of Detroit, Mich.,* No. 13–53846, 2014, http://
www.detroitmi.gov/Portals/0/docs/EM/Bankruptcy%20Informa-
tion/M.%20Kopacz%20Expert%20Report%20to%20Judge%20
Rhodes%20071814.pdf.

85 *All the city's systems seemed to bear:* Christine MacDonald, "Detroit's Property Tax System Plagued by Mistakes, Waste," *The Detroit News,* February
22, 2013.

86 *Even as power returned to elected officials:* Matt Helms, "Snyder Appoints
Review Commission for Detroit," *Detroit Free Press,* November 10,
2014; "About the Detroit Financial Review Commission," Michigan
Department of the Treasury, https://www.michigan.gov/treasury/0,
4679,7-121-1751_51556_77310—,00.html.

7. A Decent Home

89 *In October 2016, nearly two years:* The city had passed state audits:
Detroit Financial Review Commission, City Resolution 2016-13,
"Certifying the City of Detroit's Compliance with the Michigan Fi-
nancial Review Commission Act," September 16, 2016.

91 *That year the county entered 23,000 properties:* Complaint, *Morningside Community Organization et al. v. Eric Sabree,* No. 16-008807-CH, Mich. Cir.
Ct. (July 13, 2016).

91 *The volunteers told Reggie that by negotiating:* Roz Edward, "Treasurer's Program to Avoid Foreclosure, Reduce Interest Rates Ends June 30,"
Michigan Chronicle, June 20, 2016.

91 *Alternatively, no one could bid on the house:* On Detroit's land bank see Tobias
Armborst, Daniel D'Oca, and Georgeen Theodore, "Improve Your
Lot," in *Cities Growing Smaller,* Kent State University's Cleveland Urban
Design Collaborative, 2008; Jason Hackworth, "The Normalization
of Market Fundamentalism in Detroit: The Case of Land Abandon-
ment," in *Reinventing Detroit,* ed. Michael Peter Smith and L. Owen Kirk-

patrick (New Brunswick, N.J., and London: Transaction Publishers, 2015); Jason Hackworth, "The Limits to Market-Based Strategies for Addressing Land Abandonment in Shrinking American Cities," *Progress in Planning* 90 (2014): 1–37; W. Dennis Keating, "Urban Land Bank and the Housing Foreclosure and Abandonment Crisis," *St. Louis University Public Law Review* 33 (2013–2014): 93–109; Margaret Dewar, "Disposition of Publicly Owned Land in Cities: Learning from Cleveland and Detroit," University of Michigan Center for Local, State, and Urban Policy Working Paper No. 2010, 2009; Michelle Bennett et al., "Strengthening Land Bank Sales Programs to Stabilize Detroit Neighborhoods," Urban and Regional Planning Program, University of Michigan, April 2016; Erick Trickey, "Detroit's DIY Cure for Urban Blight," *Politico,* May 18, 2017; "Strategies to Rebuild Detroit's Homebuyer Ecosystem," Homebuyer Ecosystem Working Group, December 2016; Matthew Goldstein, "Detroit: From Motor City to Housing Incubator," *The New York Times,* November 4, 2017.

91 *The previous year the land bank absorbed:* Bennett et al., "Strengthening Land Bank Sales Programs."

92 *The previous year 28,000 properties:* Sarah Cwiek, "2015 Tax Foreclosure Auction Ends, but a Vicious Cycle Continues," Michigan Radio, October 23, 2015.

92 *With money provided by the tenants:* See list of tax foreclosure auction winning bids maintained by Loveland.

93 *The auction would take place:* United Community Housing Coalition, "Information Sheet," distributed at 2016 tax foreclosure counseling sessions attended by the author.

93 *Recently the aggregate value:* Ryan Stanton, "Ann Arbor Has State's Highest Assessed Property Values in 2016," *MLive,* March 22, 2017; Kirk Pinho, "A Tale of Two Cities," *Bridge Magazine,* March 20, 2017.

98 *That year, 2016, investment companies:* "Relevant News on Real Estate in Detroit," INMSA Real Estate Investments Company, November 13, 2017.

8. The Architectural Imagination

100 *City officials understood that:* Jonathan Spader, Jenny Schuetz, and Alvaro Cortes, "Fewer Vacants, Fewer Crimes? Impacts of Neighborhood Revitalization Policies on Crime," *Regional Science and Urban Economics* 60

(2016): 73–84; Richard C. Sadler and Natalie K. Pruett, "Mitigating Blight and Building Community Price in a Legacy City," *Community Development Journal* 52 (2017): 591–610; Bradley Pough and Qian Wan, "Data Analytics and the Fight Against Housing Blight," Responsive Communities, March 2017.

100 *Boarding up and securing vacant:* Aaron Klein, "Curing Community Blight," Community Blight Solutions, February 2017; Christine Ferretti and Jonathan Oosting, "Duggan Plans 'Board Up Brigades' for Vacant Houses," *The Detroit News*, May 31, 2017; Benjamin Raven, "City Will Tear Down 10K Abandoned Houses in 2 Years, Detroit Mayor Says," *MLive*, February 22, 2017.

100 *Cracking down on landlords:* Christine Ferretti, "City Pushes Landlords to Register Rental Properties," *The Detroit News*, June 10, 2016; Sarah Alvarez, "A Registry Will Help Fix Abuses in Detroit's Home Rental Market," *Bridge Magazine*, February 16, 2017. On blight ticketing, Allie Cell et al., "Understanding Blight Ticket Compliance in Detroit," University of Michigan, Data Science for Social Good Conference, September 28, 2017; Matt Helms, "City Steps Up Blight Tickets, but Accuracy Challenged," *Detroit Free Press*, March 30, 2015; Kirk Pinho, "Blight on the Landscape," *Crain's Detroit Business*, October 16, 2016; Mary Kramer, "$1 Million in Blight Judgments Against Detroit Landlord," *Crain's Detroit Business*, October 17, 2016.

100 *Detroit ranked in the country's:* "Best Markets for Buying Single Family Rentals in 2017," Attom Data Solutions, March 21, 2017.

102 *Prior to the bankruptcy Mayor Bing:* "Detroit Demolition Impact Report," Dynamo Metrics, July 2015; David McKinney, "Knocking Down Detroit to Revive It Comes at a Price," Reuters, December 15, 2015; Matt Helms and Joe Guillen, "Duggan Explains Increase in Blight Demolition Costs," *Detroit Free Press*, October 13, 2015; Joe Guillen, "Feds Subpoena Detroit for Blight Removal Records," *Governing*, May 3, 2016; Ian Thibodeau, "Attorneys Hired as Feds Investigate Spike in Detroit Demolition Cost," *MLive*, May 21, 2016; John Metcalfe, "Browse Thousands of Tear-Downs on the 'Detroit Demolition Tracker,'" *City Lab*, June 20, 2016; Erick Trickey, "Detroit's DIY Cure for Urban Blight," *Politico*, May 18, 2017; Robert Snell and Christine Ferretti, "Grand Jury Focusing on Detroit's Demolition Program,"

The Detroit News, June 13, 2017; Bryce Huffman, "Detroit Settles Claims of Overbilling in Land Bank Investigation," *On Point,* June 23, 2017; Joel Kurth, "Can Detroit Find Salvation Through Demolition?" *Bridge Magazine,* July 6, 2017; "In Detroit, the End of Blight Is in Sight," *The Economist,* September 16, 2017; "Bulldoze Away," *Detroit Journalism Cooperative,* July 7, 2017.

102 *Administration officials extended permission:* Alan Mallach, "Hardest Hit Funds Demolition Policy Change," Center for Community Progress, July 1, 2014.

104 *The lot sat next door to:* Detroit land bank's side lot program: John Gallagher, "Detroit Side-Lot Sales a Win for Homeowners and the City," *Detroit Free Press,* January 18, 2015; "Detroit Land Bank Looks to Sell Off Side Lots to Homeowners for $100," Associated Press, April 7, 2017.

104 *Unlike everyone in her husband's family:* Reynolds Farley, "Detroit Fifty Years After the Kerner Report," *The Russell Sage Foundation Journal of the Social Sciences* 4 (2018): 206–241; "Blacks, Not Whites, Now Fleeing Detroit," *Tell Me More,* June 24, 2010; Corey Williams, "Whites Moving into Detroit, Blacks Moving Out as City Shrinks Overall," Associated Press, May 21, 2015; Mike Wilkinson, "Black Flight to Suburbs Masks Lingering Segregation in Metro Detroit," *Detroit Journalism Cooperative,* December 6, 2016; Nicquel Terry, "Black Influx Changes Face of Some Metro Area Suburbs," *The Detroit News,* November 15, 2016.

105 *Only 14 percent of Detroit's third graders:* "Detroit Faces Early Childhood Literacy Crisis with Only 14 Percent of City's Children Reading at Grade Level by Third Grade," *PR Newswire,* November 13, 2017.

107 *The planning staff then carved:* On the pilot program there, see Gilbert Sunghera, "Being a Neighbor in the Hood," *Conversations on Jesuit Higher Education* 53 (2018): 23–25; John Gallagher, "Mayor Mike Duggan Kicks Fitzgerald Neighborhood into High Gear," *Detroit Free Press,* April 5, 2017; City of Detroit, Request for Proposals, Fitzgerald Revitalization Project, 2016, available at http://www.fitzgerald-detroit.com /wp-content/uploads/CityofDetroit_RFP_ProductiveLandscape .pdf; Roz Edward, "City of Detroit Releases RFPs for Revitalization of Fitzgerald Neighborhood," *Michigan Chronicle,* July 6, 2016; Keith

Owens, "Detroit's Fitzgerald Neighborhood Sees a Brighter Future," *Michigan Chronicle*, April 6, 2017; Matthew Messner, "Detroit's Fitzgerald Neighborhood to Be Completely Transformed," *Archpaper*, April 6, 2017; Alana Walker, "Mayor Mike Duggan Announces $4 Million Revitalization of Detroit's Fitzgerald Neighborhood," *Black Life, Arts & Culture*, April 2017; Larry Gabriel, "Stir It Up," *Detroit Metro Times*, April 12, 2017.

9. If You Build It

111 *Though unlike Fitzgerald and other:* Brett Theodos, Jay Dev, and Sierra Latham, "The Tipping Point," Urban Institute, September 12, 2017.

112 *Traditionally the city relied on tax:* On cities' use of this subsidy: Robert T. Greenbaum and Jim Landers, "The Tiff over TIF," *National Tax Journal* 67 (2014): 655–674; John Diamond, "Forum: Tax Increment Financing," *National Tax Journal* 67 (2014): 651–653; Rachel Weber, "Tax Increment Financing in Theory and Practice," in Sammis B. White and Zenia Z. Kotval, eds., *Financing Economic Development in the 21st Century* (London and New York: Taylor and Francis, 2014); Robert L. Bland and Michael Overton, "Assessing the Contributions of Collaborators in Public-Private Partnerships," *The American Review of Public Administration* 46 (2016): 418–435; T. William Lester, "Does Chicago's Tax Increment Financing Program Pass the 'But-for' Test?" *Urban Studies* 51 (2014): 655–674; Adam Baldwin, "Tax Increment Financing," *Economic Affairs* 36 (2016); Richard F. Dye, David F. Merriman, and Katherine Goulde, "Tax Increment Financing and the Great Recession," *National Tax Journal* 67 (2014): 697–717.

112 *The approach, which underlay the:* Joe Guillen, "Little Caesars Arena: How the Cost Nearly Doubled to $863 Million," *Detroit Free Press*, September 7, 2017.

113 *In the following years Gilbert's:* David Segal, "A Missionary's Quest to Remake Motor City," *The New York Times*, April 13, 2013; Kirk Pinho, "Gilbert Purchases 1900 Saint Antoine Building Across from Stalled Detroit Jail Project," *Crain's Detroit Business*, March 15, 2016.

114 *Quicken Loans, however, faced:* Julie Crewswell, "A Mortgage Lender Digs in Its Heels," *The New York Times*, January 21, 2017; John Gallagher, "Dan Gilbert Vows He Will Never Settle Department of Justice Mortgage Lawsuit," *Detroit Free Press*, January 19, 2018.

114 *When homeowners could not pay:* Quicken denied the charges, and when this book went to press, the case was still ongoing.

114 *He planned to build out more:* "Gilbert Wants to Build the Tallest Skyscraper in Detroit (and Public Financing to Do It)," *Daily Detroit,* February 22, 2017.

114 *Within a few years the new subsidies:* Lindsay Vanhulle, "Taking the 'Gilbert' out of the 'Gilbert Bills,'" *Crain's Detroit Business,* February 5, 2017.

115 *The activists noted a $175 million:* J.C. Reindl, "Arena Contractors Fined $500K for Not Hiring Enough Detroiters," *Detroit Free Press,* October 12, 2016.

116 *The activists lobbied for a referendum:* On Detroit's initiatives and community benefits agreements more generally: Kelly L. Patterson, Molly Ranahan, Robert M. Silverman, and Li Yin, "Community Benefits Agreements (CBAs): A Typology for Shrinking Cities," *International Journal of Sociology and Social Policy* 37 (2017): 231–247; Edward W. De Barbieri, "Do Community Benefits Agreements Benefit Communities?" *Cardozo Law Review* 37 (2015–2016): 1773–1825; Desiree Hatcher, "Detroit's Proposed Community Benefits Ordinance," *Profitwise* 3, Federal Reserve Bank of Chicago (2015): 4–8.

116 *The head of the city's economic:* "City Council Shouldn't Pass a Shakedown Tax," *The Detroit News,* October 11, 2014.

118 *mortgage market in Detroit:* Lewis Wallace, "Why There's Almost No Mortgage Lending in Detroit," *Marketplace,* October 5, 2016; Erika C. Poethig, Joseph Schilling, Laurie Goodman, Bing Bai, et al., "The Detroit Housing Market," Urban Institute Research Report, March 2017; "Strategies to Rebuild Detroit's Homebuyer Ecosystem," Homebuyer Ecosystem Working Group with Community Reinvestment Fund, USA, December 2016.

118 *About 30 of the mortgages came:* Julian Spector, "Detroit's Ambitious Plan to Jump-Start Its Housing Market," *City Lab,* February 18, 2016; Matt Helms, "New Mortgage Program Big Boost for Detroit," *Detroit Free Press,* February 18, 2016; Brena Swanson, "Lenders Work to Overcome Detroit's Appraisal Gap Roadblock," *Housing Wire,* September 29, 2016; Frank Altman, "Detroit Home Mortgage: Innovative Rehabilitation Financing," Officer of the Comptroller of the Currency, U.S. Department of the Treasury, February 2018; Ilyce R. Glink, "Beautiful Mansion Is Detroit's Biggest Sale in at Least a Decade, *Yahoo News,*

September 11, 2014; Janis Tsai, "Here's 5 Reasons to Explore Detroit's West Village," *Daily Detroit*, August 9, 2015; Amy Haimerl, "West Village Open for Business," *Crain's Detroit Business*, March 23, 2014; Aaron Mondry, "How One Block Can Change a Neighborhood," *Model D*, April 23, 2018.

10. Having Trouble Getting to a Job? Start Your Own!

126 *A New York investment bank pledged:* Tammy Coxen et al., "Detroit's Untapped Talent: Jobs and On-Ramps Needed," J.P. Morgan Chase & Co. and Corporation for a Skilled Workforce, January 2016.

126 *As city residents like Lola:* Lester Graham, "Detroiters Need Jobs and Detroit Needs Taxpayers," *Stateside*, January 30, 2014; Bill Bradley, "Detroit Losing Money from Reverse Commuters Who Don't Pay Income Taxes," *Next City*, August 15, 2013.

126 *Several bills to compel the withholding:* Paul Egan, "Bill Would Make Suburban Michigan Employers Collect City Income Taxes," *Detroit Free Press*, November 28, 2016; Chad Livengood, "Groups: Don't Force Suburbs to Collect Detroit's Taxes," *The Detroit News*, November 28, 2016; Marti Benedetti and Dustin Walsh, "Income Tax Collection Plan Riles Outstate Michigan Cities," *Crain's Detroit Business*, August 23, 2015.

126 *In Detroit, meanwhile, suburban residents:* Bryce Huffman, "Detroit Is Getting More Serious About Collecting City Income Tax, and It's Paying Off," Michigan Radio, December 19, 2016; Matt Helms, "Income Tax Crackdown Brings Detroit More Revenue," *Detroit Free Press*, December 17, 2016.

126 *Now a prominent downtown law firm:* An appeals court eventually decided that the law firm did not owe taxes for this income.

127 *To boost collection rates:* Matt Helms, "State Prepared to Collect City Income Taxes," *Detroit Free Press*, September 15, 2015.

127 *The state legislature, however, began:* Kathleen Gray, "Michigan Senate Republican: Let's Get Rid of the State Income Tax," *Detroit Free Press*, January 6, 2017; David Fair, "State Senator from Ann Arbor Reacts to Proposals for Eliminating Michigan's Income Tax," *Michigan Public Radio*, January 27, 2017; Brad Tuttle, "The Latest State Moving to Kill Its Income Tax," *Time*, January 13, 2017.

128 *Since the mid-1980s companies enlisted:* "Race to the Bottom," *The New York Times*, December 5, 2012; Emily Badger, "Should We Ban States

and Cities from Offering Big Tax Breaks for Jobs?" *The Washington Post*, September 15, 2014; Brent Gardner, "Ending the Corporate-Welfare Circus," *The Wall Street Journal*, June 5, 2016; Romina Boccia, "Corporate Welfare Wastes Taxpayer and Economic Resources," Testimony before the Subcommittee on Federal Spending Oversight and Emergency Management Before the United States Senate, June 10, 2015.

129 *Beating out Ohio, the city won:* Tom Walsh, "Chinese Fuel-Tank Maker to Build Detroit Plant," *Detroit Free Press*, July 28, 2015.

129 *A few years later Amazon would:* Daniel Howes, "Detroit's Failed Amazon Bid Should Be a Wake-Up Call," Michigan Radio, January 20, 2018; Kirk Pinho, "Detroit Misses Cut for Amazon HQ2 over Talent, Mass Transit," *Crain's Detroit Business*, January 18, 2018; Sarah Holder, Benjamin Schneider, and Alastair Boone, "The Ultimate List of Top Contenders for Amazon's HQ2," *CityLab*, September 12, 2017; Alfred Ng, "Here's What the Final 20 Cities Offered Amazon for HQ2," *CNet*, January 18, 2018; "The $5 Billion Question: Will Cities Win or Lose in the Bid for Amazon's Second Headquarters," Penn Institute for Urban Research, January 18, 2018; Joseph Parilla, "Which Cities are Well Positioned to Land Amazon's HQ2," Brookings Institution, September 8, 2017.

131 *Currently they were discussing the news:* John Wisely, "Russell Center Owner Accused of Renting Unsafe Apartments," *Detroit Free Press*, February 23, 2017; Ryan Patrick Hooper, "Russell Industrial Center Artists Scrambling to Find New Homes," *Detroit Free Press*, March 7, 2017.

131 *She had just won $45,000:* Gerald A. Carlino and Thorsten Drautzburg, "The Role of Startups for Local Labor Markets," Federal Reserve Bank of Philadelphia Working Paper No. 17-31, September 29, 2017; Margaret O'Neal, "Roadmap to ReUrbanism," *Forum Journal* 31 (2017): 41–49.

134 *Mission investors operated in Detroit:* Diana Cristina Searl, "Density and Diversity: Evaluating One CDFI's Place-Based Revitalization Strategy in Detroit's Underwater Market," Massachusetts Institute of Technology, Department of Urban Studies and Planning, 2016; Brett Theodos, Eric Hangen, Jay Dev, and Sierra Latham, "Mission Finance in the Motor City," Urban Institute, September 2017. For a more general discussion of CDFIs: James L. Greer and Oscar Gonzalez, *Community*

Economic Development in the United States: The CDFI Industry and America's Distressed Communities (New York: Palgrave Macmillan, 2017).

136 *In the 2016 presidential election:* "Reality Check: Who Voted for Donald Trump," *The Guardian*, November 2016.

11. The Motor City

137 *Forty-four years earlier Michigan:* "Why Detroit Is the Most Expensive City in America to Buy Car Insurance," *The Economist*, July 5, 2018; J.C. Reindl, "No-Fault Car Insurance in Michigan," *Detroit Free Press*, May 6, 2017; J.C. Reindl, "How Michigan Got—and Kept—No-Fault Auto Insurance," *Detroit Free Press*, May 6, 2017.

139 *Insurance there cost more:* Dana Afana, "Study Ranks Detroit Auto Insurance Rates Highest in US—by Far," *MLive*, June 8, 2017; "Nearly Half of Detroit Motorists 'Driving Dirty,'" Associated Press, July 20, 2015; Devin Fergus, "Are Auto Insurance Companies Red-Lining Poor, Urban Drivers?" *The Guardian*, July 21, 2014; David Muller, "Detroit Has Highest Car Insurance Rates in the Country," *MLive*, February 3, 2014.

139 *The proposal failed:* Chad Livengood, "Michigan House Hands Duggan Big Defeat on Auto Insurance Reform," *Crain's Detroit Business*, November 2, 2017; Kathleen Gray, "Defeat of No-Fault Auto Insurance Overhaul Doesn't End the Debate over High Rates," *Detroit Free Press*, November 4, 2017; "Detroit Mayor, Statehouse Leaders Take Another Shot at Michigan No-Fault Reform," *Insurance Journal*, October 19, 2017; Chad Livengood and Mike Wilkinson, "How Michigan's Auto Insurance Premiums Became the Nation's Highest," *Bridge Magazine*, October 24, 2017; J.C. Reindl, "No-Fault Fixes?" *Detroit Free Press*, May 8, 2017; Kathleen Gray, "4 Plans Considered to Bring Auto Insurance Rate Relief to Michiganders," *Detroit Free Press*, September 18, 2017; Kathleen Gray, "Michigan's No-Fault Auto Insurance Reform Defeated in the House of Representatives," *Detroit Free Press*, November 2, 2017.

141 *Prior to the bankruptcy, in 2007:* "What's Happening with Public Transportation in Southeast Michigan?" Michigan Radio, January 28, 2014; Sarah Hullett, "Rail Group Says It Has Money to Build System, Run It for a Decade," Michigan Radio, April 24, 2012; Mark Brush, "More Private Backing for Light Rail Plan in Detroit," Michigan

Radio, April 23, 2012; Mike Scott, "Mass Transit for Motor City," *CNNMoney*, February 15, 2010.

142 *The federal government agreed to contribute:* Ryan Felton, "How Can Detroit Improve Its Disastrous Public Transit System?" *The Awl*, August 18, 2016; Anna Clark, "Metro Detroit Has a $4.6 Billion Transit Decision to Make," *Next City*, June 8, 2016; Jen Kinney, "Detroit's Multibillion-Dollar Transit Plan Comes to a Halt," *Next City*, August 1, 2016; Frank Witsil and Eric D. Lawrence, "RTA Millage Rejected by Metro Detroit Voters," *Detroit Free Press*, November 9, 2016.

142 *"No fines, no fees":* The author has corroborated this and subsequent references to judicial rulings and court proceedings in relation to Miles from the 36th District Court and 3rd Judicial Court of Michigan and in copies of records provided by Miles on file with the author.

142 *A few weeks later a bill for drivers':* Chad Livengood, "The Latest Hurdle to Employment in Michigan? Traffic Fines," *Bridge Magazine*, August 10, 2017.

143 *City bus routes terminated:* "Detroit Transit History," Phase Two of a Study by the University of Detroit Mercy's Transit Research Team, January 15, 2013; Ryan Felton, "How Detroit Ended Up with the Worst Public Transit," *Detroit Metro Times*, March 11, 2014; Quinn Klinefelter, "Commuters Suffer as Detroit Cuts Bus Service," *All Things Considered*, March 8, 2012; Brian Thompson, "Detroit Set to Roll Out New Business and Mobile App for DDOT," *MI Headlines,* January 11, 2015; Eli Newman, "DDOT to Add 24-Hour Service, Eastern Market Bus Lines," *All Things Considered*, September 2, 2016; Bill Laitner, "DDOT Expands Service with New Buses, Six 24-Hour Routes," *Detroit Free Press*, September 1, 2016; Dan Austin, "How Metro Detroit Transit Went from Best to Worst," *Detroit Free Press*, February 6, 2015; Henry Grabar, "Can America's Worst Transit System Be Saved?" *Slate*, June 7, 2016; Nina Ignaczak, "Will Metro Detroit Suburbs Buy into Regional Transit?" *Model D*, April 7, 2015; Stephen Henderson and Kristi Tanner, "Region's Transit System Can't Get Many to Job Centers," *Detroit Free Press*, February 22, 2015.

143 *The authority then placed an initiative:* Michael Schramm, "Southeast Michigan Residents: Here's What to Know About Your Transportation Ballot Proposal," Michigan Radio, October 22, 2016.

144 *A few months later the light rail:* Laurel Wamsley, "After 61 Years, Detroit Gets a Streetcar Once More," National Public Radio, May 12, 2017; Dan Lijana and Keith Jones, "QLine Detroit: A National Model for Public-Private Partnership, American Public Transportation Association, June 13, 2017; "QLine on the Move," Kresge Foundation, May 2018; Bre'Anna Tinsley, "QLine: What You Need to Know," *Detroit Public Radio WDET,* May 12, 2017; Adrian Marshall, "Detroit's New Streetcar Is OK, But It Can't Save a City," *Wired,* May 20, 2017.

12. City on the Move

146 *Since then Reggie and his family:* "Understanding Adoption Subsidies: Michigan," State Guide, www.law.capital.edu/uploadedFiles/Law _Multi-Site/NCALP/Michigan_Subsidy_Guide.pdf; Michigan State Adoption Assistance Program, North American Council on Adoptable Children, April 2013.

148 *That day, known as spring count day:* Kate Zernike, "A Sea of Charter Schools in Detroit Leaves Students Adrift," *The New York Times,* June 28, 2016; "Student Count Day and School Funding Information," State of Michigan, 2017, www.michigan.gov/documents/mde/Student _Count_Information_514003_7.pdf.

149 *If Charles could not drive Yvonne:* "Transportation Services," Office of Student Transportation, Detroit Public Schools Community District, http://detroitk12.org/admin/operations/transportation/; Erin Einhorn, "The Extreme Sacrifice Detroit Parents Make to Access Better School," *The Atlantic,* April 11, 2016.

150 *He would have to choose between:* Jonathan Oosting, "Michigan Looks to Kill 7-Day Car Insurance," *The Detroit News,* April 17, 2017; "Why Auto Insurance in Detroit Is So Damn High, Explained," *Daily Detroit,* October 19, 2015.

150 *Had it worked, and had he:* Lindsay VanHulle, "Budget Proposal Includes Spending Cuts, Making Room for Tax Cut or Debt Payments," *Crain's Detroit Business,* April 23, 2017.

151 *In 2011 when Governor Snyder slashed:* Lindsay VanHulle, "Snyder's Michigan: Business Taxes Fall, Burden Shifts to Residents," *Bridge Magazine,* February 6, 2018; Stephen Henderson, "Governor Rick Snyder Still Can't See that Tax Cuts Alone Create a Weaker Michigan," *Detroit Free*

Press, June 1, 2016; Liz Farmer, "The Curious Case of Disappearing Corporate Taxes," *Governing Magazine,* January 2016.

151 *In May, just as the state:* Erin Einhorn, "Inside Nikolai Vitti's Early Efforts to Transform Detroit's Battered Public Schools," *Detroit Free Press,* September 17, 2017; Tyler Clifford, "New Detroit Schools Superintendent Cuts 70 Jobs to Save $5 Million," *Crain's Detroit Business,* June 27, 2017; "Dr. Nikolai Vitti Confirmed as New DPSCDS Superintendent," Detroit Public Schools Community District, May 22, 2017; Chastity Pratt Dawsey, "'Our Biggest Barrier Is Stability,'" *Bridge Magazine,* January 22, 2015.

152 *Instead of continuing with emergency:* Jonathan Oosting and Shawn D. Lewis, "Snyder Signs $617M DPS Bailout," *The Detroit News,* June 21, 2016; Emma Brown, "Michigan Legislature Approves $617 Million Bailout Package for Detroit Schools," *The Washington Post,* June 9, 2016; Ann Zaniewski, "Governor Proposes a Plan to Eliminate Detroit Schools' Debt Problems," *Governing Magazine,* May 1, 2015; "A Progress Report on Detroit Public Schools Community District Finances," Citizens Research Council of Michigan Memorandum 1145, May 2017.

152 *Democrats wanted the plan to include:* Erin Einhorn, "A Year After the Tearful Demise of a Proposed Detroit School Oversight Commission, Backers Seek Another Way to Bring Order to Detroit Schools," *Chalkbeat,* July 6, 2017; Robin J. Lake, Ashley Jochim, and Michael DeArmond, "Fixing Detroit's Broken School System," *EducationNext* 15 (2015); Beth Hawkins, "Detroit's Educational Catastrophe," *The Atlantic,* May 10, 2016; Rochelle Riley, "Why the Detroit School District Needs a Watchdog Group," *Detroit Free Press,* April 15, 2017.

153 *Delilah's school operated within:* April Van Buren, "After Six Years, Education Achievement Authority Leaves Behind Lackluster Legacy," Michigan Radio, June 26, 2017.

154 *The state-run district had not:* Tresa Baldas, Kat Stafford, Kathleen Gray, and Ann Zaniewski, "Feds: 12 Detroit Principals Stole $1M in Kickback Scheme," *Detroit Free Press,* March 29, 2016; Robert Snell, "Detroit School Principal in Kickback Case Freed on $10,000 Bond," *Crain's Detroit Business,* December 21, 2015; Jennifer Chambers, "Ex-Detroit Principal Gets Year in Prison for Kickbacks," *The Detroit News,* June 1, 2016.

154 *Lola did, however, know that:* Shawn D. Lewis and George Hunter, "Detroit School Closure Plan Draws Objections," *The Detroit News*, February 13, 2017; Erin Einhorn, "These 38 Michigan Schools Could Be Shut Down for Poor Performance in June," *Chalkbeat*, January 20, 2017; Khalil AlHajal, "Closing Detroit Schools Would Create 'Education Deserts,' Says Teachers Union," *MLive*, January 23, 2017; Chad Livengood, "Detroit District Sues State to Block 16 School Closings," *Crain's Detroit Business*, March 21, 2017; Chastity Pratt Dawsey, "Michigan Shuts Down Bad Schools. Leading States Build Them Up," *Bridge Magazine*, February 21, 2017; Natalie Fotias, "Is Closing Schools a Fake Fix?" Skillman Foundation, February 10, 2017.

155 *The new superintendent and new school:* The idea that positions were left open for budgetary reasons does not seem to have been published anywhere. The information stems from an off-the-record interview with an elected member of the school board.

13. The Campaign

158 *Over the following months, during:* Monica Davey, "Mike Duggan and Coleman Young Will Face Off in Detroit's Mayoral Election," *The New York Times*, August 8, 2017; Christine Ferretti, "Duggan, Young Set to Meet in Detroit Mayor Fall Contest," *The Detroit News*, August 8, 2017; Quinn Klinefelter, "Duggan Gains Massive Primary Win, Will Face Young in General Election," *WDET*, August 9, 2017; Christine Ferretti, "TV Ad Supporting Duggan Set to Air Tuesday," *The Detroit News*, October 2, 2017.

159 *By 2015 fewer police officers:* George Hunter, "Fewest Cops Are Patrolling Detroit Streets Since 1920s," *The Detroit News*, July 9, 2015.

159 *City officials spoke of plans:* Hunter, "Fewest Cops Are Patrolling"; Chastity Pratt Dawsey, "Facing Police Shortage, Detroit Seeks to Stop New Cops from Jumping Ship," *Bridge Magazine*, April 10, 2018; Kurt Nagl, "With Crime Down in 2017, Detroit Plans to Hire 200 Police Officers, Expand Partnerships with Businesses," *Crain's Detroit Business*, January 4, 2018; Christine MacDonald and George Hunter, "Detroit Ranks as 2nd Most Violent Big City," *The Detroit News*, September 24, 2018.

159 *The city only had the resources:* Christine Ferretti, "Detroit Land Bank Funds at Limit as Inventory Grows," *The Detroit News,* April 11, 2016; Jason Margolis, "For Sale: Detroit Land Bank Seeks Buyers for Vacant Houses," *All Things Considered,* June 11, 2015.

160 *The event, intended to pique the guests':* J.C. Reindl, "Interior of Michigan Central Station Shown to 'Homecoming' Crowd in Rare Display," *Detroit Free Press,* September 13, 2017; Tanya Moutzalias, "Detroit's Michigan Central Station Lights Up for First Guests Since 1980s," *MLive,* September 14, 2017; Chad Livengood, "Detroit Train Station Gets a Homecoming," *Crain's Detroit Business,* September 13, 2017.

161 *She had arrived at her planning:* Drew Mason, "Brightmoor Artisans Collective Unites Detroit Neighborhood," Michigan Economic Development Corporation, September 26, 2018.

161 *The city's police chief claimed:* Corey Williams, "Crime in Detroit Is Down Overall in 2016; Homicides Up by 7," *Detroit Free Press,* January 3, 2017; Tresa Baldas, "Detroit Is Once Again the Most Violent City in America, FBI Says. Chief Craig Disagrees," *Detroit Free Press,* September 25, 2017; George Hunter and Christine MacDonald, "Police: Our Data Shows Crime Fell Last Year in Detroit," *The Detroit News,* September 29, 2017; Daniel Fisher, "America's Most Dangerous Cities: Detroit Can't Shake No. 1 Spot," *Forbes,* October 29, 2015; Cleve R. Wootson Jr., "Police Chief Says Detroit Isn't America's Most Violent City, Despite the FBI's Data," *The Washington Post,* September 26, 2017; Todd Newcombe, "Crime, Not Debt, Is Detroit's Biggest Problem," *Governing Magazine,* August 2013; Charlie LeDuff, "Violent Crime—Are Detroit Cops Cooking the Books?" *Deadline Detroit,* October 19, 2017; Joe Guillen, "Detroit's Crime-Fighting Surveillance Program Expands," *Detroit Free Press,* May 24, 2016.

161 *Detroit officials' primary response to crime:* "Project Green Light Detroit," City of Detroit, https://detroitmi.gov/departments/police -department/project-green-light-detroit; Allie Gross, "Does Detroit's Project Green Light Really Make the City Safer?" *Detroit Free Press,* April 20, 2018; Will Feuer, "Controversial Project Green Light Comes to Corktown," *MetroTimes,* October 31, 2018; "What Are Those Flashing Green Lights Doing on Detroit Businesses?" *WDET,*

December 22, 2017; "City Officials, Business Partners Announce Greektown District as First Green Light Corridor," City of Detroit, January 30, 2018.

163 *Rather than boost resources for Detroit's:* "Detroit Police Chief 'Not Concerned' with Private Security Teams Downtown," *Daily Detroit,* July 6, 2016; "Private Security for Detroit Neighborhoods Urged by Community Groups," *Huffington Post,* May 18, 2012; "Downtown Detroit: Private Security in a Public Space," Michigan Radio, May 20, 2015; Laura Gottesdiener, "This Is the Part of Detroit That Most People Are Not Aware Of," *Mother Jones,* November 18, 2014; Darrell Dawsey, "Private Security in Palmer Woods Shows How Commitment to Living in Detroit Can be Taxing," *MLive,* June 6, 2011; Mark Jay, "Policing the Poor in Detroit," *Monthly Review* 68 (2017): 21–35; Brian Doucet and Edske Smit, "Building an Urban 'Renaissance': Fragmented Services and the Production of Inequality in Greater Downtown Detroit," *Journal of Housing and the Built Environment* 31 (2016): 635–657.

167 *The mayoral contest, meanwhile, grew:* Kat Stafford and Ann Zaniewski, "Young Releases Racially Charged Attack Ad Comparing Duggan to Kilpatrick," *Detroit Free Press,* October 20, 2017; Sarah Cwiek, "Detroit's Only Mayoral Debate Was Testy, Personal, and No-Holds-Barred," Michigan Radio, October 26, 2017; Jack Roskopp, "Coleman Young II Holding 'Take Back the Motherland' Rally Night Before Mayoral Election," *Detroit Metro Times,* October 30, 2017.

167 *Young aired an ad arguing:* Steve Friess, "Detroit's Mayor Seeks to Continue Urban Renewal, Relying on Unique Strategy," *The Washington Post,* October 30, 2017.

14. Report Cards

171 *The criminal charges that prevented:* Complete records available from the 36th District Court, http://www.36thdistrictcourt.org/online-services/case-inquiry-schedule, and from the Third Judicial Circuit of Michigan, https://cmspublic.3rdcc.org, and also on file with the author.

172 *Nevertheless in November 2017 Duggan:* Kat Stafford, "Election Day 2017: Mike Duggan Defeats Coleman A. Young II," *Detroit Free Press,* November 7, 2017.

173 *"There are haves and have-nots":* Christine Ferretti and Christine MacDonald, "Victorious Duggan: 'One Detroit for All of Us,'" *The Detroit News,* November 7, 2017.

173 *A clerk told him that judges:* "Judge Speaks Out Against 36th District Court Change," *Click On Detroit,* April 6, 2015; "Walk-In Docket," 36th District Court, http://www.36thdistrictcourt.org/divisions -departments/traffic/walk-in-docket.

173 *Local governments found a steady:* "Targeted Fines and Fees Against Low-Income Communities of Color: Civil Rights and Constitutional Implications," Briefing Report of the United States Commission on Civil Rights, Washington, D.C., September 2017; Dan Kopf, "The Fining of Black America," *Priceonomics,* June 24, 2016; "Investigation of the Ferguson Police Department," United States Department of Justice Civil Rights Division, March 4, 2015. On fines and fees in Detroit see Sarah Alverez, "Detroit Court Gets Tough on Traffic Tickets. County Taxpayers Get Stuck with Tab," *Bridge Magazine,* June 12, 2017.

175 *Miles's district court records predated:* David Ashenfelter, "Restructuring of the 36th District Court," Michigan Supreme Court, September 2014.

175 *"without prejudice":* Marc L. Steinberg, "Dismissal With or Without Prejudice Under the Speedy Trial Act: A Proposed Interpretation," *Journal of Criminal Law and Criminology* 68 (1977): 1–14; Gillian K. Hadfield, "Where Have All the Trials Gone?" University of Southern California Law School Law and Economics Working Paper Series 12, 2004.

176 *To reinstate his driving privileges:* Jonathan Oosting, "Michigan Looks to Kill 7-Day Car Insurance," *The Detroit News,* April 17, 2017; "7-Day Car Insurance Plans Are Popular in Detroit. Now, Lawmakers Want to Ban Them," Michigan Radio, April 11, 2017.

177 *She affixed a gold seal:* The author has a photograph of the documents on file.

177 *It featured call-in shows hosted:* "Detroit Politician Admits Bribery," CNN, June 26, 2009; "Monica Conyers Gets 37 Months in Prison," *Crain's Detroit Business,* March 10, 2010; Chad Livengood, "Detroit Aims to Mandate Project Green Light Crime-Monitoring Surveillance for Late-Night Businesses," *Crain's Detroit Business,* January 3, 2018.

180 *The preacher's house fell outside:* Joe Guillen, "Detroit's Showcase Neighborhood Project Falls a Year Behind Schedule," *Detroit Free Press,* July 6, 2018. Project delays reduced a $1.6 million federal grant by $274,000, and the city made up the difference from its general fund. City officials explained they voluntarily reduced the federal grant and made the federal money available to other city projects. By law, the money from the general fund would have to be used for public purposes. The affordable housing project would have fulfilled the requirement.

181 *At Marygrove College enrollment had:* Tyler Clifford and Kurt Nagl, "Marygrove College to End Undergrad Programs, Offer Graduate Studies Only," *Crain's Detroit Business,* August 9, 2017.

182 *Seven district managers now oversaw:* "Department of Neighborhoods," City of Detroit, http://www.detroitmi.gov/Neighborhoods; Nancy Derringer, "Detroit's New District Managers Serve as Important Ambassadors for Rebuilding City," *Bridge Magazine,* January 15, 2015.

15. The Way We Live Now

186 *Though the number of mortgages:* Joel Kurth, "Banks Are Lending Again in Detroit . . . if You Live in the Right Neighborhood," *Bridge Magazine,* March 15, 2018; "A Decade After Housing Bust, Recovery Is a Story of Location," *PRNewswire,* September 13, 2018.

189 *She had seen a few foreign:* The author does not know whether this was serious or whether she actually had a gun. Her exact words were "lock and load."

189 *Detroit had few immigrants:* Steve Tobocman, "Global Detroit Expands Efforts to Retain and Attract Immigrant Talent," Knight Foundation, September 16, 2014; "How Immigrants Are Helping Detroit's Recovery," *The Economist,* February 16, 2017; Jason Margolis, "Detroit Welcomes Immigrants to Spur the City's Revival," *PRI's The World,* September 18, 2018.

189 *In response the district manager phoned:* "Updates from the Inclusion Committee," Neighbors Building Brightmoor Newsletter, April 2016.

194 *The county treasurer declined the funding:* Violet Ikonomova, "Wayne County Treasurer Rejects Two Last-Minute Plans to Help Detroit Families Avoid Foreclosure," *Detroit Metro Times,* November 1, 2017; Christine

MacDonald, "Sabree's $200K Home Aid Rejection Spurs Frustration," *The Detroit News*, October 29, 2017; Tyler Clifford, "McGregor Fund Grants $500,000 to Help Shield Homeowners from Tax Foreclosure," *Crain's Detroit Business*, October 11, 2017.

16. I'm from the Government, and I'm Here to Help

196 *The stress of the upcoming move:* On asthma, poverty, and race, Nicole Kravitz-Wirtz, Samantha Teixeira, Anjum Hajat, Bongki Woo, Kyle Crowder, and David Takeuchi, "Early-Life Air Pollution Exposure, Neighborhood Poverty, and Childhood Asthma in the United States, 1990–2014," *International Journal of Environmental Research and Public Health* 15 (2018): 1–14; C. Andrew Aligne, Peggy Auinger, Robert S. Byrn, and Michael Weitzman, "Risk Factors for Pediatric Asthma," *American Journal of Repiratory Critical Care Medicine* 162 (2000): 873–877; Corinne A. Keet, Meredith C. McCormack, Craig E. Pollack, Roger D. Peng, Emily McGowan, and Elizabeth C. Matsui, "Neighborhood Poverty, Urban Residence, Race/Ethnicity, and Asthma," *Allergy and Clinical Immunology* 135 (2015): 655–662; Ki Lee Milligan, Elizabeth Matsui, and Hemant Sharma, "Asthma in Urban Children," *Current Allergy and Asthma Reports* 16 (2016); Delancey Gracy, "Managing Childhood Asthma as a Strategy to Break the Cycle of Poverty," *American Journal of Public Health* 108 (2018): 21–22; Helen K. Hughes, Elizabeth C. Matsui, Megan M. Tschudy, Craig E. Pollack, and Corinne A. Keet, "Pediatric Asthma Health Disparities: Race, Hardship, Housing, and Asthma in a National Survey," *Academic Pediatrics* 17 (2017): 127–134.

199 *Until the house had those things:* Kat Stafford, "Controversial Water Shutoffs Could Hit 17,461 Detroit Households," *Detroit Free Press*, March 26, 2018; Joel Kurth, "Detroit Shut Water to 1 in 10 Homes This Year," *Bridge Magazine*, December 5, 2017.

200 *"Boycott All Brightmoor Farmway Farms:"* Picture of sign on file with the author.

201 *People in the neighborhood who kept:* Theodore Pride, "Resident-Led Urban Agriculture and the Hegemony of Neoliberal Community Development," *Wayne State University Dissertations*, January 1, 2016; Sarah Williams, "Brightmoor Neighborhood Sows Seeds of Sustainability," *Mirror News*, April 9, 2018.

17. Nice Work if You Can Get It

208   *In some parts of the city property:* Christine Ferretti, "Residential Property Values Going Up in Detroit," *The Detroit News,* February 5, 2018; Kat Stafford, "Detroit Property Values Rise for First Time in 17 Years," *Detroit Free Press,* February 5, 2018.

208   *As winter dragged on prospects:* "Green Garage," http://www.greengarage detroit.com/site/; Jessica Bruder, "In Detroit, the Green Garage Is a Different Kind of Incubator," *The New York Times,* June 21, 2012; Sarah Cwiek, "Detroit Green Garage Looks for the Meaning of 'Green,'" Michigan Radio, December 15, 2011.

209   *Additionally, the city had also:* Claire Charlton, "The Future Is Now: A Glimpse into Metro Detroit's Mobility Ecosystem," *ModelD,* January 29, 2018; "The New Detroit, from 'Motor City' to 'Mobility City,'" *Inc.* [no date available]; "Ford, Techstars Select 12 Startups to Focus on Mobility Solutions as Part of 2016 Mentorship Program," *Business Wire,* June 8, 2016.

209   *The CDFI was working to apply:* Brett Theodos, Sameera Fazili, and Ellen Seidman, "Scaling Impact for Community Development Financial Institutions," Urban Institute, June 2016; Kat Stafford, "How Detroit Plans to Raise $130M to Invest in 7 Neighborhoods," *Detroit Free Press,* May 7, 2018; "Returns on Investment—Invest Detroit," New Economy Initiative, https://neweconomyinitiative.org/story/returns -on-investment-invest-detroit/.

210   *Simultaneously the staff members were:* Chastity Pratt Dawsey, "Poor People at Risk of Eviction as Tax Credits Expire and Detroit Revives," *Bridge Magazine,* August 21, 2018; Sarah Cwiek, "Detroit to Launch $250 Million Affordable Housing Fund, Strategy," Michigan Radio, March 12, 2018; Violet Ikonomova, "Can a Mixed-Income Housing Ordinance Really Help Solve Detroit's Affordability Problem?" *Detroit Metro Times,* May 17, 2017.

214   *Developers were repurposing old:* Sarah Brodsky, "Detroit Hotel Industry Expecting Major Growth in 2017," Madonna University, February 20, 2017; Jena Tesse Fox, "Healthy Hotel Pipeline Puts Detroit on the Fast Track," *Hotel Management,* June 14, 2016; "Detroit Is Going Through a Hotel Boom," Michigan Radio, April 14, 2015.

18. New Beginnings

218 *So far that year about 120:* George Hunger, "Union Chief: Detroit Losing Police Officers," *The Detroit News,* July 4, 2018; Chastity Pratt Dawsey, "Facing Police Shortage, Detroit Seeks to Stop New Cops from Jumping Ship," *Bridge Magazine,* April 10, 2018; Sarah Cwiek, "At Detroit Budget Hearings, Police Grapple with Officer Retention Issues," Michigan Radio, February 26, 2018.

219 *The jail should have closed:* Hasan Dudar, "Wayne County Jail Finally Gets a New Home in Detroit," *Detroit Free Press,* March 7, 2018; Gus Burns, "Detroit Jail Debacle Finally Sorted Out, with Taxpayers on Hook for $600M-Plus," *Mlive,* June 8, 2018; Sarah Cwiek, "Wayne County Approves Land Swap Deal, One Step Closer to New Jail Deal with Gilbert," Michigan Radio, April 6, 2018; David Muller, "County Moving Forward with Plan to Turn Over Failed Downtown Detroit Jail Site to Dan Gilbert," *MLive,* November 16, 2013.

220 *Just as the bail payment:* Records available from Dayton Municipal Court and Montgomery County Clerk of Courts and in copies of documents Miles provided, on file with the author.

221 *As Miles struggled to get:* Monica Davey, "As Detroit Sheds State Oversight, Its Mayor Reflects on Its Path," *The New York Times,* April 30, 2018; Camila Domonoske, "Detroit Released from Financial Oversight, 3 Years After Emerging from Bankruptcy," NPR, April 30, 2018.

222 *"Look, this city ended up in":* Davey, "As Detroit Sheds State Oversight."

222 *He announced a new job:* John Gallagher, "Detroit Workforce Participation Rate Is Lowest in Nation," *Detroit Free Press,* June 8, 2018.

222 *A few months into his first:* Police report on file with the author.

225 *In March Governor Snyder had signed:* Chad Livengood, "Snyder Signs Bills Wiping out $630 Million in Unpaid Driver Fees," *Crain's Detroit Business,* March 1, 2018; "Law Takes Effect Forgiving Driver Responsibility Fees," *The Detroit News,* October 1, 2018.

226 *At the barbecue restaurant Michael:* Melena Ryzik, "Detroit's Renewal, Slow-Cooked," *The New York Times,* October 19, 2010; "Phillip Cooley: Detroit Dreamer Before It Was Cool," *The Detroit News,* November 5, 2015; Noelle Lothamer, "Slows Growth: How One Cool Biz

Transformed a Neighborhood," *ModelD*, March 26, 2012; Christy McDonald, "Slows BBQ Owner Inspires Change in Detroit Neighborhood," *WXYZ Detroit ABC 7*, May 24, 2010.

227 *The president of the property company tweeted:* Christian Meyer, https://twitter.com/cdmhomesinc/status/535523734325432321.

227 *When Delilah came home from:* Stephanie Steinberg, "LifeBuilders to Restore 100 Detroit Homes in Regent Park," *The Detroit News*, May 5, 2017.

229 *Calling the towers the Renaissance Center:* Francis Desiderio, "'A Catalyst for Downtown': Detroit's Renaissance Center," *Michigan Historical Review* 35 (2009): 83–112; William J.V. Neill, "Lipstick on the Gorilla: The Failure of Image-Led Planning in Coleman Young's Detroit," *International Journal of Urban and Regional Research* 19 (1995); John McCarthy, "Revitalization of the Core City: The Case of Detroit," *Cities* 14 (1997): 1–11; Marion E. Orr and Gerry Stoker, "Urban Regimes and Leadership in Detroit," *Urban Affairs Quarterly* (1994); Colin Marshall, "The Renaissance Center: Henry Ford II's Grand Design to Revive Detroit," *The Guardian*, May 22, 2015.

229 *An education advocacy group had:* Jennifer Chambers, "Fewer than Half of Third-Graders Proficient in English," *The Detroit News*, August 29, 2017; Jennifer Chambers, "Duggan's School Bus Loop Approved by Ed Board," *The Detroit News*, May 23, 2018; Jennifer Chambers, "Bus Loop Looks to Bring Back Detroit Students," *The Detroit News*, June 11, 2018; Erin Einhorn, "A Controversial Joint Bus Route for Detroit District and Charter Schools Hits a Speed Bump," *Chalkbeat*, April 30, 2018; "10 DPSCD and Charter Schools Join Northwest Detroit GOAL Line Pilot, Connecting Detroit Children to Better Transportation and After School Enrichment," Skillman Foundation, June 11, 2018.

230 *A judge described the conditions:* Jacey Fortin, "'Access to Literacy' Is Not a Constitutional Right, Judge in Detroit Rules," *The New York Times*, July 4, 2018.

230 *Later in the summer the superintendent:* "Detroit Shuts Off Water Fountains at 106 Public Schools," Associated Press, September 4, 2018; Jacey Fortin, "Detroit Schools Turn Off Drinking Water, Citing Elevated Lead and Copper," *The New York Times*, August 30, 2018.

230 *As the country enjoyed strong employment:* Lester Graham, "Detroit's True Unemployment Rate," *Michigan Radio*, February 16, 2018.

19. Bait and Switch

233 *Local news reports of construction:* John Gallagher, "Detroit Lags on Redevelopment Due to Worker Shortage," *Detroit Free Press,* June 9, 2018.

234 *Though his record would not:* J.C. Reindl, "Detroit's Rebound Brings Surge in Downtown Security Jobs," *Detroit Free Press,* June 14, 2018.

234 *Finally the lawyer phoned with:* Copy on file with the author.

236 *He explained that in the intervening:* Michael Coyle, "Race and Class Penalties in Crack Cocaine Sentencing," The Sentencing Project, 2002; Ryan S. King and Marc Mauer, "Sentencing with Discretion: Crack Cocaine Sentencing After *Booker,"* The Sentencing Project, 2006; William Spade, Jr., "Beyond the 100:1 Ratio: Towards a Rational Cocaine Sentencing Policy," *Arizona Law Review* 38 (1996); Joseph J. Palamar et al., "Powder Cocaine and Crack Use in the United States," *Drug and Alcohol Dependence* 149 (2015): 108–116; Richard D. Hartley and J. Mitchell Miller, "Crack-ing the Media Myth," *Criminal Justice Review* 35 (2010): 67–89; Elizabeth Tison, "Amending the Sentencing Guidelines for Cocaine Offenses," *South Illinois University Law Journal* 27 (2002–2003).

237 *While Detroit lost population and abandoned:* Annalise Frank, "Business-Heavy Mexicantown Avenue to Be Remade as Shared Street," *Crain's Detroit Business,* May 23, 2018; Daniel Denvir, "The Paradox of Mexicantown," *City Lab,* September 24, 2012; Maria Elena Rodriguez, *Detroit's Mexicantown* (Charleston, S.C.: Arcadia Publishing, 2011).

239 *Beside them lay a mess:* Dana Afana, "Shipping Container Retail Spaces Open Along Detroit's Dequindre Cut Greenway," *Mlive,* May 27, 2018; "Detroit Greenway Shipping Container Project Set to Open," Associated Press, May 18, 2018.

239 *Down the street sat the Michigan:* Tom Perkins, "On Urban Farming and 'Colonialism' in Detroit's North End Neighborhood," *Detroit Metro Times,* December 20, 2017.

242 *The Berlin club's owner, Dimitri:* Sarah Hucal, "A Berlin Club Owner's Mission to Give Back to Detroit, the City That Gave Europe Techno," *ABC News,* June 1, 2018; J.C. Reindl, "German Techno Club Owner Eyes Abandoned Detroit Factory," *Detroit Free Press,* October 14, 2014; Jack Nicas, "Where Detroit Sees a Derelict Factory, Berliners See a

Techno Dance Club," *The Wall Street Journal,* October 14, 2014; Will Lynch, "Bringing It All Back Home: How Techno Is Poised to Return to Detroit," *The Guardian,* December 8, 2014; Violet Ikonomova, "Mayor Duggan Considers Proposals to Make Detroit a Destination for Drag Racing and Techno," *Detroit Metro Times,* June 28, 2018; David Muller, "Berlin Techno Mogul to Talk Plans for Detroit's Abandoned Fisher Body 21 Plant," *MLive,* November 26, 2014.

242 *Already Hegemann had sought out:* Candice Williams, "A Year into Revival Efforts, Packard Plant Cleans Up," *The Detroit News,* March 1, 2018; Dana Afana, "Brewery Planned for Historic Packard Plant Site in Detroit," *MLive,* December 8, 2017; J.C. Reindl, "Detroit's Packard Plant Rehab Breaks Ground," *Detroit Free Press,* April 28, 2017; "Revamp of Former Detroit Packard Car Plant in Cleanup Phase," Associated Press, March 1, 2018.

20. Detroit Versus Everybody

244 *On an overcast humid morning:* Cindy Burton, "Ford Says It Will Spend $740M to Bring Detroit Train Station Project to Life," *Detroit Free Press,* August 15, 2018; Kirk Pinho, "Ford Paid $90 Million for Michigan Central Station," *Crain's Detroit Business,* September 24, 2018; Tamara Warren, "Inside Detroit's Crumbling Train Station That Ford Plans to Transform into a Mobility Lab," *The Verge,* June 20, 2018; Neal Boudette, "Ford Aims to Revive a Detroit Train Station, and Itself," *The New York Times,* June 17, 2018; David Shepardson, "Ford to Invest $740 Million in Detroit Train Station, City Development Project," Reuters, August 14, 2018; Neil Rubin, "A Celebration, Not an Implosion, at Michigan Central Depot," *The Detroit News,* June 19, 2018; Kat Stafford and Allie Gross, "Ford Closer to Securing $103M in Tax Breaks from Detroit," *Detroit Free Press,* October 16, 2018; Violet Ikonomova, "Ford Agrees to $10M in Community Benefits as It Seeks $104M from Detroit," *Metro Times,* September 25, 2018.

245 *Soon self-driving electric shuttles:* Keith Naughton and Sarah Gardner, "Simple Self-Driving Shuttles Become First Robot Rides in Detroit," *Bloomberg,* June 26, 2018.

246 *Already a company in New Jersey:* Randy Essex, "Detroit Train Station: Nearby Lot for Sale, Listed for $2M," *Detroit Free Press,* June 13, 2018.

247 *Back at Robin's commercial building:* Sarah Cwiek, "In a Changing Detroit, North End Neighborhood Vies to Shape Its Future," Michigan Radio, May 12, 2016; Sarah Rose Sharp, "In Detroit's North End, Akoaki Uses Art and Design to Bolster the Community," *Detroit Free Press,* November 12, 2017; Dennis Archambault, "North End, Detroit Neighborhood East of New Center, Is Focus of Organic and New Development," *Huffington Post,* February 26, 2013; "'On the Ground' Series Examines Detroit's North End Neighborhood," *WDET,* December 26, 2017.

250 *In that neighborhood, 40 years:* Jeanie Wylie, *Poletown: Community Betrayed* (Urbana and Chicago: University of Illinois Press, 1990); David Fasenfest, "Community Politics and Urban Redevelopment," *Urban Affairs Review* 22 (1986): 101–123; John J. Bukowczyk, "The Decline and Fall of a Detroit Neighborhood," *Washington and Lee Law Review* 41 (1984).

Epilogue: We Hope for Better Things

257 *The Congressional Budget Office has estimated:* "The Macroeconomic and Budgetary Effects of Federal Investment," Congressional Budget Office, June 2016; "Estimated Impact of the American Recovery and Reinvestment Act on Employment and Economic Output from January 2012 Through March 2012," Congressional Budget Office, May 2012.

257 *By 2015 federal spending amounted:* Josh Bivens, "Why Is Recovery Taking So Long—and Who's to Blame," Economic Policy Institute Report, August 11, 2016; Josh Bivens, Andrew Fieldhouse, and Heidi Shierholz, "From Free Fall to Stagnation," Economic Policy Institute Briefing Paper, February 14, 2013; David Cashin, Jamie Lenney, Byron Lutz, and William Peterman, "Fiscal Policy and Aggregate Demand in the U.S. Before, During and Following the Great Recession," Board of Governors of the Federal Reserve System, Finance and Economics Discussion Series 2017-061, 2017.

258 *Because of state balanced budget laws:* William Tabb, "National Urban Policy and the Fate of Detroit," in *Reinventing Detroit,* ed. Michael Peter Smith and L. Owen Kirkpatrick (New Brunswick, N.J., and London: Transaction Publishers, 2015), Chapter 4.

258 *In 2011 Jeb Bush and Newt Gingrich:* Jeb Bush and Newt Gingrich, "Better Off Bankrupt," *Los Angeles Times,* January 27, 2011.

258 *In his bid for the GOP presidential:* Tim Pawlenty, "Consider Letting States Have Bankruptcy," CBS MINN, January 24, 2011, http://minnesota .cbslocal.com/2011/01/24/pawlenty-consider-letting-states-have -bankruptcy/; Rick Unger, "Is State Bankruptcy the Next Wave in Public Employee Union Busting?" *Forbes,* February 28, 2011; Jack M. Beermann, "The Public Pension Crisis," *Washington and Lee Law Review* 70 (2013): 3–94.

259 *To pre-empt emergency management:* Nathan Bomey and John Gallagher, "How Detroit Went Broke," *Detroit Free Press,* September 15, 2013.

259 *In 2001 local business leaders raised money:* Alesia Montgomery, "Reappearance of the Public: Placemaking, Minoritization and Resistance in Detroit," *International Journal of Urban and Regional Research* 40 (2016): 776–799; Brian Doucet and Edske Smit, "Building an Urban 'Renaissance': Fragmented Services and the Production of Inequality in Greater Downtown Detroit," *Journal of Housing and the Built Environment* 31 (2016): 635–657.

259 *In 2005 the scion of a suburban:* Melena Ryzik, "Detroit's Renewal, Slow-Cooked," *The New York Times,* October 19, 2010; "Phillip Cooley: Detroit Dreamer Before It Was Cool," *The Detroit News,* November 5, 2015; Noelle Lothamer, "Slows Growth: How One Cool Biz Transformed a Neighborhood," *ModelD,* March 26, 2012; Christy McDonald, "Slows BBQ Owner Inspires Change in Detroit Neighborhood," WXYZ Detroit ABC 7, May 24, 2010.

260 *In Midtown, a nonprofit development group:* Ashley C. Woods, "Live Midtown: Subsidies Drive Residential Demand, New Development in Detroit Neighborhood," *MLive,* February 8, 2012.

260 *The density of the neighborhood increased:* Stacy Crowley, "How Wayne State Police Helped Breathe Life into a Blighted Detroit Strip," *The New York Times,* February 25, 2015; Dennis Archambault, "How Midtown Became Detroit's Safest Neighborhood," *Second Wave Michigan,* January 26, 2018.

260 *Following the recent financial crisis Vallejo:* Mark Davidson and William Kutz, "Grassroots Austerity: Municipal Bankruptcy from Below in Vallejo, California," *Environment and Planning A: Economy and Space* 47 (2015): 1440–1459; Kenneth E. Noble and Kevin M. Baum, "Mu-

nicipal Bankruptcies: An Overview and Recent History of Chapter 9 of the Bankruptcy Code," *Pratt's Journal of Bankruptcy Law* 9 (2013): 513; Steven Greenhut, "Vallejo's Painful Lessons in Municipal Bankruptcy," *The Wall Street Journal*, March 26, 2010.

261 *Even among companies, however:* Adam J. Levitin, "Bankrupt Politics and the Politics of Bankruptcy," *Cornell Law Review* 97 (2012): 1399–1459.

261 *Many companies have repeatedly entered:* Lynn M. LoPucki and Joseph W. Doherty, "Bankruptcy Survival," *UCLA Law Review* 62 (2015): 969; Edward I. Altman and Ben Branch, "The Bankruptcy System's Chapter 22 Recidivism Problem: How Serious Is It?" *Financial Review* 50 (2015).

262 *For analogous reasons, bankruptcy:* Noble and Baum, "Municipal Bankruptcies"; Laura Beth Kurtz, "Responses to Local Government Fiscal Diress," Dissertation, PennState, 2016.

266 *Studies have shown that the resurgent:* "Expanding Opportunities in America's Urban Areas," Center for American Progress, March 23, 2015; Paul A. Jargowsky, "Concentration of Poverty in the New Millennium," The Century Foundation and Rutgers Center for Urban Research, https://tcf.org/assets/downloads/Concentration_of_Poverty_in_the_New_Millennium.pdf; Alaina J. Harkness, Bruce Katz, Caroline Conroy, and Ross Tilchin, "Leading Beyond Limits: Mayoral Powers in the Age of New Localism," Brookings Institution, October 24, 2017; Ely Portillo, "Charlotte, Other Cities Must Find Own Ways to Fund Programs Like Transit, Expert Says," *The Charlotte Observer*, December 5, 2017; Marvin Rees and Bruce Katz, "Putting Cities Center Stage," *Governing*, December 4, 2017; Bruce Katz and Jennifer Bradley, *The Metropolitan Revolution*, Washington D.C., Brookings Institution, 2014.

268 *The city has diverted tax revenues:* Jeffrey Dorfman, "Government Incentives to Attract Jobs Are Terrible Deals for Taxpayers," *Forbes*, September 6, 2017; Richard Florida, "Handing Out Tax Breaks to Businesses Is Worse Than Useless," *City Lab*, March 7, 2017; Henry Grabar, "Corporate Incentives Cost U.S. $45 Billion in 2015, Don't Really Work," *Slate*, March 10, 2017; William Ruger and Jason Sorens, "Tax Incentives' Bipartisan Folly," *Governing*, September 24, 2018.

269 *Brightmoor residents celebrated when:* Beth Stuever, "MSU Launches Partnership for Urban Agriculture in Detroit," *MSU Today*, November 16, 2017.

270 *Despite recent cuts, the federal government:* Robert Jay Dilger, "Federal Grants to State and Local Governments: A Historical Perspective on Contemporary Issues," Congressional Research Service, May 7, 2018; "Federal Aid to State and Local Governments," Center on Budget and Policy Priorities, April 19, 2018; Megan Randall, Sarah Gault, and Tracy Gordon, "Federal Aid to Local Governments," Urban Institute, September 2016; "Federal Grants to State and Local Governments," Congressional Budget Office, March 5, 2013.

270 *No process currently exists to facilitate:* "Final Report of the State Budget Crisis Task Force," January 14, 2014; Alan Mallach, "Facing the Urban Challenge," Metropolitan Policy Program at Brookings Institution, May 2010.

271 *Federal tax credits that subsidize:* Amanda Gold, Matthew Gerken, Carl Hedman, and Corianne Payton Scally, "Technical Documentation for 'the Low-Income Housing Tax Credit,'" Urban Institute, July 2018; Lance Bocarsly and Rachel Rosner, "The Low Income Housing Tax Credit," *Practical Real Estate Law* 33 (2017): 29; Kim McClure, "Reform of the Low-Income Housing Tax Credit Program," Statement to the United States Senate Committee on Finance, August 1, 2017; Raquel Smith, "A Seat at the Table," *Columbia Journal of Race and Law* 6 (2016): 193–210.

272 *As urban America enjoys diminishing:* Emily Badger, "As American as Apple Pie?" *The New York Times,* November 20, 2016; "American Democracy's Built-in Bias Towards Rural Republicans," *The Economist,* July 12, 2018; Jon Emont, "The Growing Urban-Rural Divide Around the World," *The Atlantic,* January 4, 2017; Emily Dreyfuss, "The Electoral College Is Great for Whiter States, Lousy for Cities," *Wired,* December 8, 2016.

272 *Reduced attention to urban priorities:* H.R. 1 (2017).

272 *Four hundred miles southeast of Detroit:* "Behind the Teacher Strikes That Have Roiled Five States," *The Economist,* May 5, 2018; Rivka Galchen, "The Teachers' Strike and the Democratic Revival in Oklahoma," *The New Yorker,* July 4 and 11, 2018; Ellen David Friedman, "What's Behind the Teacher Strikes?" *Dollars & Sense,* May 27, 2018.

273 *Less than a year after Detroit exited:* Katy Stech, "Bankrupt Kentucky City Reaches Repayment Deal," *The Wall Street Journal,* March 30, 2016; Elizabeth Campbell, "Kentucky Town Is First to File for Bankruptcy

After Detroit," *Bloomberg*, August 20, 2015; Jody Godoy, "Bankrupt Kentucky City Reaches Repayment Deal," *Law360*, March 30, 2016.

Author's Note

278 *Numerous articles were touting:* On the movement for state bankruptcy, see David A. Skeel, Jr., "States of Bankruptcy," *University of Chicago Law Review* 79 (2012): 677; Mary Williams Walsh, "A Path Is Sought for States to Escape Their Debt Burdens," *The New York Times*, January 20, 2011.

Index